D1234888

CRISES IN CALIFORNIA HIGHER EDUCATION

CRISES IN CALIFORNIA HIGHER EDUCATION

EXPERIENCE UNDER THE MASTER PLAN AND
PROBLEMS OF COORDINATION, 1959 TO 1968

By ARTHUR G. COONS

President Emeritus, Occidental College

Chairman, California Master Plan Survey, 1959-1960

President, Coordinating Council for Higher Education in California, 1965-1968

THE WARD RITCHIE PRESS • LOS ANGELES

EVERY WRITER seemingly must justify why he foists upon the reading public another book, thus using up more paper in a paper consuming, paper overwhelmed world. I have written this book for three reasons: (1) I wanted to record my experiences and views for my own satisfaction as well as for the possible significance of all of this on public opinion and policy; (2) I have been encouraged by several friends for various reasons to do so, persons whose friendship, however, may have outrun their common sense in urging me on; and (3) there is conceivably an historical value particularly as to California in this exercise of memory and collation even if there is little or no influence of this writing on what transpires tomorrow or next year or beyond.

I am writing this as personal memoirs around aspects of my life and experience which have meant much to me whether or no they have any other meaning. The story is built chronologically and substantively around my participations as an educational administrator in public life and in the policy problems of higher education and planning considerably beyond the immediate responsibilities of a college president.

It is in no sense written about Occidental College where much of my life has been cast, and for not one word of it is Occidental College responsible.

In 1955 I was elected vice president of the Association of American Colleges, then president in 1956 with the inescapable responsibility of being concerned about all major issues of public policy affecting higher education both private and public. In 1956-57 I was a member of President Eisenhower's Committee on Education Beyond the High School. In 1959 I was chairman of California's Master Plan Survey. From 1953 to 1967 I was a member of the Board of Directors of the Council for Financial Aid to Education in New York. These are the principal participations to which I refer. There were a number of others.

Writing in the first person and yet drawing in much material relevant to the subject, this is neither wholly autobiographical nor wholly historical; it contains personal opinions. I hope I have been objective where objectivity is required, and I hope also I have been sufficiently revealing subjectively so that my own biases are understood even if I have not stated them. This is not intended to be a comprehensive, scholarly treatise with bibliography and extensive footnotes and citations and with the minutiae of detail necessarily embraced by the scholar or by the staff member of a government agency; however, it is my intention to be scholarly in the sense that what is stated as fact is fact, and what is opinion is discernible as such.

Someone has asked me, Who is your audience? For whom are you writing? I write for him who wishes to read what is written. The issues are of contemporary meaning and of importance to citizens. They are also issues on which the responsible educational administrator and many professors find they must be informed. It is intended to be helpful both to the citizen and to those in education who want to know why things are as they are, or at least what I think about things as they are. Many are confused by the day-by-day flow of news about events, about the clashes of opinions, about programs and plans in higher education. Perhaps this book may be of help.

At any rate, this is a story of California's problems of coordination, structure, major issues of governance, and relationships in higher education in the past decade and some conclusions therefrom based on the experiences and observations of the writer.

Without doubt, and in spite of all constructive efforts made, higher education in California has been in a state of crisis for at least ten years, and still is. Although private higher education has been affected and concerned, the primary arena of struggle has been public higher education.

The underlying frame of reference of this book, the reason for its being, is the continuing importance of the unresolved issues of fundamental significance to California citizens. That is to say, it is the crisis once existing, the discontent behind present tensions, and the impending problems upon whose appropriate solutions according to enduring principles the welfare of the state depends, which constitute the substance of this document.

I am profoundly grateful to Dr. Thomas C. Holy, a member of the California Master Plan Survey in 1959-60 and before that a member of the Liaison Committee staff, as well as to Dr. Willard B. Spalding, director of the California Coordinating Council for Higher Education, for their helpful suggestions for improvement after reading the manuscript in initial draft. Neither is in any way responsible for anything here written. In addition, I express thanks to Keith Sexton, an associate director of the Coordinating Council, and his colleague Leland W. Myers for providing numerous specific facts and interpretations, but whose use in this manuscript become wholly my responsibility. I also thank my friend Richard Laugharn for his many constructive suggestions regarding the manuscript content and form. To Jean Paule, my secretary for seventeen years who is Secretary of the College at Occidental College, I am indebted both for typing the manuscript and for critical comments thereon. My wife Edna receives my thanks for reading and criticizing the manuscript as well as for tolerating this effort so graciously.

Finally, and most appreciatively, I express thanks to the John Randolph Haynes and Dora Haynes Foundation of Los Angeles for a grant to assist in preparation of this manuscript and in partial support of its publication. In no way is the Haynes Foundation responsible for any of the facts or opinions in this book.

ARTHUR G. COONS
NEWPORT BEACH, CALIFORNIA

April 1, 1968

TABLE OF CONTENTS

ix

CRISES IN CALIFORNIA HIGHER EDUCATION

1

THE CALIFORNIA EDUCATIONAL SETTING

CALIFORNIA'S DEVELOPMENT of a Master Plan for higher education in 1959-60 was a direct resultant of the unresolved problems of rivalry, tension, and struggle over several decades among the three public segments of higher education and also among and between them all and the private or independent segment. The chief struggle over three decades has been between the University of California and its developing system and the State Colleges and their developing system, a struggle for program, position, prestige, and power. In the background always keeping watch and themselves occasionally entering the fray on one side or another or having separate or specific struggles of their own with one or more segments have been the public junior colleges and the private colleges and universities. This is the broad sweep of the background which made the Master Plan both necessary and possible.

This is also the broad background from which spring the present unresolved problems and their tensions and pressures.

Our task will be to examine history, take note of ideas which have dominated struggles and policies, record achievements, indicate present tensions and conflicting policies, and finally suggest major problems which cannot long go unresolved. The springboard for this total effort is the Master Plan of 1959-60, now nationally and world famed, which continues to be, unless and except as changed, the primary frame of reference for organization of and planning for public higher education in California.

The huge enrollments of veterans in colleges and universities in the period immediately following the close of World War II, and later the upsurge in national life following the conclusion of the Korean turmoil, stimulated an unprecedented ferment in higher

3

education in America. No state could escape the impact of these events, but among the several states probably none experienced a more pronounced reconsideration of all the major issues related to the future of higher education than did California.

The numbers game was out in front. It was the problem of what to do about the projected increase in college age population over the period to 1975 and beyond, the possible but certainly expected increase in the percentage desiring to go to college which experience since then has borne out, the problem of the magnitude of the part-time enrollments in all four segments of higher education swelling the total burden of full-time equivalent students (that is, beyond the enrollment of full-time students). This was the major factual factor in the backdrop setting the stage for the Master Plan Survey.

Although a problem of national scope, one which had received increasing attention in educational circles all through the fifties, the severity of the problem in California was relatively much higher.

The total (full-time and part-time) enrollments in California were projected to rise from 420,000 in 1958-59 to over 1,000,000 in 1975. The total full-time only enrollments projected on a *status quo* basis as given to the Master Plan Survey from the Department of Finance as the team began its work in 1959 showed an assumed rise from 276,000 in 1960 to 661,350 in 1975.

When any private enterprise or public activity has the responsibility of more than doubling its coverage in fifteen years, with the necessity of more than doubling facilities which means capital outlay, and more than doubling the costs of current operations, it has problems, even with no account taken in either capital or current expenditures of the threat of inflation and an attendant cheapening of the dollar.

When the total enterprise is divided into four segments with three of them, the public ones, struggling, competing hard, to get as much of the "business," that is to say, the enrollment, as possible and the fourth segment, the private, desirous in general of growing but not at rates comparable to the public segments, then the problems are even more pronounced.

If it is asked, as some did naively, "But why should each public segment be so eager to get as much enrollment as possible?" the answer is that this factor, the quantitative one, is considered to be the basis of power: financial power in the size of budgets, political power in the range or extent of contact, academic power in

4

the factors of recognition, prestige, and continuing drawing power of new faculty and students, as well as the possibility on the basis of all of these of establishing a new and more inclusive status for one's own "corporate" unit.

For many years in the fifties nearly every local chamber of commerce in the state was working to get a campus of either the University or the State College system established in its area with such an educational unit regarded in the same significance as a new factory or business establishment. Here was no yearning for culture but for all the economic advantages of payrolls and purchases. Indeed, most local chambers of commerce would be shocked to learn later the degree to which the academic personnel added would hold them in contempt if they showed lack of appreciation of the significance and work of a college or university campus. New junior colleges were appreciated but not similarly to the state-supported campuses, because after all, the junior college while a good addition if achieved was still local industry in the minds of many.

California's educational programs and plans have been objects of attention not only in the United States but in numerous foreign countries, while in California for several decades the political importance of higher education has steadily mounted. Now an awareness of the major problems facing colleges and universities, both public and private, is of fundamental importance for anyone aspiring to a responsible state governmental post, either executive or legislative. And, since the junior colleges are both local and state-wide in their significance, aspirants for local leadership must also know thoroughly the issues of importance to the successful development of the junior colleges.

So widespread has been the concern of the electorate for good education at all levels and so strong has been the whole system of higher education in California, again including both public and private institutions, that a knowledge of the educational issues has become an essential of political literacy. Indeed, many a man has been judged as to his fitness by his statements and voiced attitudes on higher education, because this has become an inescapable factor of high public policy. The judgment of the electorate may at one time be guided mainly by the degree of availability of higher education, at another time it may be a question of its quality, or of its cost, while at another as in 1966 the issue may be the degree of responsibility manifest in the leadership of higher education. However, its major importance to the people remains.

5

Admittedly, electorates here and there and officials here and there may fall short, may ignore history or may misread the future, but so outstanding has been California's concern for higher education (a concern which rarely flowers except where the elementary and secondary levels of education are also taken seriously and are forced to accountability on levels of educational achievement rather than on mere parsimonious cost calculation) that no responsible leader can long disregard this concern and demand. California is not immune to demagogic political behavior, but in the long run the record reveals a popular even though sometimes naive or uninformed awareness that in this day and age no significant progress can possibly be built on anything less than the best the state can afford in higher education, even though many a citizen sympathetic to higher education's role today could not easily spell out all the reasons.

Higher education is today so much more fully reported and commented on editorially in the public press than was true a decade or more ago. No better evidence of the importance of higher education to the reader at a level above student athletics, dramatics, social affairs, and other student activities once so predominantly the concern of news reporters and journals, is to be found than the present major attention of the leading newspapers with highly informed, interested and perceptive writers and editors assigned to the coverage of the major issues today in higher education in California and the nation.

In 1959-60 as a result of much debate, discussion, and study California established a master plan for major progress in higher education. Entitled "A Master Plan for Higher Education in California, 1960-1975" it was published in 1960 by the California State Department of Education in Sacramento. That plan had within it certain ideas, principles, and proposed relationships between higher education and the people of the state, and among all the agencies of higher education with each other, both those of public sponsorship and of private character. That plan reflected not only a belief that higher education was and is one of the state's major industries but also that for the continuity at a high level of all the economy the continued support of wide educational opportunity for all qualified youth and of high quality in scholarship and teaching was and is important to the welfare of all the people. Or to put it differently, in facing the future, the state realized that higher education's continued

6

growth, development, and achievement were as they now are a primary task.

At the time in 1960, and for four or five years thereafter, nearly all of the basic premises appeared to have broad popular acceptance and were not subject to important challenge either in academia or the marketplace or political circles, nor in the executive offices or the legislative chambers. Then, for various reasons, criticism began to be evident. Some of this criticism was directed at particular institutions of higher learning or at individuals in leadership responsibility because of unfortunate developments in academic life wholly unrelated to the Master Plan in any of its principles. Or criticism was pointed to the Master Plan as such with reference to one or another of the items in that plan which for one reason or another irritated or was disliked. Then too, the Plan was simply criticized as representing the new *status quo* without any apparent or specific reason other than that "things ought to be different." In some instances of critical comment it was quite clear to the informed that the spokesmen did not know what was in the Master Plan and perhaps had not read the whole of it.

Certain principles regarding the responsibility of the state in higher education are evident to the careful reader of the Master Plan for Higher Education as presented to the California Legislature in January, 1960.

One of these principles was that the efforts in California over fifty or more years to broaden the opportunity for higher education should be advanced further in the direction of equalization of educational opportunity.

Another principle was that California should build even more solidly than before upon the University of California with its several campuses, the already numerous State Colleges, the junior colleges each supported both by its own district and by the state, and the private colleges and universities.

Another principle was that the state has a responsibility only for those persons able to embrace appropriately and willing to seek such higher education. Higher education should not grade down but grade up, with the doors of the several types of public institutions open to receive persons according to demonstrated achievement standards intended and designed to admit to the University or the State Colleges only persons possessed of the ability to make effective use of their respective facilities and

7

faculties according to their defined functions and levels of instruction; and to the junior colleges on a broad base of acceptability recognizing their specially designated range of functions. The private institutions were admonished to keep their standards of admission and required achievement high.

There were other principles dealing with costs, adequacy of faculty and facilities, the location of campuses, greater availability of state scholarships for the very able and needy with the individual student having the power of choice of institution, and other details later to be covered.

The principle which has received outside California the greatest attention, interest, and commendation has been that of promoting the broadest educational opportunity. Inside California steady and ever greater progress towards equalization of educational opportunity as a goal was taken for granted except for a very limited group of extremist diehards who were and are for various reasons against any greater public support of higher education.

As a result of the Master Plan of 1959-60, the State of California advanced further the idea that education is its primary task; that is, to usher in the future with the greatest human promise is its most important challenge. This stands in contrast to older ideas that the state's primary function is negative and not positive, namely to do the minimum only in cleaning up the failures of the past by simply using temporary ameliorative measures regarding individual human and social problems. In California today, considering both public and private institutions and all levels from the kindergarten through the graduate school, education is the major industry.

The magnitude of the problem of higher education in California was in 1959-60 and is now really overwhelming. On this question of size and of magnitudes, nearly all states are involved. California has one of the largest systems of public higher education: nine University of California campuses, eighteen State Colleges, and eighty public junior colleges.

The magnitudes of higher education in California are huge and startling indeed. The facts which follow for 1966-67 show some of these magnitudes.

In the three public segments of the University of California, the California State Colleges, and the junior colleges there were enrolled, full time and part time, over 740,000 students.

In the private or independent segment there were enrolled

over 70,000 students, which with those in public institutions made a total in excess of 800,000 students.

California higher education is an industry of nearly two billion dollars in total annual expenditures, including current and capital costs, in both public and private institutions.

Public higher education including the University of California, the California State Colleges, and the junior colleges represent an annual operating cost to the state of somewhat over $667,000,000. However, their total annual budgets will be over one and a half billion dollars for current and capital expenditures.

Capital annual outlay expenditures in public institutions currently will approach $300,000,000 including $135,000,000 only in state funds, the balance being federal or private, but at least nonstate.

There are to be considered also the millions of dollars, mostly nonstate funds, which will be expended in public colleges and universities in auxiliary enterprises such as residence and dining halls, student unions, and parking, some of this from fees paid by students.

In addition to institutionally administered scholarships, all aspects of student aid in loans and economic opportunity grants, the loan and grant funds available coming from federal programs, the California State Scholarship Commission distributed nearly $6,000,000 for scholarships.

In 1965, I stated, "Clearly these last years have deepened California's conviction that its historic line of direction in seeking to provide educational opportunity for all able and willing youth was the right one. Now the problem is to be willing to pay for it some way." At the present time the convictions of Governor Ronald Reagan and the Legislature are not so clear, and the problem of paying for what is to be done remains.

Educational opportunity is a resultant of many factors: (1) the quality of the educational programs offered (how good are the institutions?), (2) admission policies (how open are the doors?), (3) earlier educational experience (how prepared is the student to enter and carry the course he elects?) (4) the costs to the student of both institutional charges and his own maintenance at home or away from home, and (5) available financial resources (how much money does he have or can he get through work or loans or grants or scholarship to go to the institution he chooses and is qualified to enter?). For a considerable number of students there are cultural and familial factors affecting opportunity

9

which are not quickly changed, such as proper conditioning to the value of education, inspiration to the necessary willingness and discipline to acquire further education, informational awareness of the institutional opportunities available close at hand or at a distance, and a willingness of the family to forego as family income the earnings of their college-bound youth.

For many years a great corporation's television program always ended with the statement, "Progress is our most important product." The voice, together with the face and personality uttering these words so convincingly, has become nationally if not world famous. Today rightly or wrongly, a nonpartisan reporter on the California scene of higher education cannot avoid observing that there is uncertainty as to whether today educational progress is considered our most important product.

For myself, at the outset of this document, I state the conviction of a lifetime as an educator, that educational progress should be, indeed has to be, our most important product or all else will weaken or fail. We will not reach the goals of the civilization we embrace and the business and industrial economy we wish to achieve and further improve if we do not keep educational opportunity at the highest possible level. This conviction must be contagious to prevail; it must become the creed of the leaders of the state outside education, and it must be supported by other than words.

2

NATIONAL EDUCATIONAL THINKING AS BACKGROUND
FOR CALIFORNIA'S MASTER PLAN

THE BACKGROUND for understanding the developments as of 1960 and the years since is both the history of higher education in California itself, as well as the place of higher education in national thinking particularly since World War II. Let us look to the national situation before reviewing the state situation.

In 1947 the Report of the President's (Truman's) Commission on Higher Education was issued in five volumes. Then and in 1948 it became very much a matter of debate. It was an important and significant document, to which no simple analysis of its proposals could do full justice, a forceful statement of certain problems and policies. That Report looked forward to as thoroughgoing a democratization of the opportunity for collegiate education as had occurred in the previous seventy-five years in elementary and secondary education. It asked for provision of opportunity in the next decade or two for a doubled percentage of our youth to obtain collegiate education and professional training. The "ultimate goal," stated the Commission, was seen as "an educational system in which at no level ... will a qualified individual in any part of the country encounter an insuperable economic barrier to the attainment of the kind of education suited to his aptitude and interests."

This Report was of course influenced by the large increase in enrollments in the post-World War II period largely occasioned by the G. I. Bill veteran benefits. However, enrollments included many women and also nonveterans as a result of the high level of national income. In the year of that Report the registration in American colleges and universities was 2,350,000. This Report did not spring in my judgment from a fear as some alleged at the time that there would be a great falling off in college and university enrollments after the veteran registrations declined. Rather the recommendations derived from a pronounced shift which already had taken place in the opinions of both educators and the public as to (1) the requirements of an inclusive educational system in a democracy, (2) the needs of an economic system poised as the United States was then (and is now) at a high level of prosperity, and (3) the importance of education in a political organism concerned over both the moral and technical phases of its world responsibility as well as the security of its total institutional fabric.

There were new views presenting a belief that a larger proportion of our youth should be considered educable and that a cultural contagion had been set in motion by the program of veterans' education which would result in larger numbers of youth desiring and even demanding higher education.

That Report in 1947 predicted 4,600,000 students in colleges and universities by 1960. In 1966, not quite twenty years later, the actual enrollment was 5,500,000, and in 1967 was over 6,500,-000.

Three principal proposals emerged from the Commission's Report:

Tuition fees should be eliminated in public institutions for the first two years of collegiate work and for the third and fourth years reduced to 1939 levels. For private institutions the recommendation was that tuition fees be rolled back halfway to the 1939 rates. Reading such recommendations twenty years later may cause belief that the whole Report was equally as unrealistic, but one can only conclude the writers had only limited conceptions of the economic forces even then beginning their work to change all the magnitudes within the American economy. Certainly the trend of fees, both in public and private institutions, has been up not down. However, the spirit of the document in support of the lowest cost to the student of higher education consonant with the economic realities of cost was to be commended.

There was recommended also a scheme of federal scholarships for use in state-approved institutions, whether public or private, for qualified needy students at varying stipends, the number of such scholarships varying annually but up to perhaps 800,000 in 1960, with competitive graduate scholarships at $1,500 each.

These scholarship proposals did not then gain legislative support but laid a basis in public opinion for later reviews bringing developments in California, several states, and in recent federal legislation.

The third principal recommendation was federal subsidies to public colleges and universities for buildings, salaries, and current expenses. This recommendation at the time brought on a considerable debate with reference to the place of the federal government in financial assistance to public institutions possibly serving to subvert state institutions or to introduce federal control. There was also debate as to the effect of this recommendation on all nonpublic colleges and universities and with reference to the place of private institutions, which would have been doomed if such a federal policy had prevailed.

What may be of some later importance also is the fact that a person such as myself, identified in some capacity with private institutions since 1927 and after 1945 the president of a respected private liberal arts college, should become involved then and subsequently in issues affecting so profoundly public higher education as well as those of private institutions. The reasons for such concern are political, cultural, and personal, but they may serve to reflect the important controlling opinions of the 1950's and the 1960's, and will be a part of a later chapter.

In 1956 President Eisenhower appointed The President's Committee on Education Beyond the High School whose First Interim Report was issued in November, 1956, whose Second Report was filed in July, 1957, and whose final communication to the President was in late 1957. (I had the high privilege of serving as a member of that Committee.) These documents recognized certain basic premises:

"(1) We are concerned, as individuals and as a Nation, with promoting the fullest possible development of the aptitudes and abilities of our population.

(2) Our ideals and the increasing complexity of our civilization require that each individual, regardless of race, creed, color or national origin, have the opportunity to pursue education or training beyond high school to the full extent for which he or she is willing and able.

(3) The needs and demands of individuals and of society in the next ten to fifteen years will require great expansion of the overall capacity of existing colleges and universities and of other

post-high school institutions, with improvement rather than sacrifice of quality.

(4) The key figure in the educational equation is the teacher. Many more teachers both able and highly qualified will be needed. Substantial salary increases are imperative.

(5) There must be a clarification of responsibilities for providing the needed financial support to both institutions and individuals.

(6) The proper role of the Federal Government in post-high school education needs to be determined."

In the Second Report as of July, 1957, after five regional workshops had been held, and much sampling of public opinion achieved, the above premises and principles were reinforced. The Committee recommended that "vigorous efforts be made to remove barriers to the pursuit of education by all talented youth," and that "educational institutions abolish discriminatory policies and practices based on race, creed, color, sex or national origin, where they exist." It was further recommended that "increased public and private support be given to sound plans, developed at the state and local levels," to extend credit on flexible terms at low interest to competent high school graduates interested in continuing their education, that the idea of judicious use of credit in financing an individual's education be popularized, and that there be developed an experimental, federally sponsored "work-study" program at institutions of higher learning to provide 25,000 to 50,000 "notably able and needy students" with appropriate employment at fair wages in the service of the institution attended.

Other measures in assistance to students were recommended, including increased guidance and counseling, increased or initiated state scholarship funds together with postponement of adoption of federal undergraduate scholarships until, after fair trial, other sources should prove inadequate, all such scholarships, state or federal, to allow free choice of course and "reasonable" choice of institution with a cost-of-education grant to the institution (wherever feasible) based on national average institutional costs. Concern was expressed lest no or inadequate supplemental payments (above tuition and fees) would mean that an "attempt to educate more students ... would inevitably lead to a deterioration of the quality of education."

14

The need for planning was emphasized, an expansion of diversity of educational opportunities recommended, but at the same time it was cautioned that while important that educational opportunities be more accessible, this be done without diverting to uneconomic new programs resources needed for existing institutions. The expansion and support of existing institutions "should in general take priority over the establishment of new ones." The Committee strongly recommended consideration of the two-year community college to care for substantial growth in student population and also recommended further study of the opportunities in adult education. These recommendations were supported enthusiastically, particularly those in reference to the junior college, by the California members of the President's Committee (Mrs. Dorothy Buffum Chandler, James McKinney, and myself) as an evidence of California's advanced achievements in the junior college and adult or continuing education fields.

The Committee urged state and regional as well as community planning and also individual institutional planning in order on levels other than the federal government alone there be instituted comprehensive efforts to encompass a markedly increased enrollment in colleges and universities, private and public, without decline of quality of educational program. Also, attention was called to the tendency of an increasing number of high school graduates to seek further education as a result of many influences then evident.

There is no doubt in my mind but that President Eisenhower's Committee's Reports, coming within less than a decade after President Truman's Commission, markedly influenced the popular mind and both executive and legislative personnel to make possible a receptive atmosphere for the California Master Plan of 1959-60.

The Eisenhower Committee had reported the revolution in American education as being propelled by powerful forces such as, ". . . an explosion of knowledge and population, a burst of technological and economic advance, the outbreak of ideological conflict and the uprooting of old political and cultural patterns on a worldwide scale," and hence "an unparalleled demand by Americans for more and better education." It declared "without realizing it we have become a 'society of students,'" called upon "to perform something close to a miracle in the next ten to fifteen years," but the "difficulties are not so great that they cannot be overcome by the American people if they set themselves to the task."

Another study of broad influence on the public mind in reference to public policy in higher education was the product of private not public investigation. This was the report entitled "Higher Education in a Decade of Decision," published in 1957 by the National Education Association, the work of its Educational Policies Commission, chairman of which was Dr. Herman B. Wells, president of Indiana University.

This document properly recognized that one fundamental purpose of higher education "is to help realize the dream of individual opportunity," to enable youth to mature "intellectually, aesthetically, socially, vocationally, and morally." Also was stressed the fact that higher education "has been deeply influenced by the American concept of equality of opportunity," pointing out that the earlier view, namely the presumption that higher education is a privilege belonging to a small exclusively selected group, "has not taken root in American soil." It has been the American hope that "all who want to go to college and are able to do college work should have the chance to go." And as a result "special institutions ... have come into existence to meet career needs in fields valuable to the public." Or possibly to put it differently, the American college or the American university is not simply a transplanted European institution.

Raising the question as to who will go to college, the answer came clearly that "the most broadly representative group ... ever to share in higher education" is already the policy, with "selection on the basis of ability rather than class" and with "abilities which warrant college education ... not narrowly defined."

Leaping such pertinent but for our present purposes not pertinent questions as "what shall be taught?" "what research and public services" shall be embraced? and "who will teach?" the report points out that the individual institution of higher learning can no longer be as was the older European university a self-governing community, in all respects, but of necessity, and for many reasons, must engage in voluntary cooperation and coordination and especially among public institutions must possess state-wide and regional cooperation and coordination.

Reviewing the problems of the immediate future (as seen from 1957), "the American people can finance the expansion of higher education if they so desire," but with a scheme of priorities: first,

16

faculty salaries increases, "rapidly and substantially," then plant expansion, with the third need "the provision of large-scale scholarship funds." All of these dollars were to come from the then established sources: taxes, individual gifts, tuitions, fees, foundations, churches (for private institutions), corporations, and the federal government. As to the latter, "The role of the federal government in the support of higher education is neither clear nor simple; clarification of this role is one of the major tasks of this decade of decision." As to the burden on the American economy, including the responsibilities of the states, "the efforts required" and the "adjustments" were reported to be "difficult and strenuous." How prophetic this was, not only for California but for all the states of the Union and for the federal government! This report, however, stopped short of recommending a broad and inclusive program of governmental scholarships, state or federal, until "the responsibility for full support of public higher education" had been met, as indicated above.

In educational circles and in legislative halls, in the years after the flush of the G.I. Bill and veterans' care had been met, and looking forward to the anticipated waves of enrollment, the debates had gone on, year after year, as to priorities. Should provision for increased space and equipment in facilities, or for improved faculty remuneration, or for increased availability of student aid in loans, scholarships, or work opportunities take precedence? Or what combination would be the wisest planning? The realists favored concern first for facilities and faculties, the idealists, whose warm human motivations had to be praised, pleaded for student aid even if the opportunities provided were to prove less than ideal. However, for over a decade as it worked out, the logic of facilities and faculties as first concerns prevailed, and only in the late fifties and sixties did federal aids to student finance and state programs for scholarships and student aid seize central public attention.

Nevertheless, even in the mid-fifties, and among the membership of the Eisenhower Committee on Education Beyond the High School, there were those who pleaded for the adoption of the veterans' aid program for all students augmented by the Soviet principle of complete support from governmental sources of all students qualified for approved college and university programs. This was based on the doctrine that such full subsidization not simply may have been earned as was the feeling about war veterans but would prove of advantage to the whole society

17

3

THE SITUATION IN CALIFORNIA IN 1959:
PRIOR STUDIES AND PLANNING
EFFORTS IN CALIFORNIA

IN 1958-59 A SITUATION DEVELOPED in California which because of
its dramatic character became a matter of broad awareness both
within and beyond the confines of the state. The trends of
thought and action of the past in California as well as of those in
the nation as a whole came to sharp focus in the tensions and
struggles then made evident leading to an insistent demand for
action.

There had come to pass a phenomenal rate of population
growth which later caused California to be the nation's largest
state, there was a very considerable increase in economic well-
being as well as general prosperity with a rise in per capita
income, and there was an increase in the percentage of high
school graduates and college age youth desirous of attending
college. None of this was kept a secret. The newspapers were full
then as now with the magnitudes of changes occurring or impending.

Competition for dollars, for students, and for new functions,
programs, and campuses was rapidly increasing between and
among the various segments of public higher education. There
was also competition among localities for new campuses with
chambers of commerce, city councils, mayors, and legislative
representatives active in promotion of specific areas or sites for
institutions. The location of a college in a city or town seemed the
assurance of a realtor's paradise for profits in related community
development. Land use planning and profits eclipsed concern
among many for appropriate educational planning with prophetic
insight.

19

After a decade of phenomenal growth in the State Colleges, then under the relatively loose and unsystematized administration as provided by the State Superintendent of Public Instruction and the State Board of Education, it was understandable that these institutions individually and as a sort of system had aspirations for additional recognition, prestige, and status as well as functions, for greater freedom from noneducational supervision such as was represented by the close interest of legislators in the details of budgets, administration, and teaching, for greater opportunity for faculty research and for authority, carrying with it financial support, to grant doctoral degrees. In short, these aspirations, not left unvoiced by some State College presidents and other administrators, were to be satisfied in their minds by transforming the State Colleges into California State University to rival for funds and acclaim the prestigious, long-established (1868), world-famous University of California.

The State Colleges had been a problem in one way or another for twenty to thirty years. With the close of World War II and the heavy influx of veterans as well as the changes occurring in California society and economy, the character of the State Colleges began to change in several very evident ways. From 1948 to 1959 the State Colleges doubled in enrollment. During that same period the junior colleges increased by about 80 percent and the University did not gain appreciably; indeed from one basis of measurement the University declined. As a natural result the aspirations of the State Colleges for greater prestige and recognition, for broader functions and new programs and for new campuses, were strongly voiced. There were changes in the quality of the faculty appointed, and several persons in the leadership of the State Colleges became restless under the continuing influence of the earlier and long-existing image of the State College in higher education circles, in the minds of the electorate and public officials, as well as in their own self-regarding attitudes.

In addition, apart from pursuit of the interests the Colleges had in common, there were rivalries for programs, support, and position between and among the various colleges, some of which reached the level of close contact for support with various friendly legislators.

The State Colleges have had a long and honorable history. The oldest is San Jose State College, which celebrated in the 1967-68 academic year its 110th anniversary. Originally established in San Francisco in 1857 for teacher training it early became known as

20

California State Normal School, and was moved to San Jose in 1871. Like its later sister normal schools its name in 1921 was changed to a teachers' college, i.e., San Jose State Teachers' College. Under the jurisdiction of the State Board of Education in a general way after 1899, but with local governing boards, the teachers' colleges in 1920 were clearly placed under the State Board of Education and the State Superintendent of Public Instruction with a concomitant abolition of the local institutional boards. Thus the Legislature moved in the direction of developing a state-wide system of teachers' colleges, and of course of developing coordination among the various programs which up to that time had been developed. As a result, these teachers' colleges began to wield an influence in teacher education and selected aspects of higher education to which these institutional leaders conceived their functions were related. Their growing emphasis on the necessity of study in the liberal arts and sciences as an essential part of the preparation of teachers for the schools initially at least brought cheers from other segments of higher education. Teacher training was to become teacher education.

It was soon realized, however, this broadening of the curriculum, clearly needed and justified, was to become the basis for a steadily broadening curriculum in these colleges. In 1935 the Legislature renamed the teachers' colleges state colleges, specifically approved the organization of curricula for career purposes other than teacher education by eliminating the course requirements in education for graduation, but continued the stipulation that the primary function of these colleges remained the training of teachers. In the internal politics and administration of these institutions the faculty in education frequently remained in actuality the most influential, and at least in legal concept this seemed appropriate, but time here also brought its changes. With growing enrollments and expanding curricula often rationalized quite effectively as a logical extension of its primary function of supplying the state's public school system with teaching, supervisorial, and administrative personnel from the kindergarten through the junior colleges, the vocational, professional, and liberal academic programs multiplied considerably. Also, with very flexible admission standards considerably below those of the University of California and of a number of private institutions, enrollments continued to grow, and this growth sustained the broader programs developed.

It was small wonder, therefore, that other segments of higher

21

education, including the University of California, the junior colleges, and the private colleges and universities should begin to ask as to whither these State Colleges were bound. In fact, not only were enrollments and academic standards a matter of direct concern but also the potential significance of these regionally oriented, seemingly more politically influential, State Colleges suggested the possibility of a marked transformation of the pattern of higher education in California. Nor can it be denied that the educational philosophies of the State Colleges and those of the University and several private universities and colleges varied considerably, though in differing degrees from one State College to the other. In addition, the depression of the thirties and the uncertainties of a world at war caused broad concern to be manifest.

This is all a part of the background for the many studies of the problems of higher education in California from 1932 through 1959, referred to below.

The University of California in 1958 had elected a new president, Dr. Clark Kerr, then Chancellor of the University of California, Berkeley campus, to succeed Dr. Robert Gordon Sproul, who had been president of the University since 1930. A sense of impending changes within the University had been in the air for several years. The growth in strength of the other campus of the University of California, at Los Angeles, then the only other general campus along with Berkeley having a full university program, and at Davis, Riverside, San Francisco, and Santa Barbara, but especially at Los Angeles, had brought new problems annually. Many UCLA leaders in the latter years of President Sproul's administration were openly critical of alleged unnecessary excessive centralization of authority in the President's office, or of too large authority or preference enjoyed by the Berkeley campus.

The non-California reader should understand that the conception, both in California and outside the state, of the University of California has always been Berkeley. This conception prevailed when there were two campuses other than Berkeley, namely at Davis and San Francisco. It prevailed even after the Los Angeles Normal School was taken over in 1919 to become the University of California, Southern Branch, later known as the University of California at Los Angeles (now the University of California, Los Angeles campus), embracing a program far beyond a normal school or teachers' college. Nevertheless, the University was

22

Berkeley and Berkeley was the University. Today nearly fifty years later, both faculty and students at the Berkeley campus will answer to the query about identification either "Berkeley" or "the University of California" not mentioning Berkeley because in their minds synonymous. This is the theory that only Berkeley is the "University of California" and all other campuses, but not Berkeley, require separate geographical identification. The balance of the University of California in 1964 and thereafter has paid the price of this self-regarding tendency at Berkeley. It has been a kind of academic snobbery in part justified by the facts, and in part significantly myopic and anachronistic.

Also, the reader should understand that the Regents of the University of California have status of long standing of a semi-independent or autonomous character set forth in the Constitution of California, as a public trust or corporation not subject to the Governor or the Legislature except as to extent of financial support. In addition, there is a strong constitutional assurance, along with the public school system, of priority of claim on the state's revenues. Regents, other than those serving ex-officio, are appointed by the Governor each for a term of sixteen years and not subject to removal. The intent of those drafting the constitutional status of the University's Regents was to avoid the potential political intervention in the conduct and governance of University affairs, in faculty selection, curriculum coverage, student life, and general institutional behavior. The day-by-day influences of partisan politics should be eliminated in order to assure that continuity of academic freedom in pursuit of truth and in teaching which has been shown to be essential for intellectual progress. The framers of the California Constitution could not foresee but possibly almost probably had some hint that powerful economic, political or other interests could later emerge which might seek to control, directly or indirectly, the nature of the University's interpretation of accepted truth.

As early as 1956 when the retirement of President Sproul was known to occur within a year or two, one president of a private college in California (myself) speaking about the problems of the University indicated that the Regents in seeking a successor to Dr. Sproul did not know, indeed had not defined, so it seemed, what was to be the post of President of the University for which they were seeking an incumbent. In my judgment, the man to be chosen should fit the post as conceived by the Regents rather than simply to allow the new man chosen to develop the presidency and the internal relationships of the University pretty much as he conceived, even though the Regents would be in continuing counsel with him and might finally approve what the President would recommend.

Whatever transpired, the issues already evident in 1956 had not been composed with full inner harmony by 1959, although there was the expected sense of promise with a new, experienced, and informed president at the helm. Hence, along with an external united front with reference to growth and development regarding new campuses, the University like the State Colleges had its own internal struggles for programs, position, and power, as well as sometimes strained community relationships with nearby State Colleges and independent institutions. This was the immediate background of the University's position as the necessity of composing a master plan for all public higher education was mandated in 1959 to the University and the State Colleges by the Assembly Concurrent Resolution No. 88.

While the reasons for the mandate for the Master Plan in 1959 are found later in this chapter and implied in many other treatments of the problems, essentially the mandate derived from a legislative belief that the conflict among public institutions of higher education had got out of hand and required a long, hard, and steady look in search of reasonable solutions and economy to the taxpayers.

The third element in the situation in 1959 was the then status, general attitude, and problems of growth of the public junior colleges. The junior college had existed since postgraduate programs in high schools were legislatively permitted in 1907, with the first such institution established at Fresno High School in 1910. The junior college as it developed came to lean for financial support both upon the state and the local district. The local district supporting a junior college as time passed became either a high school district, or unified school district, or a specially formed junior college district when the latter became permissible by legislative action.

Up to the early 1930's, the curricula of the thirty-five junior colleges formed by that time were predominantly composed of courses closely paralleling the work of the first two years at the University with administrators and faculty keeping a close eye on University requirements for the so-called junior certificate. However, the educational functions of the junior colleges were markedly broadened by the 1930's to include technical and voca-

24

tional instructional programs intended to be terminal with the close of the fourteenth grade. Thus the groundwork was laid to cause the junior college to become as it has been recognized a truly unique institution for California, as well as one which has increasingly been copied for the programs of community colleges developed elsewhere in the nation.

Since my attendance at Fullerton Junior College from 1916 to 1918 inclusive, for my freshman and sophomore years in fully transferable collegiate and university work, I personally had held and voiced high respect for the junior colleges of California conceived and conducted as junior colleges. Hence, I had some idea from experience and the background of general respect of the place the junior colleges held and could hold in the development of public higher education.

By 1959 there were sixty-three public junior colleges being conducted by a slightly smaller number of districts with a total full-time enrollment of over 90,000 students. By contrast, in the 1967 fall semester the comparable figure was 213,496.

For a number of years the idea was brought forward by various spokesmen for junior colleges that these two-year institutions should be developed into four-year colleges under one or another scheme of financing but almost always with the state to participate heavily. Hence, profound concern existed among both the University as well as State College leadership as to the likelihood of such an eventuality markedly changing their own level and character of support; and the private colleges were almost unanimous in opposition.

These junior colleges conversely were vitally interested in the policies to be pursued by the State Colleges and the University of California with reference to institutional expansion, admission of freshmen and acceptance of transfers, and the financial burden on the state insofar as their own chances of increased support were concerned.

Of course, although in no way directly related to public policy in higher education, except as a constitutional tax-exempt position was enjoyed for all property exclusively used for educational purposes, the private, independent colleges and universities were observing all the developments in public higher education through the postwar period with a variety of reactions as to what was good for higher education as a whole and what impact public decisions would have on the welfare of their own institutions in particular.

25

The politics of planning public higher education in California have often been depressing and outright disgusting, legislators seeking advantage for their own bailiwicks without regard to the logic of probable population increase, future need, or the recommendations of responsible educational authorities or leaders. One example of this was a Senate bill in 1955 to establish eight (at one time it was to be ten) new State Colleges, all but one of these to be located north of the Tehachapis and hence where political power in the Senate at that time was located but not where any sensible logic would dictate. Fortunately, that bill was killed.

In 1958 and 1959, therefore, a sense of insecurity about the future, a kind of fear as to what might happen, was clearly present in each public segment of higher education; and this was seriously affecting the attitudes and concern of the private segment of higher education as these independent colleges and universities thought about future enrollments, faculty recruitment, gift dollars, and possible if not probable impact of all the struggles then evident on the level of public expenditures and the resultant necessary or inevitable tax load on the economy. Clearly all of this had important political significance. State officials cannot long condone needless economically indefensible duplication of facilities and programs; nor can they be unmindful long of major segments of public opinion.

In addition, the private institutions (Stanford, University of Southern California, University of San Francisco, Loyola University of Los Angeles, California Institute of Technology, Pomona College and the other Claremont Colleges, Occidental College, Mills College, and others) happened to have as trustees, presidents, or among their alumni persons importantly placed in influence or in the total power structure of the state so that considerable heed to their voices perhaps above that earlier accorded had to be given. The political strength, existing and potential, of the private institutions had been demonstrated in the legislative passage in 1955 of the enabling act to create the California Scholarship Commission.

As later official reports showed, the private institutions, as to the use of space and even in some instances personnel, according to the norms or standards adopted, had unused facilities. This fact, together with other considerations, undoubtedly played a significant part in causing the Legislature to pass the act creating the California Scholarship Commission calling also for state scholarships in specified numbers to a named amount of financial aid

26

for able and needy youth with free choice by the student of the institution to which he would go and use the scholarship aid provided. (Free choice of institution was recommended in two later official study reports.) This measure had been almost universally supported by the independent, private colleges and universities and was the means then and later as expanded of causing a sustained and increased use of private college facilities and faculties at great saving to the state over against the per capita cost to the state had these same students attended public institutions. This is not the place for an inclusive statement of the State Scholarship plan. Suffice it here to indicate the awareness existing that the load on the state and the citizens of California would have been even larger than those projected in the various studies prior to or later in the Master Plan Survey if all the private institutions were markedly weakened or eliminated. Various legislators frankly said they saw no reason for the state to take off the backs of the students and their parents and of donors, alumni, churches, corporations, foundations, and others interested, the burdens they were for the most part willing to accept.

The California State Legislature in 1959 had before it numerous proposals for reorganizing the structure and control or coordination of public higher education. In fact, there were introduced in the 1959 Legislature a total of twenty-three bills on higher education. Such legislative concern was not without expectation, not only because of the seriousness of the situation, but also because of the many reports, studies, and plans which had been made in earlier years.

Like many other states California has long been concerned about its needs in higher education and the appropriate relationships among the various segments, so that its needs will be met in the most efficient and economic manner. As early as 1899 there was created the California Educational Commission of seventy members to make recommendations for its improvement. In the intervening two-thirds of a century there have been many studies of public higher education in California under legislative authority as well as others by the institutions themselves and under state agencies. A brief statement on several of these intervening studies is included here.

The first of these studies was the Suzzalo Report in 1932 prepared by President Henry Suzzalo of the Carnegie Foundation for the Advancement of Teaching. This study and report came about through the leadership of President Robert Gordon Sproul of the University of California and as a result of the efforts being made in the Legislature to establish regional four-year public colleges and universities under the State Board of Education, the import of which in time would markedly affect the University of California's development. The Suzzalo Report's recommendations included a proposal to place all public higher education in California under one authority, namely, the University of California Regents. The depression of the thirties, as well as lack of agreement, brought little results from this report. One resultant, however, was the enactment in 1933 of a law providing for a State Council for Educational Planning and Coordination, but this agency soon ceased to function effectively and has not met since 1945. The legislation creating it was later repealed. It is not to be confused with the Coordinating Council for Higher Education established by law in 1960 which is presently functioning.

The Strayer Report in 1948, entitled "The Survey of the Needs of California in Higher Education," headed by Dr. George D. Strayer of Columbia University, was generally a reasonably comprehensive study and had considerable impact on educational opinion but received only limited legislative support.

The McConnell Report of 1955, called "A Re-Study of the Needs of California in Higher Education," was a thoroughgoing excellent document which had profound effect on educational and general public opinion in the state and to which the Master Plan Survey of 1959-60 was greatly indebted both for facts and ideas. Also, the 1957 additional centers staff-study, entitled "A Study of the Need for Additional Centers of Public Higher Education in California," was a further precedent careful review and of great influence.

Hence, the Master Plan Survey report of 1959-60 was built on the edifice of fact, analysis, and principles in previous studies plus new data, as well as upon new unprecedented agreements among the several segments as to policies for the future. The Master Plan Survey resulted, as has been indicated, from Assembly Concurrent Resolution No. 88 introduced in 1959 demanding at once (i.e., in eight months) a charting of the course for the future of California higher education, and especially for the period 1960 to 1975. The basic issues were the future role of the junior colleges, the State Colleges, and the University of California and how these three segments should be governed and coordinated to avoid duplication and waste.

The legislative resolution was addressed to the then existing

Liaison Committee, an *ad hoc* body which had earlier been established between the University of California Regents and the State Board of Education for the State Colleges as an agency of counsel and conference, study and planning with a limited staff. The Master Plan Survey team was responsible to the Liaison Committee and was composed of one representative each from the University, the State Colleges, and the junior colleges, plus a liaison staff representative from the University of California and the State Colleges plus a California Junior College Association representative. In addition to these six persons in effect representing public segments of higher education, there was one representative chosen by the Liaison Committee to represent private institutions after consultation with the Association of Independent California Colleges and Universities. The chairman of the Master Plan Survey team, myself, had been chosen in early June, 1959, and before the others above indicated were named, by President Clark Kerr and Superintendent of Public Instruction Roy Simpson, and although some persons of strong tendency to believe in economic determinism considered the chairman a representative of private higher education, he considered himself primarily a representative of the general citizenry as will later be explained.

It is quite clear that the Master Plan team did not start from scratch. It inherited a wealth of material in notes, discussions, recommendations and proposals from previous work. In spite of the later extensive favorable publicity attending the acceptance of the recommendations of the Master Plan (i.e., most of them), the members of the Master Plan Survey team would be among the first to recognize their debt to the wisdom, foresight, and specific action of the Liaison Committee which had been in existence since 1945 and to which the Survey team reported in 1959. Apart from the various studies mentioned, the Liaison Committee had developed a continuing staff of which T. C. Holy and Arthur Browne of the Master Plan Survey were members, and had had extraordinary success in obtaining acceptance and support for its recommendations from the two Boards which had created it and from the Legislature. Furthermore, it had been instrumental prior to the passage of A.C.R. No. 88 in obtaining support from the two governing boards towards helping create a climate favorable to the Resolution's passage.

Also, on April 15, 1959, on recommendation of the Liaison Committee, the two governing boards had declared that no new

State Colleges or campuses of the University, other than those already approved, should be established until adequate junior college facilities had been provided in the areas where new campuses would be located. This was to obviate strong political pressure from districts without junior colleges whose citizens wished to avoid local property taxation for a junior college but who were quite willing to have higher education provided to their young people wholly at state expense.

In addition, both the Board of Regents of the University and the State Board of Education had declared that no new State College or University campus should be established without prior approval of both boards. The two boards had also gone on record favoring state aid for capital outlay for junior colleges whenever state finances might permit it.

All of these declarations foreshadowed proposals later to be formulated by the Master Plan. Along with this recognition of wise action it must be recorded as unfortunate, however, that the position of the Liaison Committee had been weakened by certain actions of each board, clearly of mutual concern, which had been taken unilaterally in violation of existing agreements and before consideration of such matters by the Liaison Committee.

An important evidence of the significance of the work of the Liaison Committee as well as of its staff is evident in the general outline of a Master Plan study which that committee had adopted on June 3, 1959 as a guide to whatever study or survey team might be appointed. This outline involved queries as to probable size of enrollments in 1975, projections to 1975 for all four segments of California higher education and for each State College and University campus, both on the existing basis and as possibly modified by the Master Plan. There were also queries whether admission requirements should be modified, and as to appropriate differentiation of function in the light of "present and prospective" circumstances, and as to a recommended priority list and time schedule for establishing new University and State College campuses, with approximate location designated. There was also a question as to the needs for additional junior colleges both at once and by 1970, and where they should be located.

The Liaison Committee's guidelines raised a number of questions about the estimated cost to the state for public higher education both as to capital outlay and annual operation; and what proportion of the financial costs, capital and current, of junior colleges should be borne by the state.

Also asked was "How many lower division students who would normally enroll in a State College or University campus can be shifted to the junior colleges, and how can the districts meet additional costs resulting therefrom?" The reader should note that no query as to the desirability of such a policy action was written in this question. It appears that in the light of previous reports and discussion in California desirability was taken for granted. Also one suspects that uncertainty as to the state's ability to bear all the costs of the two other public segments as they might otherwise develop even though not yet defined created for many persons an *a priori* favorable judgment on the wisdom of diverting some lower division students, one way or another, to an as yet undetermined number, to the junior colleges.

There were questions as to how much of the cost of public higher education should be borne by the students, and whether the present fee structure should be altered. A query about "what economies can be effected in the operation of the existing institutions?" with the admonition, "consideration should be given to economies in current operation, in capital outlay, and in the use of physical facilities," seemed to invite very careful inspection since there was no self-protecting "if any" clause after "economies." This query really opened the door to consideration of year-round operation and to avoidance of duplication of function or facilities wherever possible as well as to the principle of diverting students to some extent from the most costly (to the state) to the least costly (to the state). To the careful reader then and now these questions as well as the way in which they were worded suggested a high degree of cost-consciousness.

This guide to study contained questions about California's ability to pay for the future development of its public higher education and what were the probable supplemental (nonstate) resources which might be tapped.

The final query was clearly a major one: "What plan is recommended for the organization, control, and administration of publicly supported higher education in California?"

Thus was the stage set for the drama of struggle, of reasonable analysis and discussion, of significant agreement, and finally of strong influence and decisive impact which the Master Plan for Higher Education in California came to represent.

4

THE BACKGROUND OF THE MASTER PLAN'S CHAIRMAN:
NOTES REGARDING EDUCATIONAL POLICY

I OFTEN WONDERED why I was chosen as chairman of the Master Plan Survey. Of course, only President Clark Kerr and Superintendent Roy Simpson could answer that query. I never asked either of them, but in 1965 President Kerr wrote to a friend about my selection for this responsibility in these words, referring to 1958-59:

> ".... when we seemed to be threatened with real anarchy in the public higher education sector of the state, Roy Simpson (then superintendent of public education) and I appeared before the Legislature and asked that higher education be given a chance to work out its problems before any outside agencies sought to devise solutions. We were given one year to develop a plan. After a meeting to discuss setting up a study committee to work on the problems and give us advice, I said to Roy Simpson that I had a nominee for the chairmanship of the committee: Arthur Coons. Roy said that he was just going to make the same suggestion to me. To our great pleasure, Arthur agreed to serve, and it was under his statesmanlike direction that the Master Plan for Higher Education in California was developed."

For me, the story began in an immediate sense in the first week of June, 1959. I was called at Occidental College on the telephone by President Clark Kerr of the University of California to inform me that he and Dr. Roy Simpson, California Superintendent of Public Instruction, an elected constitutional official, had agreed to request me to become the impartial chairman to lead a survey team of representatives of public higher education to report to the Liaison Committee (explained elsewhere) to fulfill the responsibility of composing a master plan for California's public higher education under the terms of the Assembly Concurrent Resolution of 1959 recently passed by the Legislature. As Clark Kerr explained my role I thought of it as not unlike a referee of a court or a master in chancery but in a different sense since time was of the essence and negotiation and active leadership to achieve a plan were required. It was clear I would be under the necessity of trying to get the "warring" factions into sufficient agreement fast enough to fulfill the Legislature's demands.

It is not easy for the president of a private liberal arts college or university to take on the kind of responsibility as well as honor proffered to me. So I asked for a little time to consider it, but as was obvious, time was of the essence in the matter, and the University, and the State Colleges, and indirectly the junior colleges, were against the wall threatened with no or minimal budgets for fiscal 1961 if no or an inadequate or unsatisfactory report were filed by the required date in January, 1960.

There were two Occidental trustees strongly opposed to my accepting this call to public service, one predicting openly in a Trustees' meeting that it would result in a severe damage to my health. (I had had my first heart attack in May, 1957; he was right—I had my second in January, 1960.) I was, however, under considerable pressure to accept.

One pressure was inside myself; I wanted to do the job. One pressure was my inner certainty that if this responsibility could be fulfilled well, it would redound to the good of Occidental College which had in so many ways been my life.

One factor but not pressure was the number of University of California Regents on the Occidental Board of Trustees (then three: Edward W. Carter, Dorothy Buffum Chandler, Samuel B. Mosher; later three others: Jesse W. Tapp, Edwin W. Pauley, and John R. Mage, the latter while president of the University of California alumni). Mr. Carter said to the Occidental Trustees in June, 1959, that if this Master Plan were done well, it would without doubt be a model to the West if not to the entire nation. (He proved to be a prophet.) Neither Mrs. Chandler nor Mr. Mosher interposed objections, believing that I, and only I, could decide whether I had the strength to do the job, but each while eager for the University also had misgivings about the effect on me. Mrs. Chandler and I had worked together on various assignments of the President's Committee on Education Beyond the High School, and she had known of my inability in 1957 to finish my duties within that committee because of hospitalization in May, 1957.

Dr. Kerr and Dr. Simpson had said it would take only two to three days per week, i.e., about half my time. They were poor prophets. I found after acceptance that it took most of my time to read, become informed, be prepared, plan for meetings, conduct them and then remember thoroughly what had transpired. During those seven months of 1959, I kept the Occidental College faculty reasonably informed of what I was doing, not everything, of course, but enough to let them feel a sense of participation, and also to get reactions from some on the major issues.

There is a sense in which it may be said that unwittingly I had prepared the ground for being chosen. In 1955 I had spoken in Berkeley before a meeting of an association of registrars on the need for a dual system of public and private higher education. In October, 1955, the Association of American Colleges Bulletin carried as an article a speech given earlier before that body on "Is There a War between Public and Private Colleges?" In December, 1955, I spoke before The Annual Conference on Higher Education in Michigan at Ann Arbor on "The Dual System of Higher Education." Much of this had appeared in print. However, the record runs further back, an expression of views about which I find few if any regrets.

Possibly, however, it would be useful to review the statements which I had made and the positions which I had taken with reference to public higher education, indeed most of the issues of higher education in the past twenty years.

In March of 1948 and again in August of 1954, I placed myself on record publicly as to the essential necessity, if we would be educational statesmen in our American pluralistic society, of providing adequate support through established channels for both public and private institutions of higher education so that both might work to provide fulfillment of the needs of our people. In 1948 I was speaking before the Los Angeles Bar Association, and in 1954 the Los Angeles Rotary Club. In the latter case I followed by a few weeks a presentation by President Robert Gordon Sproul of the University of California, his address being on public institutions and mine on the future of private colleges and universities.

To the Bar Association in 1948 under the title "Standard Bearers of Educational Freedom," among many other things, I said: "On this question (the question of freedom in education), the first words I would say would be in appreciation of the powerful contribution of the public higher educational institutions to the development of American democracy. We have a great pride in and respect for the large and significant need for public education. I ask no decline of interest in and legitimate support for publicly supported and controlled institutions of higher learning." To be sure, my address was a defense of and plea for support of private institutions but without "inveighing against public higher education." I said further that this is not a case of "either-or" but an instance of "both-and," in thinking about "the effect of social and economic policies upon private as well as public institutions which have already by their fruits demonstrated their scholarship, their democratic effectiveness and their loyalty to the culture of the western world."

In August, 1954, with the title "Whither America's Independent Colleges?" I said, "Let me say at the outset that (in developing the role of the independent, private or church-related institutions) you are not going to get from me any partisan statement that seeks to set up a conflict with public higher education, that seeks to defend as if there were a battle on." I indicated that a few insufficiently thoughtful, too ardent advocates of independent institutions had voiced such views. I declared, "As a citizen and educational leader, I am proud of the greatness of the University of California in all its inclusiveness, of the contribution which it has made to the culture, prosperity, and general welfare of California."

At that time also I said, "Also I rejoice in the high level of educational opportunity and advance to which our farsighted public policy has moved us among the states in the development of the state colleges and the junior colleges."

Similarly, then, I repudiated the viewpoint, already being heard from some private collegiate spokesmen that "public institutions should be repressed so that the independent institutions could expand either in number or size." The incontrovertible facts about population growth were already outrunning the rate at which private institutions could possibly finance increased enroll-

35

ments, and in addition it was evident certain private colleges believed they would lose their existing essential character if any appreciable change in size were adopted.

Clearly, I hope, I stated that the future problem of caring for the new waves of young people in higher education, beyond what private institutions could plan to enroll, had to become a responsibility of the state but that the state's problems of finance and facilities would become compounded if the private colleges and universities were allowed to "be weakened in their effectiveness."

Again I spoke of my pride in our California state system of higher education. "I want them all to be strong and to fulfill their required and essential functions." A plea was made for what has become the statesmanlike attitude as to "the complementary, mutually respectful character" of the dual system of higher education.

In 1955 with reference to "The Costs of Higher Education in California in the Decade Ahead," as stated in a public address before the California State Chamber of Commerce, I raised a series of questions about costs and California's ability to pay:

(1) Are we properly assessing all of the costs of other public services for dependents, defectives, delinquents, penal institutions, roads and traffic, parks and recreation which will have to be embraced along with schools, colleges, and universities which will fall on the taxpayers sooner or later, and impliedly compete annually with the colleges and universities for public funds?

(2) Are not many persons assuming that a mere quantitative increase of the population will bring with it the economic power to provide for all needs, failing to recognize that the composition of that population as to age, resources, skills, etc., is of greater importance?

(3) What are the economic potentialities and limitations of California's economy?

(4) Are we properly assessing the costs of public higher education with some eye to the principle of paying for benefits received? Or as was otherwise stated, should not fees be charged, balanced by adequate scholarships for the truly deserving and needy, which come nearer to costs of the higher more costly level educational efforts, which will be of such great value to the individuals benefited in the form of intellectual capital? (This was a viewpoint regarding tuitional fees at the costly high levels but not at the lower division or perhaps undergraduate levels

which I had held and voiced since I had been a member of the Economics faculty at UCLA from 1924 to 1927.)

A similar viewpoint which I stated in 1954 was as follows:

"That our nontuitional or low-fee tax-supported colleges are basic to our society, few will seriously deny. I have wondered whether every aspect of the very advanced graduate instruction in research and the professions should be available in the University on such near-gratuitous terms. Should not higher fees be charged for the higher work?"

In addition in 1955 I stated that the fees charged by state institutions to out-of-state students should not be less than the characteristic fees charged by other states to their out-of-state students.

Other viewpoints stated in 1955 were as follows:

"As an educator I cannot oppose the ultimate development of increased residential facilities at state institutions. However, I do believe the principle should be firmly embraced that such residences should be self-liquidating, that rental rates should not be established that constitute subsidization of students at the expense of the taxpayers.... On this point of state educational financing I for one am concerned, and shall watch carefully what is planned, and shall oppose as I may be able any state residential program which is not sound finance from the standpoint of the taxpayer."

Also, in 1955, and to avoid waste of public funds, I argued that "with increasing enrollments on the way, citizens have a right to look with disfavor on any activity at public expense which seeks to increase the enrollment in a particular state institution," the point being that "staffs for recruiting students appear unjustified. High school counselors can be fully informed otherwise about the academic curricula available in public institutions. Why should any state institution seek to build its enrollment at the expense of any other state institution? Should it not be enough to be prepared to take those who choose to come?"

In the fifties there were some voices arguing that since the imminent tidal wave of students was about to overwhelm all education and the costs of public higher education were going to be so high, some efforts might be made to repress the force of the wave by raising educational standards everywhere, i.e., even in junior colleges, and thus eliminating the need to cover the costs of some persons' education. This idea, a throwback to aristocratic theories of education I opposed as anachronistic and out of harmony with essential democratic concepts of an open door for development of all personal talents.

Then, too, there were others who wanted standards of requirements for teachers and class and laboratory equipment reduced, primarily to save money. On all of this argument I took the position in April, 1955, before the Orange County School Trustees Association that we faced a new level of the sea not simply a surging tidal wave, and that neither California nor America would accept any reduction of quality in education. I also argued the situation would probably be worse before it would improve because of the transitional problems to ever higher levels but that neither public nor private higher education could avoid holding their sights as high as possible, proceeding to provide equipment and libraries on a planned basis starting at once, of using older teachers beyond retirement and apprentice teachers under master teachers, and of actively recruiting everywhere for the teaching profession. Also, I urged a review of the faculty salary question comparing 1954-55 levels with 1936 to 1940, and indicating the need for added respect for the teacher at all levels by the press, parents, and community and political organizations.

The problem of bringing together in effective combination in institutions and systems the quantitative and qualitative aspects of rapid growth continued to plague our minds in California as elsewhere. In November, 1956, speaking to the topic of "Preservation of Educational Ideals and Standards in a Period of Rapidly Increasing Enrollments," before the Western College Association meeting in Sacramento, California, I suggested the necessity of bold projection of new patterns of higher education and commended our capacity for adaptation. Some suggestions were; "developing a common minimal basis of entrance to college," "raising admission standards in many colleges," "stiffening academic procedures especially after general education and for admission to the upper division and for the collegiate degree" along with "cutting programs in terms of time involved," and strengthening the junior colleges in quality. All of this was intended to be related to "developing clearer conceptions of what we are all striving to do." This address was an appeal to seek the achievement of greater maturity among our students not through administrative prescription but by "full faculty participation in self-criticism in seeking out and cutting out the soft spots." "There is in my mind no doubt but that remedial work must go" pushing back to the secondary schools "basic language and mathematical and scholastic skills"; and on the other edge of the academic spectrum "engage more of the gifted students in independent study, directed reading, individual project work ... but they must not be completely neglected by their teachers as students in independent study sometimes are."

In 1955 and 1956 I was vice-president, then president, of the Association of American Colleges, the oldest of the intercollegiate bodies in the United States, and an organization at the time having approximately 800 members, of which the majority were private institutions. This organization annually and through its elected commissions has given continuing consideration to the major issues facing higher education.

In another chapter is mentioned my participation as a member of President Eisenhower's Committee on Education Beyond the High School. I became identified with the essential ideas of that Committee's Report and as broadly as possible participated in conferences and programs both leading up to the Committee's conclusions and resulting from the publication of its deliberations.

The experience of working with the Association of American Colleges, beginning with one of its major committees from 1951 through 1952, then during the six-year period from 1952 to 1958 as a member of its executive committee, then as an officer through two years, and finally as the immediate past president on the executive and other committees, as well as the other participations on a national level, including the National Commission on Accrediting, 1948 to 1953, the Board of Directors of the Council for Financial Aid to Education, 1953 to 1967, and as a vice-chairman in 1960-61 of the American Council on Education, I count as of very great importance in allowing me to gain informed and reasonably broad views of the diversities in American higher education. All of this experience was of immense helpfulness in the work of master planning in California as well as in the coordinating process since 1960 which has resulted from it.

5

THE MASTER PLAN SURVEY TEAM IN ACTION

APPROACH TO THE TASK of chairman of the Master Plan team in June, 1959, required that some lines of possible direction be set forth. While indicating at the early meetings of the team that we should present only items or recommendations on which unanimous action or at least "no dissenting voice" existed, I knew inwardly without being told that limits did exist as to the possibilities of agreement on many issues. Already, at the April, 1959, meeting of the Board of Trustees of Occidental College over two months before I was chosen as Master Plan chairman, I had reported on the state educational scene and had voiced a note of despair as to the possibility of reasonableness being the dominant note of the near future; but to accept this attitude as chairman of the team would have meant defeat from the start. One had to carry on in the hope that there could be achieved a reasonable solution. The best device seemed to be to proceed not by making proposals as if my mind were already made up but by asking questions. It soon became evident that this was the better procedure to follow.

In the light of these misgivings it seems appropriate to include the following statement from the January 29, 1960 letter at the end of the team's labors transmitting the Master Plan report to the Liaison Committee and of course also, because of its complete support, to the Legislature:

> Despite widely divergent views held by different members of the team as to how higher education in California should develop, the sixty-three recommendations made to the Committee were approved by the team *without a single dissenting vote.*

The membership of the Master Plan Survey team as initially appointed was:

From the California State Colleges: Glenn S. Dumke, President, San Francisco State College; and Arthur D. Browne, Specialist in Higher Education, State Department of Education;
From the Junior Colleges: Howard A. Campion, Associate Superintendent, Los Angeles City Schools, Retired; and Henry T. Tyler, Executive Secretary, California Junior College Association;
From the University of California: Dean E. McHenry, Professor of Political Science, University of California, Los Angeles, who then also was a part-time special assistant to President Kerr; and Thomas C. Holy, Special Consultant in Higher Education, University of California.

At the first meeting of the team the question of private institutional representation was raised. I took the position that, although I was the president of Occidental College, I was not functioning in the role of a "representative" of private higher education, but primarily I was striving to be objective, balanced, fair and judicial to represent the whole people, and that this sort of conceived "role" for me was important because we did not yet know how the whole experience would come off, i.e., whether we could get sufficient agreement. I indicated the day might come when I would have to set forth a "master plan" as my own without full agreement from the team. Hence, it was proposed there should be chosen one representative of the independent colleges and universities.

The seven members unanimously expressed the hope that Robert J. Wert, Vice-Provost of Stanford University, might be chosen. President Kerr and Superintendent Simpson agreed, obtained the consent of the Liaison Committee and also the full cooperation of the Association of Independent California Colleges and Universities, and as a result within a matter of days Dr. Wert became an active, full member of the Master Plan Survey team, making a total of eight.

Several aspects of procedure and relationships deserve mention because they had a great deal to do with the ultimate acceptance of the Master Plan report by the Liaison Committee and the two boards (i.e., the Board of Regents of the University and the State Board of Education).

One of the first decisions to be made was whether the meetings of the Master Plan Survey team would be open to the public or closed. The team believed it would be impossible to carry through the work of planning, of necessity involving the frankest discussions, if every meeting were open and subject to reporting in the public press. I took the position firmly that I would not serve as chairman unless the team's work could be regarded as research and study, and that all meetings would be closed. On this the team was sustained, and no outsiders were admitted to meetings except as invited. Not all persons were satisfied, and there was some talk of invoking the Brown Act, named for former Speaker Ralph Brown, which required open public meetings by public bodies, but no molestation occurred.

Another decision was to establish cordial relations with the Assembly and Senate Committees on Education. To do this Keith Sexton, of the staff of the Assembly Committee on Education, was chosen. He was asked to attend most of the sessions of the team and many of its subcommittees' meetings, keeping selected persons of the two legislative houses informed and maintaining contact with the Governor's staff, channeling back to the team reactions to ideas as proposed.

Relations with the press had to be maintained on a cordial and informative basis. In general, not until the latter weeks of the work of the Survey team did the representatives of the working press manifest great interest in asking for interviews or briefings, or off-the-record interpretations except as coverage was given to certain planned public hearings or meetings with interested special groups. The cordial relationship developed stood the team in good stead in the final presentation days, and the team came to respect the knowledgeability, understanding, and general helpfulness of the press personnel assigned to cover our work.

At one time as the report drew near to completion certain members of Governor Edmund G. Brown's staff asked to attend our meetings or to have the team review its findings with the Governor before the final report. Rightly or wrongly I refused both of these requests and was sustained by my colleagues but did brief these secretaries rather extensively on how our deliberations were moving. Their principal interest had to do with structure and whether or no the Master Plan Survey team intended to recommend a single board, and whether or no broadened functions for the State Colleges were to be recommended. I had felt very strongly that it would have been impossible to keep from the public press awareness either of the Governor's staff in attendance at team meetings or of a conference by our team with the Governor himself, and that some doubt as to the independence and nonpolitical sincerity of the team's recommendations would inevitably follow if either of such moves were made no matter how well intended.

Another procedure was to consult broadly. There had already been set up in December, 1958, a joint advisory committee to the joint staff of the Liaison Committee which was used. Also were appointed various technical committees on (1) enrollment projections, (2) selection and retention of students, (3) adult education, (4) California's ability to finance higher education, (5) costs of public higher education in California, and (6) institutional capacities and area needs. Hearings were held in various regions and with various interested groups, particularly with the junior colleges, private institutions, and those concerned with adult education.

Finally, a precedural factor, internal to the Master Plan Survey team itself was the informal setting up of *ad hoc* committees, each to keep an eye on all the various activities of the team and its technical committees and external relationships. This device proved most useful. For example, Dr. Wert accepted the chairmanship of the team's working committee on junior college problems, and Keith Sexton worked along with him, thus developing within the team's operations a non-junior college expertise to work along with the professional expertise of Messrs. Campion and Tyler. Similarly, other assignments helped all members to obtain perspective on the wide range of topics necessarily embraced.

Admittedly and quite frankly, in commencing work on the problem of structure I had earlier developed a predisposition in favor of a single board for all public higher education in California, a control board of inclusive and extensive authority and power. Although the student population and institutional magnitudes involved in 1932 were very considerably less than 1959, the Suzzalo Report did recommend a single board for public higher education. The idea had long been in the public domain of ideas but not embraced in other reports. (How as chairman I finally came out in full support of three boards with a coordinating council to function between and among them and with private institutional participation should be of interest in the theory and practice of public administration of higher education. This will be found in a later chapter.)

Possibly some further word about the personnel of the Master Plan Survey team, other than what appears in the titles above, would be useful. Doctors Browne and Holy were already members of the Liaison Committee's staff, participants in one or more previous analyses of California higher education, clearly informed professionals with expertise in higher education. Dr. Henry Tyler once head of Modesto Junior College had become in a sense "Mr. Junior College" himself as the informed and effective staff leader of the California Junior College Association, enjoying broad confidence among persons related to the junior colleges and beyond in other sectors of education. Dr. Howard Campion was for a period of years the central figure for the junior colleges under the superintendent in the Los Angeles City School District, and was highly respected in university and college circles.

Dr. Robert J. Wert, himself an alumnus of Stanford University (A.B., M.B.A., and Ph.D.), had been at one time assistant to the president of Stanford University, later an executive associate of the Carnegie Corporation of New York, then had returned in 1959 to Stanford University in the post indicated and also as a professor of education. He had been made vice-provost. Since 1959 he has been chairman of the American Council on Education, president of the California Coordinating Council for Higher Education, a consultant of the Ford Foundation, and in many national and state educational activities. At Stanford he became dean of undergraduate education, then incumbent of an endowed chair in higher education, resigning in 1967 to become president of Mills College in Oakland.

Dr. Glenn S. Dumke prior to his presidency of San Francisco State College had been Dean of the Faculty and Professor of History of Occidental College. An alumnus of Occidental in 1938, he had taken his Ph.D. in history at UCLA and began teaching history at Occidental College in 1940. Promoted to the deanship of the faculty in 1950 his administrative abilities caused him to be chosen in 1957 president of San Francisco State College. Superintendent Roy Simpson told me one reason he placed Dr. Dumke at the head of the list for San Francisco State College was Dumke's strong experience in and identification with liberal arts education as well as his own scholarship, and in recognition of the high quality of the San Francisco State College faculty. In the years since 1960 he has served as vice-chancellor and since 1962, chancellor of the California State Colleges. For many years both while at Occidental College and at San Francisco State College

44

he was chairman of the commission on membership and standards of the Western College Association and later a member of the National Commission on Accrediting. He is author of several books on California and Western American history.

Dr. Dean E. McHenry was a graduate of UCLA, earned an M.A. from Stanford, and took his Ph.D. at the University of California, Berkeley campus. He had taught at Williams College, Pennsylvania State College, and UCLA in political science prior to being promoted to professor in 1950. He had been dean of the division of the social sciences at UCLA and department chairman as well as a state-wide academic assistant to President Clark Kerr. Subsequent to 1960 he was made state-wide dean of academic planning for the University of California and then became in 1961 chancellor of the newly established campus of the University of California at Santa Cruz where he also is professor of comparative government. A widely known author of books in political science, he had participated in studies of South American universities for the Ford Foundation, and in the survey of higher education in the Kansas City area. Also, he had served as director of the Nevada State University Survey.

Some intimations of how broadly conceived were the responsibilities of the Master Plan Survey team have already been given in other earlier chapters. Also, reference has been made to the preparatory outline submitted by the Liaison Committee in 1959, which technically speaking, constituted the frame of reference of the work of the Master Plan Survey. Then, too, there were the specific items of reference within the Assembly Concurrent Resolution No. 88. Reference to the document itself, that is to say, "A Master Plan for Higher Education in California, 1960-1975," reveals the way in which the Master Plan team regarded its responsibilities and dealt with them. A recital of major topics upon which recommendations were formulated or with regard to which material and extensive data were submitted gives more tangible meaning to the work of the Master Plan Survey and of its discussions. The chapter titles of the Master Plan report are as follows:

Structure, Function, and Coordination
Students: The Problem of Numbers
Students: The Problem of Quality
Institutional Capacities and Area Needs
Faculty Demand and Supply

45

Adult Education
Costs of Higher Education
California's Ability to Finance Public Higher Education, 1960-75
Will California Pay the Bill?

A section on conclusions is found at the close of the last-named chapter, and in addition are included in the Master Plan report the actual legislative actions on the Master Plan recommendations, primarily the Donahoe Act of 1960, as well as the report of the Joint Advisory Committee on Differentiation of Function Among the Publicly Supported Segments, as amended by the Master Plan Survey team.

The exact order in which these topics were presented in the report should not be taken to indicate that agreement was reached seriatim upon each before going to the next topic. Nor should it be concluded that the particular order of presentation of these topics and recommendations necessarily indicated the priority of concern or priority of importance of basic principles.

In addition to the Master Plan Survey report itself, and the work of the Joint Advisory Committee to the Liaison Committee appointed in December, 1958, there were the reports of the technical committees established within the Master Plan framework, each of which was broadly representative of all segments and for each of which there was a responsible chairman who carried the report through all stages of discussion, preparation, and final report to the Master Plan Survey team itself. The membership of all such technical subcommittees is listed in the Master Plan report. These technical committees, the titles of their reports, and their chairmen were as follows:

Projections of Enrollment for California's Institutions of Higher Education, 1960-1975, Carl M. Frisen of the California Department of Finance, chairman

Selection and Retention of Students in California's Institutions of Higher Education, Herman A. Spindt, of the University of California, chairman

Adult Education in California, Oscar H. Edinger, Jr., President of Mount San Antonio Junior College, chairman

California's Ability to Finance Higher Education, 1960-1975, Joseph O. McClintic, Professor, San Diego State College, chairman

The Costs of Higher Education in California, 1960-1975, Arnold E. Joyal, President, Fresno State College, chairman

Institutional Capacities and Area Needs of California Public Higher Education, 1960-1975, Lloyd N. Morrisett, Professor, University of California, Los Angeles, chairman

Apart from members of the Legislature or the Governor's office, a total of over 100 persons from state agencies, the State Colleges, the University of California, the junior colleges, and the private institutions, and including secretarial assistance provided, participated in achieving the above reports and the Master Plan report itself. To the best of my knowledge, all services rendered were co-opted with the consent of the agencies and institutions with which these persons were affiliated. Only direct expenses were paid by state bodies, and probably under the rules existing not all of the expenses incurred. So far as I know, not one person received any extra reward or compensation, and this also includes myself since the honorarium (on a per diem basis) paid for my services was not received by me as income but was turned over at once to Occidental College. After all, during those seven or more months my availability for my Occidental duties had been sharply limited. The total cost of the 1959-60 program of master planning was almost entirely in direct expenses and relative to the total resultant and to other comparable studies very modest indeed.

The Master Plan Survey team met in full session thirty days between June and December, and this does not include committee or technical committee meetings and consultations.

6

FUNCTIONS, GOVERNANCE, AND COORDINATION

How THE UNIVERSITY, the State Colleges, and the junior colleges were to be organized and governed, what responsibilities each was to possess, and how they were all to be kept in orderly relationships to each other was the central and most important item for the Master Plan Survey to settle.

Since 1960, as might be expected with a document as inclusive and in regard to which so many interests had been involved, there have been many differing interpretations of what "the basic principle" of the Master Plan was. Some have indicated that it was the principle of differentiation of function between and among the several public segments of higher education. Others have considered it the adoption of unmistakably selective principles of admission for students in the several segments. (One Eastern leading private university president indicated to me his firm belief that this was the fundamental aspect, but clearly selective admissions is related to differentiation of function.)

Others have stated that the basic principle was the adoption of the tuition-free principle for public higher education (although the chairman of the Master Plan team was a strong advocate of the adoption of tuition in at least two of the public segments). Others have indicated that the establishment of an open door for talent, with unquestioned educational opportunity to care for the problem of numbers, was the primary point. Others have indicated that the abatement of conflict between and among the various localities and various institutions with reference to capacities, student enrollment, and institutional needs constituted the element upon which the basis for peaceful relationships could be maintained.

Others have argued that the concern for cost to the state was the guiding principle underlying all elements, but especially the principle of diversion of students to the junior college with a gradual magnification of the role of the junior college in caring for the post high school collegiate youth and the search for lower division academic viability.

While not in any manner denying the importance of these items as a part of the total problem, the judgment of the Master Plan team finally was that the interrelationships between structure, function, and coordination constituted the essential factors upon which were erected the plans and programs devised. Hence, this was made the first substantive chapter in the Master Plan Survey.

The opening paragraphs of Chapter III of the Master Plan on "Structure, Function, and Coordination" set forth the nature of the problem in the following excerpts. "Although structure, function, and coordination are each sufficiently important to warrant a separate chapter, they are discussed together because of their intimate interrelationship. . . . It became obvious that no one of the three problems could be settled alone; the solution of each required determinations for the other two." The agreement that was reached was in fact a delicately balanced consensus among the three public segments and was to be seen as essentially a "compact." The team wrote: "It must be fostered and refined, and care must be exercised that modifications do not emasculate it." It was further stated: "A 'package' acceptable to all segments required compromises." Hence, a frank recognition of the needs and desires of each segment and of relative priorities among them was an essential starting point for the kind of negotiations and extensive consultation that developed.

The organizational control of California public higher education prior to 1960 had emerged basically from the fact of differentiation of function. Elsewhere the position of the junior colleges will be discussed as a separate overall problem of provision for higher education, but immediately it had to be recognized that there was a high degree of decentralization and high responsibility upon the part of junior college administrations to the local districts within which they had been created and from whose tax bases had come the major portion of the support for the junior colleges through the fifty years of their development.

Conceived as a part of the system of public education as stipulated in the Constitution, the State Colleges had a varied history, and while specifically reporting to the California State

Board of Education had been subject to considerable control by various state agencies with regard to functions of administration and management that would normally have been within the powers and operations of a single governing board.

Very early in the Master Plan Survey the question was asked, If the State Colleges were to be given the substantial autonomy for the development of administrative authority for themselves apart from all other aspects of the public school system, that is to say, apart from the junior colleges and secondary and elementary education as comprehended under the responsibilities of the California State Board of Education, where should the administration and control of the State Colleges be located? Should there be a separate board created to administer the State Colleges? Should they be placed under a single newly created constitutionally composed board responsible for both the University of California and the State Colleges? Or should the State Colleges be placed under the existing Board of Regents for the University of California? Furthermore, were there to be a separate board for the State Colleges, should that board itself possess constitutional status with a structure similar to that obtaining already for the University of California and which would therefore possess substantial autonomy from the direct state controls which had been so harassing to the State Colleges? Or should that newly created State College Board of Trustees be statutory in origin? Furthermore, were the Master Plan team to recommend either a new single board or absorption of the State Colleges as a separate system under the University of California Board of Regents, how would the functions of the State Colleges insofar as they differed both as to level of instruction or as to inclusiveness of subject matter be adequately protected and not subverted? And especially did this appear a problem if the University of California Board of Regents were to be the agency of control.

Although many issues were involved, it seems clearly evident that what the Master Plan Survey team did recommend constituted the most effective solution to the problem. Let us allow the Master Plan report to speak for itself, in these words:

> "After the first months of consideration, the Survey Team concluded that three major possibilities for restructuring the state higher education deserved more thorough consideration: (1) a single governing board for both the state colleges and the University; (2) a

superboard over the governing boards; and (3) two
separate but parallel autonomous governing boards. . . .
The first two were rejected and the third adopted."

Actually, in the discussions of the Master Plan Survey team a
good deal of attention had been given to the possibility of placing
both the University and the State Colleges under a single governing board. Some members of the Survey team insisted they would
advocate a single board plan unless the differentiation of functions could be written out in some more secure form than then
existed. Other members preferred stronger coordination rather
than a single governing board. It was continuously being borne in
mind by members of the team that the existing situation in 1959,
being marked by undue competition, fragmented responsibility,
unnecessary duplication, and lack of coordination, called for
strong and effective preventive measures.

The one board plan was the chief alternative to the separate
but parallel boards. The final report of the Master Plan Survey at
the joint meeting on December 18, 1959 of the Regents and the
State Board of Education recommended approval of the principle
of separate but parallel boards of equal constitutional autonomous authority and did so receive unanimous endorsement from
both those boards.

I believe that at no time did a specific version or draft of a
single board plan receive more than partial acceptance within the
team. Undoubtedly some University people thought the Regents
would assuredly or necessarily constitute the one board but with
perhaps some enlargement of personnel deriving from State College representation. Undoubtedly also, the State College personnel conceived of this single board as being wholly new with no or
few carry-over members. And without doubt, all members of the
team assumed that if there were a single board, it would have
constitutional autonomy like unto the Regents.

Quoting again from the Master Plan report:

"The one-board plan was abandoned because it might
result in (1) loss of the benefits of countervailing power
and lead to concentration of enormous authority in a
single board; (2) opening up the possibility of a leveling
effect, without net gain and perhaps with some net loss
in over-all distinction of the institutions involved; (3)
lessening the amount of attention board members could

51

devote to a given problem because of their responsibility being spread over such a huge system, making the board in effect legislative rather than governing; (4) neglect of some aspects of higher education and (5) leaving the junior colleges out of the coordination."

A superboard standing above the existing governing boards in matters of common concern was given consideration as an alternative to a single governing board, with the expectation that that superboard would provide the required coordination. The Master Plan Survey team reflected in its discussions a concern over whether this type of coordination would provide adequate initiative and freedom to individual institutions with the possibility of diversification of performance of assigned function as might be achievable under two state-wide governing boards.

Early in the experience of being chairman of the Master Plan Survey I received many ideas about structure and function. Most of them came orally. There were Regents who at least initially were strongly moved in favor of a single board for all public higher education in California. There were those also who had profound doubts. There were State College leaders and faculty who strongly shared the desire of some of their vocal presidents, one of whom was President Malcolm Love of San Diego State College, for the creation of California State University to embrace all the State Colleges and to parallel the University of California; but there were also persons more often professors within that system who did not share that objective. I remember distinctly a professor in San Francisco State College whom I received in the President's Office at Occidental College who came to see me to voice viewpoints considerably different from those being set forth by his own President Glenn S. Dumke in Master Plan Survey meetings. This particular professor claimed to represent a considerable body of State College faculty opinion (but who knows on such things what is "considerable" and of what strength "opinion" is?) which desired that the colleges not expand upward in functions, not be forced into "research" and be allowed to keep teaching central in function and professional purpose in the colleges.

Three very important reasons, the one administrative, another educational, and the third political caused me as chairman of the Master Plan finally to abandon the earlier held possibility of a single board for the State Colleges and the University.

Consider first the administrative. Already there were under the Board of Regents campuses or programs at Berkeley, Los Angeles, Davis, Riverside, Santa Barbara, San Diego, San Francisco (both the medical college and the affiliated Hastings College of Law), and at Mount Lick Observatory, quite apart from Los Alamos Laboratory in New Mexico. In addition two new campuses were to be established (which within a year or two it was decided would be located at Irvine and Santa Cruz), and the further prospect of two more in process of development by 1975. The task of administration of this complex already appeared staggering, and the pressures for decentralization and local campus autonomy elsewhere referred to were already a challenge to President Clark Kerr of the University.

Already, also, in the State Colleges there were campuses at Humboldt, Chico, Sacramento, San Francisco, San Jose, San Luis Obispo, Fresno, Los Angeles, Long Beach, the Kellogg-Voorhis campus near Pomona, San Fernando Valley, San Diego, and the four State Colleges authorized by the 1957 Legislature, only two of which had been established by 1959, namely, those in Alameda and Orange Counties. The two yet to be established were later located at Sonoma and at Turlock. This system of colleges was sadly in need of coordination with a centralization of authority sufficient to establish a degree of responsible control and supervision together with vigorous leadership which had not for various reasons in those years immediately before 1959 sufficiently come to pass. The administrative task of developing a cohesive State College system was in itself a huge order. It had to be capable of a unified approach to the Governor and the Legislature, thoroughly aware of the importance of the functions assigned to it; yet also it had to be possessed of a sufficient continuum of the decentralization and campus autonomy, already possessed but about to become chaotic if not organized, so as to maintain and develop vitality and creative educational embrace of the tasks assigned. Furthermore, it was believed that four to six new colleges would become necessary by 1975.

The administrative task of combining all that was then in existence as well as that envisaged along with clear differentiation of function between the two segments, already existent and presumably continuing, seemed to be so overwhelming that two boards seemed necessary.

From the educational standpoint, it appeared impossible to protect and secure the respective educational functions of the two systems, i.e., the State Colleges and the University, unless there were two separate organizations, i.e., two boards. The educational and scholarly traditions of the State Colleges and the University historically have been different; in general this differentiation had received the approval of the people of California over many years. Furthermore, the newly agreed differentiation as well as overlapping functions to be found in the Master Plan recommendations had been accepted. It appeared that neither segment could run the risk of having its proper functions and roles as defined sacrificed to the interests or functions of the other segment. Neither segment trusted what might happen to its responsibilities were there a new single constitutional board, and the State Colleges were not willing to trust their future status were their segment brought under the existing Board of Regents of the University.

Finally, there were the political problems and they were mainly three: (1) So long as a single board were planned, whether new or the Regents of the University of California themselves, legislative approval appeared difficult if not impossible because of some already existing and expressed lack of satisfaction in legislative circles over the constitutional autonomy and freedoms enjoyed by the University; (2) Even if the Legislature passed the necessary constitutional amendment, there was the danger of not carrying a favorable vote by the electorate for various reasons; and (3) There was the danger of creating constitutionally with insufficient checks and balances a kind of autonomous political "Frankenstein's monster" whose board and president would conceivably have a potential political influence, throughout the state even though politics were abjured, which might transcend even partisan power. Or to put it differently, with the possibility of community influence in over thirty centers throughout the state, was there not the possibility that a new "center" of political power could come to pass markedly influencing the outcome of elections for governor, other executives, and the Legislature itself?

There is also always the problem of the quality of personnel composing lay boards. For all boards possessing major authority over higher education in either coordination or management, it is not easy to find qualified lay members to represent the public. It takes a lot of time and attention of mind to achieve a sufficient mastery of the problems in question, i.e., really to know what it is all about, and then to develop the basis of judgment. One cannot

54

assume that always in recompense for the prestige of membership this price will be paid. The larger the area of responsibility of a given board the greater the problem of finding qualified working members and also the greater the risk to public welfare.

Another assumption with reference to a single board of control supposedly to replace coordination is that this is the theoretically sound structure, that it leads to a simpler, more direct administrative structure and a clear, untrammeled process of decision making. This is open to question. The problems of central responsibility are many and are not simple. Autonomy would continue to be urged with reference to many items of educational import, would continue to be worked out item by item within the necessary atmosphere of give and take of the university and college world, and all of this constitutes coordination of one kind or another. Coordination is a function which some agency must always fulfill.

The man who gave up the most, who made the greatest sacrifice of authority and power when he did not have to do so willingly but who did so with statesmanlike understanding and good grace, was State Superintendent of Public Instruction Roy E. Simpson. A constitutional and elected officer, he might have tried to hold out to keep the State Colleges under his control. He might have fought the creation of a separate Board of Trustees for the State Colleges or have sought to negotiate a continuing important participation of some kind for himself or his office; but he did not.

Early in the Master Plan Survey he had assured me he desired in no way to stand in the way of the best structure and organization for the colleges and pledged me his thorough cooperation to "get out from under foot" for their good whenever the appropriate agreements had been reached for their future governance and control. Hence, I knew early that one segment would not likely have two voices on this point.

In all frankness, however, I should state that Dr. Simpson looked with misgivings for the sake of the historic, primary functions of the colleges upon the possible development of a single board for all public higher education such as had been proposed in the Suzzalo Report in 1932, and which others had at times supported. His devotion as I saw it was to the State Colleges and their functions as then developed, conceived, and supported in law and finance and not necessarily nor at all to the idea of another state university system. At any rate as I understood him he had more confidence in a new board than the

University Board of Regents, on which he sat also in his constitutional capacity, to fulfill faithfully the mission of the State Colleges as he conceived it.

In the matter of structure and function, as well as requisite coordination, the tension mounted during November and early December of 1959. This was the period of negotiation in the attempt to achieve a "package" that would provide on the one hand optimum educational service to the state and on the other hand would adequately receive support from the respective boards and subsequently from the legislative and executive departments of state government.

Indeed, in December, 1959, we had reached a crisis. Scheduled to report what had appeared at our meeting at Stanford University in early December (2nd to 4th) as firm agreement on functions, structure, and specific plans, I discovered from Dr. Dean E. McHenry, the University representative, and Dr. Glenn S. Dumke, already informed, that the University (Dr. Kerr) was not yet willing to accept what I had thought understood and agreed to. In committee counsels only but clearly and decisively I "blew my stack" to the Master Plan Survey team but principally aimed at President Kerr through Dr. McHenry. Since we were scheduled to make a final report to the Liaison Committee of the two boards for preliminary review on December 7 and 8 in Berkeley, and since the heart of the whole plan lay in the items which now apparently had to be renegotiated, and being personally determined to make a report even if it were only my own, I told my colleagues that I would let the meeting convene at the appointed time on December 7 and spend the first day covering, partly out of announced order and context, the items on which there was agreement. And this is what I did. I told no one what I would say when I ran out of "agreements."

As we neared the end of the first day, all in the presence of the public and the press, I indicated the agenda for the next day, and stated that although unanimity was yet to be achieved on certain points, in any event I would make a report the next morning. Whether as a result of this statement or no, the early evening found President Kerr and Dr. McHenry, Superintendent Simpson and President Dumke, and myself closeted in a sort of "summit meeting" in President Kerr's office in University Hall, the statewide office building in Berkeley. We were now at the summit.

Meanwhile, I had held a press conference to review the day and anticipate the next, and to indicate I would hold a press conference the next morning before the opening of the conference session. In that afternoon conference, asked as to my estimate of the possibility of agreement among the "giants" on the major items, or as one person indicated, "who gets the crown jewels," my reply was in a very pessimistic vein. This went out all over the state to the press and constituted an important setting for the evening's meeting. As we met, President Kerr wanted to know why I felt as I did, so I told him. I thought I had been let down but, actually, he seemed to feel that McHenry appeared to have agreed to too much, or rather, and straightforwardly, he (Kerr) was not willing to accept the structure planned (namely, the State Colleges Board of Trustees and related items regarding authority and functions) and support the proposals in the Legislature and to the public, especially constitutional status for a State College board of trustees, unless and until he had further assurances from Superintendent Simpson and Dr. Dumke especially regarding division of labor and differentiation of functions. Immediately I sensed the strategic value of his previous action in stalling on the University's support to the program seemingly agreed.

Two issues loomed large in President Kerr's mind. From the beginning of the Master Plan Survey discussions President Dumke had argued long and hard for adequate state support of faculty research in the State Colleges, even though initially at a minimal level, and participation as appropriately qualified for the State College faculties in doctoral graduate work. These two items (a) State College faculty research and (b) State College doctoral work were the chief items brought forward by President Kerr for discussion.

At once I made clear that I as an educator had to be in support of opportunity for the college faculties whether on state funds or federal or foundation support to engage in research appropriate to their functions as teaching institutions and under appropriate administrative and budget controls, and that I intended to make my support publicly known. I also stated that he (President Kerr) as an educator also could not fail ultimately to support the principle of faculty research being allowed and supported to some degree in any institution seeking to remain at a level of scholarly excellence even if its primary function were teaching not research. For the moment Dr. Kerr agreed to the principle but stated all details needed to be spelled out. For me this meant

57

no dissent to the principle, and hence I could announce the principle as agreed. The next morning I did.

As to participation by State College faculties in doctoral programs, my own position had been (i.e., in Survey committee discussions) less than sanguine as to how this would or could work out even if the qualifications for such work existed in the college faculties on which I admittedly had some doubts. Some colleges clearly had faculties of greater scholarly quality than others, and no simple generalization was valid. Also, the factor of cost would quickly rear its ugly head so soon as doctoral instruction were added to any State College faculty man's load, no matter how willing professors might be initially to take on voluntarily an added load during a developmental or in their minds a transitional state. Such possible willingness had been expressed by State College representatives; yet no one really believed such an assumption valid or if so, tenable.

By way of review for perspective it should be understood that the discussion of the doctorate focused attention to the relative strength of the several leading State Colleges such as Fresno, Los Angeles, San Diego, San Francisco, and San Jose, which included faculty personnel quality and physical equipment. It was clear that changed academic practices, new personnel, and considerable new money would be necessary to bring departments and colleges to levels comparable to the University of California, but all this was with full respect for the strengths brought forth and for which these State Colleges and one or two others had developed broad reputations for distinguished scholarly work and teaching.

At one time it was reported to me that a University officer had approached President Dumke with the proposal of working to the end of getting San Francisco State College transferred to the University system, and this in spite of the constitutional prohibition regarding such a transfer. I cannot declare this for a fact or claim to know whether this actually happened. It was also reported to me that Glenn Dumke rejected this proposition, and if this has any substance, it is to his credit that he did not seek what some would have interpreted as personal and institutional improvement at the expense of his presidential and institutional colleagues.

I later was informed that indirectly approaches sponsored by the University were made also to San Diego and San Jose State Colleges' leaders, but without avail.

At any rate, I did see to it that the Survey team did discuss the possibility of transferring from the State College system to the University the five or six oldest and strongest colleges and recommending a constitutional change to achieve it. This would then leave except for Chico and Humboldt the newer colleges as primarily undergraduate and limited to the M.A. degree, such as Alameda, Fullerton, San Fernando, Sonoma, Stanislaus, the two California Polytechnic campuses, as well as any others to be recommended for early establishment. No agreement could be reached on this major suggestion. Interestingly enough, it has never received any important publicity, but it continues to be an idea worthy of consideration.

Various alternatives which had been therefore considered were again reviewed at this summit conference:

(1) The University of London idea: namely, the use of the University of California faculty as an examination board for a University degree for which a State College faculty would prepare its students. This had been and was rejected by both Presidents Dumke and Kerr. President Dumke was thus seeking institutional recognition, not simply doctoral work available at a State College.

(2) The appointment of selected State College professors qualified for graduate work as adjunct professors for special service for the University of California faculty and campus nearest to the particular State College and for use primarily as State College students might apply to such professors for advanced work in the professor's field. While considered possible it had no appeal, and this too was rejected. Actually, nothing prevented then or now such individual actions except University willingness and State College permission. Again, however, this lacked the element of institutional recognition and left primary decisions with the University. However, it is still a valid device for using where desired such superior resources as the State Colleges possess.

(3) The development under University of California auspices of special doctoral seminars in areas where State College faculties were geographically contiguous for the purpose of using in such seminars the special skills and knowledges of such State Colleges professors. While occasionally appropriate on an *ad hoc* basis, this was rejected on an inclusive basis for reasons similar to those above, and as not sufficiently an answer to the aspirations of

certain State College faculties or faculty groups. Yet the joint doctorate between University of California, Berkeley, and San Francisco State College approved in May, 1967, in the study and teaching of handicapped, retarded, and other types of exceptional children is an example of such special skills.

(4) The development of a joint doctoral plan. Here the sparks of interest were evident; hence it was pursued for an hour or so.

President Kerr outlined the possibility of such an arrangement if the principle itself were approved. President Dumke said "keep talking." It became evident that a possibly mutually agreeable "modus vivendi" might emerge even though details of a "modus operandi" were yet to be worked out. Agreement seemed in sight. The next question, however, I was forced to ask, on the basis of previous experience, and knowing something of the authority on academic matters vested in the University's Academic Senate, North and South, "Will the Academic Senate approve?" President Kerr realizing the inexorable elapse of time and the impending morning meeting volunteered to consult by telephone with leaders of the Academic Senate at once. (Within the University of California, as in most long established, highly reputed institutions of higher learning, both through historic practice as well as by formal recognition in institutional by-laws, the faculty is organized with power to pass upon many items of academic importance, including curriculum content and the requirements for degrees. In the University of California the title is Academic Senate, and at that time for graduate work it was organized into Northern and Southern divisions. Generally, such a faculty organization elects its own officers or works under designated deans, and defined committees and procedures.)

I returned to my room at the Durant Hotel and nearly two hours later had a telephone call from Dr. Kerr to the effect that sufficient support seemed available to allow a tentative commitment on the joint doctorate, i.e., a willingness to work to see how it could be set in motion. An effort to see how something *can* be done is always more promising than extensive arguments *ad nauseam* as to why something cannot be done. An endorsement of the principle had been achieved.

Hence, the next day's meeting was saved from a monologue by its chairman, or any *ex cathedra* statement which, momentarily attracting the attention of press and public, would have been of little usefulness so long as agreement were lacking.

At next morning's meeting the decisions about the "crown jewels" were announced. The Master Plan was saved, and plans laid to perfect language and details so far as possible for the public meeting of both full Boards (Regents and State Board of Education) for the 17th and 18th of December when Governor Edmund G. Brown would be in the chair. It was at this later time that the report of the Master Plan Survey and its recommendations were fully approved by both boards for transmission to the Legislature as required by the 1959 Assembly Concurrent Resolution mandate.

At the close of the December 18 meeting in 1959, President Kerr and then others graciously paid tribute to me for the successful outcome of the seven months of deliberations. In response I acknowledged the debt of the whole state, its people, and its government to the members of my team and all the persons who had assisted. And I went further possibly than was called for. Dr. Kerr had referred to the whole report as the Coons plan. I indicated that the total resultant came from no one person, that all my team and both he and Dr. Roy Simpson also deserved high recognition. Then addressing Governor Brown who was still in the chair and to whom one of the press had directed a query as to whether he would support the whole action of these two days in the Legislature, and having received a reply of only partial commitment, I stated that if he, Governor Brown, would support this plan fully in the forthcoming legislative sessions, we would all forget about calling it the Coons plan and it would become the Brown plan. At any rate, I am glad the Master Plan is known by its real name and does not bear the name of any individual, because truly I believe that the credit for the successful completion of the Master Plan belongs to more than any one person. However, *Time* Magazine gave the credit to President Clark Kerr (a cover story, October 17, 1960) with no mention of Dr. Roy Simpson who certainly deserved mention. *Time*'s article had, however, a paragraph or two of comments about my part in it all.

Hence, as outlined, a kind of breakthrough was finally achieved in mid-December, 1959, when the representatives of the State Colleges and the University finally were able to agree on the general terms of a compact designed to settle the outstanding problems of the machinery of government, division of labor, and coordination, and from which emerged the idea of a coordinating council for higher education, later to become statutorily created.

The Survey team was convinced that if this compact were put into effect, it would engender efficient and economical operation of all three segments of public higher education, declaring, "California simply must put its higher educational house in order," and the private segment could move forward to embrace its opportunities and accept its responsibilities with greater assurance than had theretofore been true.

Whether or no all that was anticipated to be achieved has been achieved must be the subject of other portions of this study. However, it must be recognized now years later that the intervening period of time has provided in hindsight a certain awareness of the efficiencies in foresight then possessed, while at the same time it has yielded actual experience capable of being carefully weighed, dealing with the situation since 1959.

The Master Plan team having reached finally a balanced statement of differentiation of functions to which there was unanimous agreement, believed that this statement of functions should be written into the Constitution, and that it should not become solely a matter of statutory action. My own profound belief was that unless there were the greater degree of protection provided by the Constitution against sudden change in the functions of one or more segments, such as might possibly result from a strong political action expressive of either the State Colleges or the University, the possibility of achieving stability in public higher education in California would be markedly reduced. Furthermore, there would be a stronger arm existing in the possession of the coordinating council for higher education if, given the task as it likely would be of interpreting and making decisions with reference to differentiation of functions, its statement of functions were written into the Constitution.

In the early months of 1960 things in the Legislature looked bad for important provisions of the Master Plan. In mid-March in the Senate Committee on Education, Senate George Miller (D–Martinez) made clear his belief that the Legislature was unwilling to give up control of the State Colleges, stating that this was a general view in both Assembly and Senate. To me, then ill, and unable to participate in the struggle at Sacramento to have the Master Plan accepted as written, this seemed like a mortal wound to the Master Plan. As I reflected on the situation at the time and then coupled what happened initially with what happened finally, I realized that legislative politics were beyond me; they still are.

Senator Miller now receives among others, but in an especial way for himself, great credit for the Donahoe Act, for the establishment in law of the Master Plan. Yet initially he proposed taking out of the then proposed constitutional amendment many of the powers of the proposed new board of trustees for the State Colleges, favored taking out the coordinating council, then proposed adding three general public members to it, and also favored no specific indication of how the University should be represented, with the idea that all of these proposals should be cared for by statute. The Miller amendments were voted upon favorably by the Senate Committee but only after a masterful defense by Senator Donald Grunsky (R—Watsonville) of the Master Plan proposals themselves, particularly that of constitutional status. To him personally I shall always be grateful, because he sensed what the Master Plan was seeking to do in developing genuine freedom for the State College segment of higher education.

The situation in which the State Colleges were left by the proposed Miller amendments was extremely difficult. The really powerful board of trustees as provided by the Master Plan would not come to pass. The substantive elements which might go in the Constitution, except for functional differentiation, were reduced to practically nothing. The very carefully forged balance of interests would be broken. The possibility of placing the whole fabric of understanding and agreement as we had conceived in the Constitution was down the drain. The Legislature in its battle for its own prerogatives and powers was close to condemning the state of California to continued struggle over the powers of the State Colleges which otherwise would have been relatively frozen in the Constitution. It seemed to me that the Master Plan was gone. I knew that the State College presidents were ready to arm and mobilize. I knew that President Malcolm Love of San Diego State College, one of the strongest of the presidents, was not enthusiastic about the differentiation of functions compromise and especially the joint doctorate proposal. I knew also what had been prior to the Senate Committee's actions the votes of the faculties of the various State Colleges, with Alameda, Chico, Humboldt, San Fernando Valley, San Francisco (only four negative votes in the faculty), San Jose (only one negative vote in that faculty), and Orange County overwhelmingly in favor of the Master Plan provisions, with Los Angeles and Sacramento State Colleges voting against the Plan, and with Long Beach and San

63

Diego yet to vote and report. I knew the feeling even before this faculty vote that there was a danger the Legislature would prove to be pro-University and anti-State College; and this is what really was happening.

Even a last-minute effort from the Liaison Committee, which met in emergency session to attempt to salvage as much as possible of the conceived Master Plan, pleading at least for personnel controls for the proposed new State College board even if of statutory origin, did not receive much hearing. There was considerable State College sentiment to support a pullout of the impasse by calling for continuing interim study.

Finally, Senator Hugo Fisher (D—San Diego) proposed an amendment which really was the *coup de grace*. This was to remove from the constitutional amendment proposal just about everything else remaining, principally the functional differentiation, arguing that if the Legislature did not wish to divest itself of control of the State Colleges, then it should not place the functions of the Colleges in the Constitution but retain control of that aspect as well. This appeared reasonable to all legislators at that moment, but it marked a failure to bring to an end the conflict over functions. Perhaps there were State College presidents who wanted it that way, striving to keep flexible for future legislative action, and hence for their own later political influence, the range of functions for the State Colleges. It seems incredible that any responsible State College leadership would have been in favor of the original proposals and amendments of Senator Miller, but not impossible or incredible that there was such support for Senator Fisher's action.

Indeed, in an address at the Chicago Conference on Higher Education in March, 1962, Dr. Lyman Glenny, of Sacramento State College in speaking on "The New Administration of Higher Education in California," pointed out the political influence of State College personnel in 1960 in the Legislature's considerations. He stated, "Differential functions and the protection which the university wanted were also provided by legislation. However, in taking these actions the legislators were greatly encouraged by various individuals and groups of faculty in the state college system who feared that a new autonomous governing board might void many of the rights and privileges that had been wrung from the old State Board of Education and the various state agencies. They also opposed the freezing of state college functions into the constitution at the very time when faculty

64

research, professional curriculums other than education and granting of doctors degrees seemed within reach through legislative action. Unlike the chief administrators, the college faculties were unwilling to bargain away any share of these aspirations for full university status merely to obtain a governing board with constitutional autonomy."

The net result, therefore, was that the entire program of the Master Plan became lodged in statute in S.B. 33 which was Senator Miller's bill and included by mutual agreement with Senator Fisher the allocation of functions provisions for the State Colleges of the Master Plan. This is the bill that passed the Senate, and became in effect the Donahoe Act after Assembly ratification. Hence, everything that really counted was put in statute rather than in the Constitution where it ought to have been, the State Colleges were left still politically controlled as the legislators wanted, and the field left open for further battle over the functions of the State Colleges. With all my respect for the abilities of certain legislators such as Senator Miller and Senator Fisher, as well as my personal friendship, I would be less than honest were I not to place on them and their colleagues, including Assemblymen, and not on so-called weaknesses of the Master Plan, the responsibility for what has transpired since 1960 in continuing pressure of the State Colleges for the doctoral degree, and in other functional debates.

When S.B. 33 was passed by the Senate, it was sent to the Assembly on March 29, 1960. The bill was assigned to the Assembly Education Committee, and the bill was immediately set for a hearing on April 4. Several members of the Assembly Committee had amendments to the bill which they planned to introduce. In order to expedite the passage of the bill, the Chairman of the Committee, Assemblywoman Dorothy M. Donahoe, requested that all amendments to be considered be given to the staff so that multiple copies of the proposals could be made and would be in front of every member of the committee at the time of the hearing. This was a move to forestall the adoption of some amendments and then sending the bill out for reprint before final action could be taken.

To the best of my memory, there were four sets of amendments: (1) one by Assemblyman E. E. Elliott to provide some protection for vocational education in the junior colleges (defeated); (2) some technical amendments by Carlos Bee (adopted); (3) amendments that were sponsored by the California Civil

Service Employees Association that would have transferred those employees currently in state service primarily working on State College matters to the new State College Trustees (defeated); (4) that section of the Act regarding State College functions— "Presently established two-year programs in agriculture are authorized, but other two-year programs shall be authorized. . . ." (adopted).

On the morning of April 4 it was decided that Dorothy Donahoe was not well enough (she had become ill over the weekend) to chair the hearing of the Assembly Education Committee. Vice Chairman Charles Garrigus (with the help of Keith Sexton) took over and chaired the committee in a four and a half hour hearing. Dorothy Donahoe died about an hour following the close of the hearing.

The bill was referred to Ways and Means. Amendments were included to provide funds for the Council and the Trustees.

On April 5 the bill was heard and voted on the Assembly floor. At Senator George Miller's request the bill was amended to become the "Donahoe Higher Education Act."

Considering the later emergent political influence of Jesse Unruh, I do not remember his playing any specific role publicly, or even behind the scenes; instructions were given, however, to keep him fully informed.

Regrettably, at the time in 1960 but not since, some State College persons voiced their belief that the University had got just what they wanted, namely a weaker, dependent status for the State Colleges. I did not believe this then nor do I now, because the University also lost security by what transpired. I hope someday some research student of the legislative process inquires into not only the influence of State College presidents on what transpired but also on the activities of the University's representatives. Possibly there were some persons identified with the University, even though I was assured if so no one of consequence, who believed it would be advantageous to the University not to have the State Colleges like the University in the Constitution as a public corporation, and who preferred the statutory rather than constitutional resultants. If this was true, they too if involved directly must share in bearing the responsibility for the continuing conflicts over functions and status which have come about since 1960.

The new and separate Board of Trustees for the rapidly expanding system of State Colleges to transfer them from the State Board of Education was set up in July, 1961. In a sense for the first time a system of State Colleges existed in law and in fact. This was to achieve a needed centralization and responsibility within an evident existing decentralization and diffused responsibility. And there had been an oral recommendation also that for the University the trend in decentralization to balance an already existing centralization should continue. The University will be discussed later.

As indicated the Master Plan had recommended constitutional status as a public trust or corporation for this Board of Trustees for the State College system to be parallel in status to that already enjoyed by the Regents of the University of California for the University. The Legislature chose not to give the State Colleges such constitutional status and hence not to refer such to a popular vote; hence the State Colleges' Trustees Board became only statutory in origin. Probably, the feeling of leading legislators about such constitutional independence was strongly influenced by the dissatisfaction or disenchantment of some of them regarding the University's status. Also, there was an unwillingness to give up a continuing detailed voice on the colleges which the Legislature had exercised for so long. A Chancellor for the State Colleges and a state-wide administration under him and the Trustees became statutorily a new administrative operation to replace but also to go beyond the old State Board of Education which had theretofore been responsible. Even such a board would reduce to some degree the prerogatives real or assumed of legislators.

The results since 1960 have not been wholly harmonious. Some of the State Colleges had already developed their autonomous status so far under the old State Board of Education and the State Superintendent of Public Instruction, neither of which could spend much time in supervision, that their presidents and faculties have not always taken kindly to the measures of Chancellor or Trustees necessary to develop something like a system, something like central responsibility and central representation. Some rather acrimonious public criticism has been evident at times, emanating from faculty or student groups and in an instance or two, presidents.

By 1962, after the first State Colleges Chancellor, Dr. Buell Gallagher, resigned, he was succeeded by Dr. Glenn S.

Dumke. Dr. Lyman Glenny, a well-informed professor of government and observer of administration and coordination, of Sacramento State College, who in that year became an associate director of Illinois' coordinating council, was quoted by Leo Rennert, then an education editor of the *Sacramento Bee,* to the effect that the new chancellor would be involved in "a three-way power juggling act with the faculty, the campus presidents, and the trustees." Glenny also predicted, wrote Rennert, that although faculty protests had been the most publicized of his problems, "the potential challenge of the presidents to Dumke's decision-making authority may be just as significant a factor."

The case made by the Master Plan report for the Trustees to have autonomous authority and responsibility in financial management for the State College system was therefore *ab initio* not fully accepted and continues in part a moot issue, but less so with each succeeding year. The pressure of the Department of Finance and of legislators continues in spite of efforts continuously being made for changing the trend to give the State Colleges Trustees such authority and responsibility. Probably such status will never be achieved satisfactorily to place a higher wall between capitol and campus until constitutional status is accepted by the Legislature and the people. In my judgment the current Constitution Revision Commission headed by Judge Bruce Sumner and the Joint Legislative Inquiry on Higher Education headed by Speaker Jesse Unruh cannot escape a decision on this issue in the very near future.

Of course, reflection at the time and subsequent events have shown that all was not lost. The fiscal and personnel positions of the State Colleges were improved somewhat even though not sufficiently. The State Colleges board did come into existence and the stature subsequently achieved under this new board and its chancellors and staffs has been remarkable. The State Colleges thought for a few weeks in spring, 1960 that their position was going to become worse than it had been before the Master Plan, but it was improved and there was created a framework for common action and for responsible leadership.

The full responsibility of the Master Plan team to handle the questions of structure, function, and coordination could not have been embraced had there not been a plan for a coordinating council. The Master Plan recommended a coordinating council of twelve (three each from the junior colleges, the State Colleges, the University, and the independent institutions). The Legislature in its wisdom in passing the Donahoe Act added to the membership three persons representing the general public to be appointed by the Governor.

The Master Plan concept of a coordinating council, with no general public representatives, but with three members each from the three public higher education segments and three from the private institutions, was labeled at the time by some political scientists as a "special interests" council. It was likened to government regulatory bodies in public utilities or industries which have often become representative of special interests and as such to be spurned as a matter of public policy on the doctrine that the public interest is not likely to be discovered on the basis of a compromise of special interests. In the case of the coordinating council projected it was being assumed by these political scientists that the only logical resultant would be compromise of otherwise special interests and no genuine search for the overriding public interest. The Coordinating Council as created had three appointed members from the general public, and therefore this council was not wholly a "special interests" council. In my judgment the record of the Coordinating Council shows that on net balance it has not been a mere "special interests" council.

Further evidence of the attitude of the State Colleges after the Master Plan legislation took effect was to be found in the initial positions of the State Colleges' representatives taken in the Coordinating Council. The Master Plan was not Holy Writ, it was not like the Ten Commandments, it was not a Mount Sinai version of the laws of God. Some such language was on the lips of Dr. Don Lieffer, onetime secretary to Governor Brown, a professor of San Diego State College and an early central administrator of the State Colleges system, in early Coordinating Council meetings.

So also a little later with the new Chancellor of the State Colleges, Dr. Buell Gallagher. Here was a man prepared to fight. I had dinner with him as a guest of a State College trustee on the first night he and his wife were in California. On the way home I voiced to my wife my misgivings about his attitude.

At the beginning the State Colleges' view seemed to be that the Master Plan was "just another survey of higher education" in the long California scene, a document which though statutorily enacted was subject to revision if possible. It seemed to me that the interpretation of the Master Plan by the State Colleges threatened that the Master Plan was not to be lived up to in spirit as well as in the letter. So, as is my wont, I spoke my mind. The

State College position regarding the Master Plan began to take on at least vocal acceptance and initial cooperation and compliance only with the selection as State Colleges Chancellor of Dr. Glenn S. Dumke, himself one of the eight Master Plan Survey members, who succeeded Chancellor Gallagher in 1962.

It was truly a great disappointment to me that the Legislature did not create the State College Board of Trustees through a constitutional amendment, but rather only through statutory action. As a result, the relationships within the Coordinating Council which was provided for by that Act between and among the University, which was in fact a constitutional body, and the State College Board of Trustees, together with the State Board of Education and whatever relationships it might bear for the junior colleges, were rendered less easily embraced than would have been true had the State College Board been given constitutional authority. In the plan, the proposed coordinating council was to have advisory functions to review operating budgets and capital outlay requests, to interpret as indicated heretofore the functional differentiation between public segments, to study the needs of the state for new facilities and programs, and as an advisory body to have the authority to advise the Regents, the State College Trustees, the Governor, the Legislature, and other appropriate state officials regarding all of these matters.

The success which the Coordinating Council for Higher Education has had in the period since 1960 when it was formed has depended not only upon the degree of cooperation and goodwill existing between and among all of the members thereof, but also upon the fact that very capable directors and technical staff have been in charge of the responsibility of gathering data, of bringing to bear available information, and of making recommendations which have clearly not been dictated by segmental domination. In general, the acceptance rate of Council recommendations has been high. In my personal judgment, the Coordinating Council would have been a failure had there not been the functioning of an impartial director and staff, and had there not been the courage which has been manifested to portray the basic and essential character and nature of the problems involved.

Also, in my judgment the Coordinating Council has been strengthened by the Legislature's wisdom in adding in 1965 three more, making a total of six, representatives of the general public to the membership of the Council, making the Council a total of eighteen members. Much, of course, depends in the Council as in the various other boards on the quality and behavior of gubernatorial appointments.

On the matter of centralization versus decentralization, no specific action was recommended to the Regents in the Master Plan report as such as to the University of California or the policies of President Clark Kerr, due to the strongly expressed opposition of University representatives. There was, nonetheless, much oral comment on the need for careful balance between the decentralization desired by nearly all campuses as an offset to the once high centralization under President Robert Gordon Sproul as well as for the centralization necessary to maintain Regental ultimate authority and responsibility. In 1959-60, therefore, discussion of the State Colleges plan inevitably focused much attention on the University of California. Already by 1959, President Kerr and the Regents had made some moves to decrease the degree of centralization already in existence, and this trend continued but not to the degree desired by some campus chancellors and faculties or some Regents.

In 1964 autonomy received a strong push from an unexpected source. Most readers are aware of the student riots, demonstrations, and participations, including both on-campus and off-campus disturbances, at the University of California, Berkeley campus, beginning especially with the opening of the fall term of 1964. The Free Speech Movement and its 1964-65 leader Mario Savio made headlines throughout the world. In early 1965 the confusion was compounded by the addition of the Filthy Speech Movement, less inclusive than the other contemporaneous F.S.M., but of profound influence.

Both these movements and also subsequent developments greatly affected the University's personnel, organization, and financial support in the administrations of both Governor Brown and Governor Reagan.

One is tempted to write at length on the small-scale but truly upsetting "rebellion" or "revolution" or at least rule and convention defying outbreak in the academic world, which the Berkeley situation was, but to do so is outside the main context of this book. It is, however, one of the major facts in the whole story of higher education today. Only a few highlights may be mentioned which affected issues germane to this document. The controversies with students brought into focus the problem of the relationship of the chancellor of the Berkeley campus and the president, Dr. Clark Kerr, whose office in Berkeley in University Hall where the state-wide administration is located was across the street from the Berkeley campus. The Berkeley chancellor since 1961 had been Dr. Edward W. Strong. He was virtually made a scapegoat in late 1964 for actions in which he was not alone at fault but for which the Regents and President Kerr in not clarifying or changing rules and procedures must also bear some portion of blame. Then Martin Meyerson succeeded Dr. Strong as acting chancellor but later left to become president of the University of Buffalo; and he was followed by Dr. Roger Heyns who was brought from the University of Michigan. In my judgment, the degree of intervention or participation in the crisis if not day-by-day then week-by-week by President Kerr would not have been tolerated at the University of California at Los Angeles nor probably at most other campuses. The campus chancellor's position at Berkeley was undermined and as a result required redefinition and clarification for all campuses.

In my judgment also, the faculty at Berkeley manifested a lack of responsibility, a failure to cooperate with the administration in achieving reasonable discipline or solutions to student problems of an extreme character, a failure to police its own membership to the end of its responsibility to the people, and a sensitivity bordering on outright distrust in reference to the Constitutional authority of the Board of Regents.

Furthermore, the resignation to the press, or more precisely the announcement of an intention to resign at the next Regents' meeting, by President Kerr and Chancellor Meyerson on March 9, 1965 represented a serious mistake in judgment, even if it is recognized that at the next Regents' meeting President Kerr was induced to remain. Later, and before the famed January, 1967 dismissal, a testing of President Kerr's continuance as president did come and in this instance he was continued.

One must be naive indeed to be unable to see a close connection between this series of events all heavily charged with emotion and the resultant political developments of 1966, the crises in budgetary finance with both Governor Brown and Governor Reagan, and the questions of the University's decentralization and the place of the Regents and the President in overall governance.

The struggles on questions of centralization and decentralization within the University of California in recent years are now familiar to many. The Byrne Report to the William E. Forbes Committee of Regents, which was one resultant of the University

72

of California controversies of 1964-65, in the spring of 1965 recommended and urged a great increase of autonomy for the nine campuses, a degree of autonomy beyond that which had been acceptable to the Regents as a whole or to President Clark Kerr. (Jerome C. Byrne, an attorney of Beverly Hills, had been retained for this special study.)

At their July, 1965 meeting, the University's Regents approved in principle proposals by President Kerr for further decentralization of Regental and administrative authority to Chancellors beyond what theretofore had existed, but apparently not so extensive as the Byrne Report recommended. President Kerr's recommendations were chiefly a formalization of then existing practice; and the eight areas in which this decentralization was to function were nonacademic personnel, academic programs, administrative personnel, admission, business services, public ceremonies and recognitions, student housing and other loan construction projects, and summer sessions. A number of other areas of responsibility were left at that time undecided. President Kerr clearly believed the extent of decentralization already in effect exceeded what the Byrne Report stated the situation to be. At any rate a speeding up of the rate and process of decentralization beyond that evident prior to the controversial year of 1964-65 was set in motion.

In 1966 the University of California issued a document entitled, "Development and Decentralization: The Administration of the University of California, 1958-1966." As President Clark Kerr wrote to me personally, "This is what has been called 'no progress.'" In this document there is a foreword quoting from President Kerr in April, 1962: "The University has, over the past several years, undertaken the first major reorganization in its history. But this is not the end of the story. Organizational forms should always be subject to further study. They should survive only as they serve well the purposes of the institution. They should be changed whenever the change will be beneficial to the University." In this document the reorganization of the University in the period covered was reviewed in two major phases: the first primarily concerned with the transfer of personnel from the University-wide office to the campuses, and the second primarily with the transfer of authority and responsibility from the Regents to the administration.

No simple summary of this document is possible. However, it was declared that three central policies are fundamental to the organization of the University: (1) There will continue to be one University of California as provided in the Constitution of the State of California, (2) the Board of Regents will retain its historic position as the final governing authority of the University, and (3) the University will continue to support and be guided by the Master Plan for Higher Education, with five basic instruments of University government to sustain and implement these policies: (1) the academic plan, (2) the long-range physical development plan, (3) the fiscal plan, (4) the capital outlay program, and (5) the operating budget. In addition there was a declaration which was fully approved, "Each campus is encouraged and aided by the University to develop its own personality, its own style, its own character, its own sense of destiny," but of course all of this was within the review and approval of the Board of Regents, with "the whole University" to be "united in purpose and basic principles" such as standards for faculty and for admission of students.

As a result of many developments, including all that had occurred up to 1966, the Board of Regents has become less an administrative board and more a policy board, and the University as President Kerr indicated has become less a monolithic structure and more pluralistic in character.

In my judgment, the answers are not all in. President Kerr saw the need for "more intensive review of the decentralization of authority and responsibility at the campuses, in both administrative and academic matters." Before I left the presidency of Occidental College in June, 1965, and somewhat after the strong thrust of the Byrne report for autonomy if not independence for the University campuses, and after I had heard one University campus Chancellor declare himself in the presence of many persons (I would name him but he may since have regretted his statement) that there should be nine universities rather than one, I stated to the Occidental College faculty that there existed real danger that there would no longer be a single set of University standards, which through decades had influenced all higher education in California, but now nine, and then ten and eleven and maybe twelve. I declared to them that with all our academic tendency to regard highly the possibilities of autonomy and diversity we in private higher education could not sit by calmly and observe bench marks possibly destroyed, and that I for one intended to continue for the sake of both the state and the academic world to struggle for an unquestioned centrality of

74

responsibility for all elements of the University of California no matter how many departures of personnel from administration or faculty should become inevitable. There cannot be many presidents, only one; nor many Boards of Regents, only one, for the University of California. Yet many differing relationships may exist within such a structure largely dependent on the persons involved and the scheme of organization developed.

In this connection the events of 1964, 1965, and 1966 lent some point to some words written by McGeorge Bundy* regarding the historic controversy of Woodrow Wilson as president of Princeton University with Dean West of the Princeton Graduate School, which related, as Bundy points out, to the then failure of the Princeton Trustees to be clearheaded as to their relationship to the President and to his subordinates, some of whom strangely had direct access to the Trustees. Here is a quotation:

> "To Wilson, in defeat, the basic question was one of the final control of Princeton University, and the question thus created in his mind never left it thereafter. It is a fair generalization that when this question is sharply posed at any American university, something is wrong. In our universities, public or private, power has no single source. In a happy university nearly everyone is likely to think that he and his immediate companions are the center of the institution; when unhappiness occurs, there will necessarily be a painful awakening for some—and perhaps for all... The truth is, as Lowell [A. Lawrence Lowell, onetime president of Harvard] used to point out, that in a university no one has or should have final control over everything."

The above principles are not unrelated to the problems of relationship of the Regents and the President to the Chancellors of the University of California's various campuses.

From the standpoint of planning and coordination, too great a degree of decentralization within a segment or among segments can jeopardize effective coordination and future planning. Autonomy while not the same as independence is often interpreted as the same. It often appears in the interest of campus officers and

*In *An Atmosphere to Breathe—Woodrow Wilson and the Life of the American University College.* Pamphlet No. 2 (1959)—Woodrow Wilson Foundation, page 9.

faculty to wrest more authority and power from centrally responsible bodies, or to behave and speak as if independence were a fact. However, this is always a short-run view. The need of coordination and future planning within a given segment remains, and the confidence of the Governor, the Legislature, and the people that responsible and effective administrative performance exists will always remain. There cannot be independence and at the same time continuous responsibility on control of costs.

Hence, we come to the biggest dilemma presented by the magnitudes of current problems in every state in the Union. This is the question as to how far the development of central policy for the state or the segment of various systems can go and reasonably expect significant and willing institutional cooperation in fulfillment. And finally, how may be defined the area in which each campus or institution may go with its institutional autonomy in pursuit of individuality so that diversity and the sense of progress and participation exist, while maintaining the integrity and significance of the management and coordination structure of the state, with equal concern for costs in each unit of operation and no wide variations of teaching or administrative costs that are not readily explainable, and likely to prove acceptable.

Autonomy is sought within each segment, but what does it mean? Clearly it is not independence, but just where are the lines to be drawn? The rising problem of student revolt in the years since 1964, at least a demand for voice and participation, has focused attention on the problem of university and college governance in a way and to a degree which the students in the Free Speech Movement at Berkeley in September, 1964 and later hardly could have foreseen. Certainly their prevision was not greater than that of the University's president, the campus chancellors, and the Regents. But the problem remains and will remain for some time. No simple nostrum can be made universally applicable. One may hope that the continuing application of historic American social processes in the formation of opinion and action will prevail and that we shall be spared greater if any resort to force and violence. For there really is no final answer. There is no way out; there is only a way on.

76

OTHER MAJOR ACHIEVEMENTS IN MASTER PLANNING AND COORDINATING HIGHER EDUCATION IN CALIFORNIA 1959-68: AND SOME UNRESOLVED ISSUES

THERE WERE and have been other major achievements of the Master Plan of 1959-60, which the Legislature with Governor Brown's support adopted, and of the Coordinating Council which the Master Plan recommended be created. Many of these other important features of the Master Plan as subsequently implemented in part or in full were of a distinctly stabilizing character. A number of these Master Plan provisions did not require legislative action; others did for consent or for finance. Chief among these other features were:

(1) The junior college in California was limited by statute to the two post-high school years, that is, they were not to become four-year colleges.

(2) A clear statement of the differentiation and also the nature of the overlapping of functions of the University of California, the State Colleges, and the junior colleges was adopted in the Donahoe statute.

(3) A procedure for setting up a joint doctoral degree program between the University and the State Colleges was agreed to, and to this date two of such programs have been established and are functioning; and soon possibly two others will be functioning.

(4) The admission standards for the University of California and the State Colleges, including transfer policies and procedures from junior colleges, were raised on a differential basis and were by 1965 in full effect for both systems.

(5) Approval was given to the principle of diverting by 1975 (and in that year fully) 50,000 entering students to the junior col-

leges in order to accommodate the prospective flood of students in the State Colleges and the University and to protect the state's cost.

(6) Another important principle was that of a 10 percent decline in the University and State Colleges in the proportion which the lower division is of the total undergraduate enrollments from the 1958-59 percentages to the 1974-75 percentages (i.e., from 50 percent to 40 percent). Obviously, this was not to mean any arithmetical decrease over the years to 1975. Regretfully, progress on this recommendation has been slow. More progress has come in the State Colleges than in the University.

(7) An increase in the percentage of state support to the junior college districts was recommended. On this, the results as yet are meager.

(8) Full coverage of the state with junior college districts, or as within the tax base for junior college operations, was also recommended by the Master Plan. This effort for full coverage geographically or financially has made important progress but is not yet an accomplished fact.

(9) A greater utilization of the facilities of independent institutions through an increase in the number and maximum scholarship grant amount under the California Scholarship Commission program was provided for. This program had begun in 1954-55 and has continuously received both general approval and legislative and gubernatorial support. (The student awarded a state scholarship chooses the institution he will attend.) The degree of expansion or increase had not been as great as independent institutions particularly have desired until 1967 when the Legislature passed the Bear bill (A.B. 1765) providing for a doubling of the then authorized available scholarships, a measure which Governor Reagan signed. In 1966-67 the total number of state scholars was 6,027, including 2,651 new awards and 3,376 renewals. The total awards for 1967-68 already made before the Bear bill was passed was 6,902 including 2,746 new awards. This whole program has been a significant and statesmanlike educational development.

(10) In 1959-60 two new State Colleges and the start or improvement of three University campuses were recommended and approved.

During the Master Plan Survey very considerable attention was paid to the projections of possible enrollments on the various campuses already in operation. For example, the projection of

Carl Frisen of the Department of Finance on a *status quo* basis
for the University campus at Berkeley for 1975 was 46,550. Yet a
reasonably dependable analysis conceived of the Berkeley campus capacity as 27,500. Where were the others, roughly 19,000, to
go? It appeared that by 1975 over 7,000 could be enrolled at
Davis in addition to what otherwise would occur at Davis, and
3,500 at the new University campus on the south central coastal
area, since established as the Santa Cruz campus. Hence, it
appeared that there would remain a definite later need for another University campus serving the Bay region to care for a
minimum of 8,000 to 8,500 students. Internal University diversion
might care for the initial impact of this unassignable load, but
ultimately a new campus would seem to be inevitable.

Similarly the *"status quo"* projection for UCLA for 1975 was
53,450. With a recommended campus ceiling set at 27,500 this
meant that diversion to other or to new campuses would be
necessary. In 1959 such "diversion" as accomplished in part
naturally by student choices and also administratively seemingly
could be achieved by campus absorption as follows: (a) to a
new campus in the southeast Los Angeles metropolitan area or in
Orange County, since in fact the Irvine campus, 12,000, (b) to
an expanded San Diego campus 6,350, (c) to the established
Riverside and Santa Barbara campuses 2,950 and 2,100 respec-
tively, beyond what these campuses on a *status quo* basis would
attract. Thus, efforts were made in planning to avoid extreme
student concentration on already established well-known campuses and to make the University's program and resources more
broadly available, with a decided increase of regional identification and visibility of the University.

In 1964, 1965, and 1966 further new campuses were recommended to the Legislature and the Governor by the Coordinating
Council, both for the State Colleges and the University, either for
early implementation or as representing "definite ultimate need."

(11) A state graduate fellowship program was recommended
which, however, did not become fully operative after years of
legislative consideration until 1967.

In the Master Plan discussions, one major issue was whether or
no there existed or was likely soon to exist a lack of capacity for
advanced graduate study. The State Colleges alleged there was a
serious shortage and therefore the State Colleges should be allowed to enter the doctorate field. Of course, the University's
position was that such expansion at the State Colleges should

stop at the master's level. It was therefore imperative to get a sample of such capacity. The University undertook to supply estimates of its own capacity without substantially increased cost to accommodate additional doctoral candidates, and it seemed desirable to get some inventory of private graduate school capacities.

One distinguished private institution estimated it could in five years expand its doctoral candidates by 5 percent or about 30 to 35 students. (Actually, since 1959, this same institution has expanded its graduate registration by 10 percent.)

One other major private university wrote that with its present faculty it could absorb about 700 more graduate students, half of whom might be doctoral candidates. About four or five departments, however, were specifically excepted, being already heavily enrolled.

Estimates in the Master Plan Survey team varied from 500 to 1,500 available doctoral candidate places in private institutions.

Other information provided to me personally further convinced me that a considerable increase of doctoral candidates, probably about 1,000 students, could be achieved in the private graduate schools provided the factor of tuition and fees were cared for. An availability of such financial assistance from the state through a state graduate fellowship program clearly would be far less costly than graduate doctoral work expansion in the State Colleges.

In the University of California estimates also were made and data provided. At least 2,000 places appeared available. As I studied the situation, the doctoral output of the University was a product of many interrelated factors. One of these was the average time required to complete on a full-time attendance basis the doctoral programs chosen and as assigned; but the time required itself was the resultant of the degree of student application as well as of professorial requirements, availability of data, library and laboratory resources, and possible necessary field research, apart from other factors. Some delays seemed preventable. Also, some professors liked to have around reasonably readily available the "slave" labor of graduate students. Some unfortunate situations were shown up. There was one department in a social science field with 154 graduate students of whom 60 were doctoral candidates, and at the last graduation there had been 5 degrees only conferred. Assuming the doctoral candidates really were promising, clearly that department needed to speed up the process somehow, somewhere. In such instances the University was its own worst enemy. Capacity to accept additional doctoral candidates in part depended on the methods of the graduate faculty in getting graduate programs completed.

(12) Adoption of the principle that the cost of services not related to instruction, i.e., not related directly to the student's educational program, should be covered by fees assessed against the students was a feature of the Master Plan of 1959. This meant also that housing, feeding, parking, and many other items should not be subsidized by the state.

(13) Students who are residents of other states (and one-sixth of the University of California enrollment generally is from outside the state) should pay tuition fees sufficient to cover the average teaching expense per student. (In a later chapter these fees and later controversies over tuition for residents will be discussed.)

(14) Adoption of year-round operation as it might prove feasible was a Master Plan recommendation and is now in process of full implementation, except as limited by insufficient or postponed budgetary appropriations.

This issue helped to reveal the leadership role the Coordinating Council has played at various times. In mid-1963 the University was moving to place several campuses on year-round operation, and considering whether to adopt a trimester system or a quarter system. Similarly, it appeared that the State Colleges might move in this direction, and various schemes of year-round operation were proposed. In this threat of confusion and possible chaos in academic calendars for California, the Council requested both segments to refrain from taking any definitive action until the matter could be studied, and with the junior colleges, private institutions, and high schools consulted in this study. This was agreed to by the State Colleges and the University, and full consideration and consultation ensued.

In January of 1964, the Coordinating Council adopted a policy urging year-round operations and adoption of the quarter calendar as the most appropriate means of accomplishing this policy as well as of coordinating with the junior colleges and the high schools. The University and State Colleges governing boards subsequently adopted this policy, and the Council then advised the Governor and the Legislature to support the State Colleges and the University with planning funds in the current budget year and to increase the institutions' operating budgets for the following year or years to cover the once-only costs to convert, campus by campus, to year-round operation. In doing this, the Council also advised the Governor and the Legislature as to the anticipated long-range substantial savings in capital outlay likely to result, or about $105,000,000.

(15) The creation of a Coordinating Council for Higher Education in California representative of the three public segments, private higher education, and the general public derived from the Master Plan, as already mentioned in the last chapter. It has been making great progress and is considered by many one of the outstanding educational and political (in the nonpartisan sense) developments in recent years. In a sense, it is the redeeming feature of the Master Plan if certain provisions of the Master Plan prove untenable. The provision for a Coordinating Council causes it to be a continuing master planning and coordinating body. Otherwise what for one moment seemed wise might later have become most illogical, static, or rigid. The Coordinating Council is a mechanism for review and alteration if necessary. The law gives the Coordinating Council three primary tasks, both in coordinating and as an advisory board to the Governor and the Legislature:

(a) Review of budgets and capital outlay requests of the public segments and advice on the general level of support sought;
(b) Interpretation of the functional differentiation among the segments and assurance that each is playing its proper role, all of this being a quasi-judicial function;
(c) Planning the orderly growth and development of higher education in California together with recommendations on the need for, and location of, new State College and University campuses.

The advice of the Coordinating Council for Higher Education in California is provided to the Governor; to the Legislature; to the Regents of the University of California, the Board of Trustees of the California State Colleges, the junior colleges' governing board, and to the private colleges and universities as well.

From the standpoint of costs to the state and the taxpayer of all public higher education, California made moves in 1959-60 which if followed faithfully can and will provide educational opportunity as desired by the people on bases less costly than probably would have been true if there had been no Master Plan and no

Coordinating Council. To summarize, the recommendations looking to this end of controlling costs (although some were not
wholly so motivated) are: (1) considerable diversion of lower
division students to the junior colleges, even recognizing greater
state aid, (2) avoidance through delineation of functions of
duplication of facilities, (3) stating capacities and locations of
existing, authorized, and new campuses, (4) assessment of student fees as indicated, (5) use indirectly of independent institutional facilities through the California Scholarship program, and
later the new Graduate Fellowship program voted and signed by
Governor Brown in July, 1965, (6) adoption of year-round calendar, and (7) orderly review of all new programs and campuses.

In 1959-60 the capital needs of public higher education were
delineated as being of such magnitude beyond general revenue
support as to require bond issues; three such bond issues mostly
for higher education have since received the approval of the
electorate (i.e., prior to 1968). It is now being questioned
whether California can go on a pay-as-you-go plan, in whole or in
part, which probably will require a willingness to tax beyond
anything that has occurred. This question is related to the broad
issues of finance elsewhere reviewed in this book and specifically
to the financial policies of Governor Ronald Reagan.

In the judgment of the Master Plan Survey team in 1959, each
segment of higher education would gain from the sum total of
recommendations then presented:

As for the junior colleges, there would be increased recognition
in significance, a larger role quantitatively, a greater possibility
that more of the better students would attend junior colleges, a
voice and a vote in coordination procedures, and, finally, the
possibility of additional state aid to operations and construction
costs.

As for the State Colleges, they would gain the efficiency of
freedom found in greater flexibility, a stronger board, a necessary,
though limited role in research, and a participation on a joint
basis with the University in doctoral programs. Flexibility, research, and the joint doctorate have been slow in coming to
realization to the extent intended.

As for the University of California, it would gain a protection
of its essential standards, a primacy in advanced graduate and
professional education, and a renewed sense of security.

As for the independent colleges, they for the first time, except tor the Master Plan Survey and its committees, significantly would be recognized in state-wide coordination with the opportunity of authentic voice bearing upon policies directly affecting their welfare.

By and large, and above all, the State of California and its people, it was believed, would reap the largest gains: in economies already mentioned, in educational decisions being placed, where they ought to be in higher education in a free society, outside of direct political influence insofar as possible but in all public higher education of course under the ultimate control as to the level of support as determined by the Governor and the Legislature.

In 1959 I stated: "I dare to believe that California, with a tripartite system of public higher education long admired by other states, does not now appear to be headed for destruction in unbridled competition, but, rather, will show the way to even further division of labor and sharing of facilities, and a realization of common cause that can be a model of cooperation for other states and for the nation. There is a sense in which it may be said that if these actions now recommended are taken, California will again pioneer in the field of higher education." I dare to believe that now, and that California will continue to do just that, despite political developments and the crises of 1966, 1967, and 1968 that may have appeared to create an alternative conception.

The Coordinating Council for Higher Education has been increasingly aware of the growingly more commonly accepted principle of college education for everyone who can benefit from it. Its own assessment leads it to believe that it is the desire of the people of California that California should excel in the quality and availability of its public and private higher education. The people generally are aware also that the size of enrollments in California higher education is continuing and will continue to grow at a notable rate, but public and private concern for the maintenance and improvement of quality has persisted. The people are interested not just in minimal efforts at educating their youth but beyond that in providing the very best education possible for the coming generations.

This underlying belief in higher education which has had deep historical roots has run parallel in the years 1964 to 1968 with an equally vocal concern for accountability and for eliminating foolishness. There has been great confusion of opinion and frustration as a result of the activities in demonstrations and other forms of student defiance of campus and governmental authority particularly since the Berkeley movements which began in 1964. The popular desire has been to recognize the rights of students as citizens but to expect of students recognition of their responsibilities as citizens and of the essential functions of the University and the colleges. There have been excesses; as a result extremist expressions of control and even of retaliation gained political strength and acceptance by leading politicians.

No doubt longer exists but that both the State Colleges and the University have suffered serious setbacks in public acceptance as a result of the events of recent years; yet all is not lost. There may yet come genuine good in stable progress from this total experience. Reflective as it has been of the pendular swings of which opinion is capable and of the fixities in polarity of opinion in certain elements of the population, it but duplicates again what has occurred before in American life, what has been true nationally and politically during the same period of years and what may be expected someday somewhere to erupt again.

One of the primary purposes of the Coordinating Council for Higher Education as it conceives its mission is to work to insure that quality in higher education will not only be maintained, but strengthened, even as the quantity of enrollments increases. Some politicians and even powerful business leaders have claimed that enrollments must be limited in order to avert deterioration in quality. Their claims often are based on the principle that quality and quantity in higher education are incompatible. More likely reason has been a desire to avoid the taxation which pursuit of both goals demands.

Some advocates of what they call the "democratic" principle claim to believe, especially in crisis, that quality should be sacrificed in order to keep open for all the doors of opportunity. This too is a false dichotomy. It is neither good democracy nor good economy nor good education nor downright good common sense to accept the mediocre in order to achieve inclusiveness. Both principles remain: the need of opportunity according to ability and willingness, and the availability of education to as high a level of achievement as one may be able to embrace.

As Dr. Willard B. Spalding, when director of California's Coordinating Council, has said, "We can indeed be proud that California's system of higher education, while accommodating more students than any other similar system in the world, has produced and maintained a level of quality in its institutions that is also unparalleled.

"The Coordinating Council for Higher Education constantly seeks ways to insure that quality and quantity in higher education will continue to be compatible, and that quality continues to improve regardless of the number of students involved.

"For one thing is certain: California institutions of higher education will be compelled by public demand to admit many more students than are now served. And it is clear to the Coordinating Council that changed practices are required to preserve and enhance the quality of education. But such changes should not be feared. Rather, they should be welcomed as needed innovations in an area of society where creative advances are continually necessary and appropriate. The Council believes that the ability to encourage and adopt changes will remain a dynamic and outstanding characteristic of higher education in California. The Council works to encourage such changes in the colleges and university, although its efforts are, by statute, largely recommendatory."

During the early years after acceptance, the California Master Plan and its system of higher education were frequently cited and commended, so frequently no record could cover it all. Some comments and evidences of interest from outside California regarding the Master Plan as achieved are some indication as to the importance if not general praise attending the Master Plan's introduction.

Time magazine for October 17, 1960 reported extensively the developments in higher education in California, under a cover story honoring President Clark Kerr, and reporting the major facets of the Master Plan.

In April, 1962, the Committee on Higher Education of Great Britain, under the chairmanship of Lord Robbins, visited California, flying directly to San Francisco and then to Los Angeles without first stopping on the eastern seaboard. The purpose of their visit, in the light of their own mission to recommend regarding reform and expansion of higher education in the United Kingdom, was to study California's recent developments up to that time. In San Francisco Lord Robbins and the committee and staff were entertained by President Clark Kerr and visited institutions there representative of the four segments. In Los Angeles, Lord Robbins and the forty persons with him were my guests at the California Club for luncheon with forty educators from the southern area, and as in the north the mission visited selected representative institutions including Occidental College and the Claremont Colleges. The five-volume report of the Robbins Committee was published in 1963.

In a report dated January, 1963 (page 18) to the European Organization for Economic Cooperation and Development at its Paris meeting there is a statement: " . . . development plans of the California type are of special interest. They seem to us to represent the most advanced effort to construct a system of mass higher education (for a tripled enrollment by 1975) while maintaining a quality of research and education at the top which is unsurpassed anywhere among OECD countries and probably in the world. . . . While the contribution of private institutions is not ignored, this emerging structural framework provided by the state may be the appropriate model for higher education in a society based on the culture of science and technology."

In the magazine *Science*, for March 11, 1963, an editorial commended and recognized the possible international significance of California developments.

In July, 1963, *Reader's Digest*, in an article by Ben Hibbs, entitled "California Builds Big for Education," broad national recognition was evident for what had transpired in California, labeling the Master Plan "ambitious" and the whole higher education system "working mightily to meet the skyrocketing needs of tomorrow," and declaring, "Since its earliest days, California seems to have been more passionately committed to public education than most states." This article did make a statement, however, not wholly borne out by later events when it said, "The state constitution gives the university autonomy, there is no political meddling with its management, and the university's Board of Regents is a hard-working, non-partisan body."

Representatives of the trustees of North Carolina, and of the central higher education body of Georgia, as well as of Texas visited for review; I met with most of them.

87

8

THE COORDINATING COUNCIL IN ACTION
AND INFLUENCE

PURSUANT TO THE PROVISIONS of the Donahoe Act, the first meeting of the Coordinating Council for Higher Education was held October 3, 1960. Governor Brown expressed a strong desire to be present upon the occasion of the initial meeting of the Council. He had appointed the three public members called for by the Donahoe Act, and he had also chosen from panels submitted by independent colleges and universities the three representatives of the private institutions. After all, the achievement of such a high degree of unanimity in the Legislature in 1960 in the passage of the Donahoe Act was very much to the credit of Governor Brown as well as to those senators and assemblymen who had stood so loyally with him in the very substantial support which had been given to most of the recommendations of the Master Plan Survey, and of the respective boards which had accepted it.

Prior to the meeting of the Coordinating Council for the first time, Governor Brown asked me if I would allow him to see that my name was placed in nomination for the presidency, to become the first president of the Coordinating Council. I refused, indicating to him that my health would not permit it, and also indicating to him that I doubted very much that my health would allow me to be present for that first meeting. As it turned out, I was not able to be present because of my physical condition at the time, but in spite of my statements I was elected president. Information was conveyed to me by telephone while the Council was in session, and I immediately resigned. At the time, I expressed my strong belief that the person ideally prepared and positioned for leadership in the Coordinating Council was Dr. Robert J. Wert of Stanford University, who had shown such imaginative and knowledgeable participation in the work of the Master Plan Survey and whose helpfulness and fairness of judgment were appreciated by all segments of higher education.

At the November 7, 1960 meeting I explained my inability to serve as president for personal reasons, whereupon Dr. Wert was elected president to serve until July 1, 1962, and also Mr. Warren Christopher, an attorney of Los Angeles, who had been appointed a representative of the general public on the Council was elected vice-president.

By the spring of 1961, a director of the Coordinating Council staff had been chosen in the person of Dr. John R. Richards, then Chancellor of the Oregon State System of Higher Education. In 1964 Dr. Richards resigned, and during the presidency of Warren Christopher, who succeeded Dr. Robert Wert in 1963, Dr. Willard B. Spalding, at the time associate director of the Council staff, was chosen director. Previously Dr. Spalding had been an administrator with the Oregon State System of Higher Education, then chairman of the Division of Education of Portland State College immediately prior to coming to the Coordinating Council. His earlier background includes the superintendency of schools in several cities in the east and later in Portland, Oregon, and he also served at one time as Dean of the College of Education at the University of Illinois.

I was elected vice-president of the Council in 1963 and continued to 1965, when, having retired from the presidency of Occidental College, Governor Brown appointed me as one of the three new public members made possible by the legislative enlargement of the public member group on the Council in that year. Likewise, at that time I was elected president of the Coordinating Council.

For a child of less than ten years of age, from conception to birth and growth to accepted maturity, the record of the Coordinating Council for Higher Education is a distinctly good one. Dating its legal birth from the Donahoe Act of 1960 and its recognized parentage and conception in the Master Plan Survey of 1959, its genealogy must include the Liaison Committee which had preceded it in the function of necessary adjustment and accommodation of strong parallel systems of higher education to each other.

Born in the struggles and contentions of 1960, its first months and its first two or three years brought forward problems of organization, of relations with staff, and of the relationships of the staffs of the various parallel systems with each other. Also there were raised inevitably both by mandate of the Master Plan, or carry-over from the Liaison Committee's work, or by legislative or executive request many of the thorny issues of the systems' operations which had been set aside during the achievement of "no dissent" in the Master Plan and executive and legislative acceptance thereof. Such issues as the interpretation of new admissions standards or the dates when applicable, or the exact meaning in operation by the Council of "level of support" in budgetary review, are but examples of the testing of procedure, temper and attitude and strength not only of the contending segments but also of the Council staff's recommendations and of the capacity of the Council's deliberations to reach a viable, reasonably acceptable line of forward action.

At the beginning Dr. Lyman A. Glenny, professor of government at Sacramento State College, was critical of the Master Plan. In 1962, he was quoted as stating it to be "largely a blueprint in search of implementation because its enforcement arm—the coordinating council—lacks sufficient muscle and has forfeited its judicial responsibility." He declared it was powerless "to prevent log rolling and deals which may or may not be in the public interest." He also interpreted early Coordinating Council decisions such as the one for the time being validating earlier Liaison Committee decisions as a continuing intention of the Council to allow the University and the State Colleges to settle various mutual problems by themselves without the Council's review or sanction, and he was reported as calling this "a limited interpretation of its own powers." In the November, 1961 Council meeting I myself voiced my own disturbed mind over the possible disposition without Council consideration of old Liaison Committee agreements by a process of bilateral settlement by State College and University representatives. The actions finally taken seemed to be weakening to the Council, but subsequent events have proved them not to be.

Early in the Council's life developed the need for understanding the role of the Council's staff. Here one stumbling block was the conception carried over by Regents, State College trustees who had served on the State Board of Education, as well as President Kerr and State College administrators of the role of Liaison committee staff. In the latter case the staff were employees of the two respective segments and therefore not expected to stand out apart from the respective segment's administrative viewpoint except on matters of fact. The Liaison Committee possessed a very competent professional and technical staff but seemingly were expected to present their policy recommendations initially through the procedural arrangements of the segment before presenting them in such form as would cause them inevitably to become public or so as to cause too obvious a conflict. That is to say, neither the President of the University or the Superintendent of Public Instruction for the State Colleges expected ever to be caught by surprise. Hence, it was early argued by some that Council staff documents should be seen in advance and their recommendations known before given a public airing; and as a result it was argued the Council staff should engage in a mediatorial role seeking in advance to bring conflicting views into some kind of at least temporarily acceptable accommodation.

These issues were important. Clearly, the doctrine of surprise would or could lead only to continuing friction. Clearly, the doctrine of prior consultation, mediation, and possible avoidance of apparent conflict might lead to unfortunate results: accusations of "behind the scenes" deals, or of one segment blocking any action at all (especially the University with constitutional status if the Regents refused to consider a matter), or of one segment starting backfires against Council staff facts, recommendations, or opinions by seeking *ad interim* through the media of communication to influence public opinion.

To establish and protect the professional independence of the staff while at the same time not establishing for them a role of technical or professional tyranny over their employers (such as has occurred so often in organizational structures) was therefore important. Affected would be the quality of the personnel appointed and employed. Affected would be their continuity in office and the possible rate of turnover of such personnel.

At the beginning and reasoning *in abstracto* no clearly delineated line of staff behavior to meet all possible future situations could be formulated; it was necessary to get on with it. Much would depend on the staff personnel themselves. And much would depend on whether the director and his staff would so conceive their roles as to be hurt or threaten to resign if overruled, i.e., if his or their recommendations were not accepted.

The post of director was given by law in the Donahoe Act, on recommendation of the Master Plan Survey, a somewhat protected status to assure some genuine professional independence.

That protection was that ten of the initial fifteen votes on the council would have to be affirmative for his removal.

The first director, Dr. John R. Richards, appointed in 1961 had held a post where although his task was clearly one of coordination he had had no authority above him save the Governor and the Legislature of Oregon. Thoroughly qualified professionally, it was soon clear he intended to perform at only a minimum level a mediatorial role, if expected. Accustomed to come to grips with a problem in both fact and principle, he proceeded to do just that. The separateness of the director and the staff from any segment was established, possibly at times more rigorously than necessary. As time passed, however, the wisdom of full prior consultation of Council staff with segmental personnel and staffs became evident. Also the desirability became recognized of full personal contact of the director with leaders of any and all segments without undue worry about the suspicion or fear of someone that X was receiving more personal attention than Y, and with the doctrine of no surprise adopted as a virtual rule, the position of the director and of the Council staff moved to one of higher respect.

This latter achievement, however, it must be stated, is more if not most to the credit of Dr. Willard B. Spalding who in 1964 succeeded Dr. Richards when the latter had resigned as mentioned, to accept a post as executive vice president of the Institute of International Education in New York.

In the period from 1964 to the present, the degree of cooperation of the director and the staff both with segmental staffs and with the staffs of executive and legislative departments and committees at Sacramento has been outstanding.

Neither the director nor the president of the Council (Dr. Wert, Mr. Christopher, or myself) has conceived of himself as the top or ranking spokesman in California for higher education in any real sense even though at times others (educators, writers, journalists, ceremonial lists) have sought to make such appear to be so. The key to the success of the director and to the role of president of the Council is at all times to recall that the Coordinating Council is an advisory coordinating body, participant in fundamental decisions affecting administration and operation but not the administrator of any system of higher education.

Any such body as this Council commencing a new role must of necessity go through a period of time of discovering its own roles, methods of operation, procedures of approach, and must also develop appropriate relationships upon its part with its staff.

At first, in the workings of the Council, an attempt was made to bring all matters bearing upon the work of the Council before a full meeting of the Council itself. As time passed, however, the wisdom of using the committee structure seemed to the membership to be more efficient and satisfying. Accordingly, a committee structure has been utilized, the present committees being Committee on Educational Programs, Committee on Finance, Committee on Physical Facilities, Committee on Council Relationships and Procedures.

Similarly the staff has been organized, as would be expected, according to the major subject factors for consideration, the exact character of the staff organization and assignment of duties being subject, of course, to the decision of the director. Reassignment of staff duties has occurred upon several occasions since 1960, in the light of new functions assigned and of new personnel added.

Use of the committee structure and, therefore, the review of all major staff reports in committee meetings prior to the regular meeting of the Coordinating Council as officially called, has both positive and negative features. In general, and especially in the past three or four years, well over a quorum of the Coordinating Council personnel have characteristically been present for the meetings of the committees, the interest of the entire membership of the Council having been quite inclusive rather than exclusive. Accordingly, there have been times when it has appeared a waste of time not only to have a review of the matter fully before the appropriate committee as would of course occur but also on the subsequent day or at a later time to have review of the same report and allow for discussion if desired before the Council as a whole.

Furthermore, when there is full or substantial Council participation in the committee meeting as such in discussion or otherwise, it has appeared to some that the restriction of voting action within the committee to the members of that committee itself may at times have caused the Council as a whole to have been prevented from recording its own judgment more fully. As a result, but also because of calendar problems, from time to time the process has been varied, and meetings of the whole Council have been held where all subject matter materials have been submitted directly to the Council as a whole, not sitting as a committee of the whole, but simply as the Council itself. Accordingly, over the period of the life of the Council thus far, a variety of procedures has been employed.

Relationships with and acceptance by the members of the Legislature have at all times been of great importance. In the master planning days of 1959, contact and communication were maintained through the presence and partial substantive participation in the deliberations of the Survey team by Keith Sexton, then staff assistant to the Assembly Committee on Education. In one sense this was one of the wisest actions of the Master Plan team, because the information transmitted by Mr. Sexton made possible reaction which could be assessed. It also meant that key legislators of both houses becoming gradually informed were never finally taken by complete surprise.

From 1960 to 1966 the head office of the Coordinating Council for Higher Education was in San Francisco as a convenience to staff and to members in travel. In 1965, however, decision was reached on the strong recommendation of the director, Dr. Willard B. Spalding, to establish the head office in Sacramento as soon as feasible in the budget year 1966-67. This action with the increased contacts available to and with legislators and their staffs has been valuable and significant for the future of the Coordinating Council.

For one who has had an intimate and direct part in the origin and development of the Coordinating Council for Higher Education to this hour, the steadily increasing acceptance of and respect for the Council has been most gratifying. New responsibilities have been placed upon it by both executive and legislative branches of government; and the rapidly increasing role of the federal government in support of higher education in one manner or another since 1962 created a need for an agency of the state government capable of functioning as a nonsegmental, impartial body. The Coordinating Council for Higher Education was made to order, and in nearly every instance was designated by executive order or by law to function as the agency to administer and distribute federal funds and programs.

The federal programs of greatest importance have been the Higher Education Facilities Act of 1963, and of the Higher Education Act of 1965, Titles I and VI. The State Technical Services Act program was assigned to the University of California, but Governor Brown requested the Coordinating Council for Higher Education to review its program and report to him and requested that the Coordinating Council for Higher Education president be a member of the Advisory Council of the State Technical Services program. This has since been changed. The Coordinating Council is represented by an appointed member.

Quite apart from the lubrication of the machinery of higher education by the federal programs, the confidence in the Coordinating Council for Higher Education by Governor Brown and the State Legislature was indicative of a status achieved and is of considerable historical importance. The Legislature indicated it would not act on any recommended new campus of the State College or University segments without prior approval and recommendation from the Coordinating Council for Higher Education, and so far has held to this policy. On several occasions both as to budgetary and specific faculty salary increases the Legislature has chosen to follow the recommendation of the Coordinating Council rather than the *ex parte* recommendation of a specific segment. The number of such instances is multiplying.

In relationship to the Governor's office, the writer has the problem of recording his contacts with both Governor Brown and Governor Reagan. (I write only vis-a-vis the period from 1965 to the present date since my presidency of the Council dated only from July 1, 1965; yet I am not unaware of most of what transpired from 1960 to 1965 inclusive since I was a member and was vice president during the years 1963 to 1965). Governor Brown apparently held the Coordinating Council for Higher Education in high respect and sought out or received its president (in person or by telephone) in conference on many problems of higher education and at numerous times from 1960 through 1966. The policy was to keep him informed, to receive suggestions if any, but not to allow him to dictate or even significantly to participate in decisions except as his own position was acceptable to the Council as a whole. In the case of Governor Reagan, it proved almost impossible to establish contact with him until over a month and a half of his administration had begun and then only after several requests from myself.

For the record, let the following be stated: The day after Governor Reagan's election I as president of the Coordinating Council for Higher Education got in touch with A. C. Rubel, the individual whom I knew best among those who were in the press indicated as close to him and his advisers on governmental organization and policy. I had known Cy Rubel for many years. He had been a trustee of Occidental College. He indicated at once an awareness of the Coordinating Council for Higher Education as to functions and personnel, and agreed to carry personally my message of a desire to place the staff of the Coordinating Council for Higher Education and myself at the Governor's service for appropriate counsel in terms of the statutory responsibilities. From this I never heard another word.*

On December 1, 1966, I wrote to Governor Reagan on several matters, including the substance of the conversation on November 9 with one of his chief advisers, and referring to it. This letter although acknowledged as to one of the items in my letter and appropriately so referred, on the other issues including functional relationship, proffered counsel and general helpfulness, was never heard from again.

On January 13, 1967, I again wrote to Governor Reagan in the same vein, this time by a voted instruction of the Coordinating Council for Higher Education at its January 6 meeting. By mid-January Governor Reagan or his Director of Finance had met on January 3, 4, and 5 and later with officials of the State College system, and of the University regarding budgets for 1967-68 and in reference also to his proposals regarding tuition. No representative of the Coordinating Council for Higher Education had been called into any of these conferences. Hence, the letter of January 13 was exceedingly pertinent and timely, again offering availability for counsel as to facts and indicating prior procedure and policies. From this letter there was no acknowledgment or response until the afternoon of February 9, 1967, and arrangements were then made for an appointment on February 21.

(On the morning of February 9 the *Los Angeles Times* carried an interview with me critical in the light of the Master Plan of the apparent budgetary position of the Governor, supportive of his tuition principle, and suggesting budgetary totals that might fulfill the minimum of Master Plan principles. See details in a later chapter.)

Meanwhile, the members of the Coordinating Council for Higher Education, other than those representing the State Colleges and the University of California (who, of course, had been in consultation in one manner or another with the Governor since January 3), that is to say, the six public members and some of the representatives of the junior colleges and private institutions,

*Mr. Rubel was deceased May 31, 1967.

were distressed as was also the Council staff over being so decidedly and manifestly bypassed by Governor Reagan, he seemingly taking for granted as they saw it the sort of advice he would receive were the Council as a whole consulted, and rejecting it in advance. These public members and others believed the Reagan administration suspicious of the Council because all six public members had been appointed by Governor Brown.

It is understandable that Governor Reagan as Governor-elect, and after his inauguration as Governor, was pressed from all sides by problems of widely diverse nature and requiring planning for the whole state. However, since he immediately consulted the two responsible administrative boards, namely the Regents and the Trustees, on budgetary matters, it seemed to the majority of Council members unfortunate that a month and a half passed after he took office before he did actually consult the Coordinating Council in any aspect of these pending fiscal matters.

Later I was to discover by the Governor's own admission on February 21 that he scarcely knew what the Coordinating Council for Higher Education was for, what it was created to do, what its history had been, and how it could be of help to him. Quite apart from the significance of these developments as any indication of the knowledge and capability of the Governor, this entire experience was a thoroughgoing revelation of the then existing experience, maturity, and knowledgeability of the Governor's staff. Primarily, I hold the Governor's staff responsible for failures fully to be informed and to inform the Governor.

With reference to these experiences during January, February, and March, 1967 vis-a-vis Governor Reagan's budgetary proposals in public higher education, several items are of conceivable interest and importance to gain full perspective so far as the Council's functioning was concerned. In the first place, the action of the Coordinating Council for Higher Education with reference to the budgets of both the State Colleges and the University on anticipated new work load for 1967-68, on new and improved programs, on selected capital outlay items, and on salary and fringe benefits increases for faculty had already been acted upon either before the election in November or at the Council's November meeting after the election results were known. These reports of course had gone to both the Governor's office and to the Department of Finance and were in these officers' files. The initial conferences with the State College and the University personnel in January showed little if any awareness of the existence or substance of these recommendations on the part of the Governor or his representatives.

Secondly, it did not escape the notice of the twelve members of the Council who had not been involved with the Governor's or the Director of Finance's budgetary conferences that the six who were directly or indirectly involved, representing the University and the State Colleges, made no suggestion that the Council be drawn into consultation, so far as is known to these Council members or the Council staff. This seemed to be a lack of confidence on the part of these two major public higher education segments as to the role the officers and staff of the Council would play, or as to the viewpoints they would express.

Thirdly, when the Council adopted unanimously all the principles set forth at its February 21, 1967 meeting which in very large measure supported the State Colleges and the University (if not in their initial requests at least in their secondary or downwardly modified sums), these two segments must have regretted their failure to suggest earlier that the Council be involved. The position of the Council as a whole was strengthened in the eyes of the Legislature, and there must have been some effect of the Council's actions on the Governor and his staff. On support or opposition to the tuition principle the Council was not unanimous, but on recommending that it should not be a part of 1967-68 budgetary planning the vote was unanimous. This too did not escape attention.

In failing to draw the Council into the deliberations, the State College and the University segments had relied each on its own strength, except as reported concerted reactions may have been agreed to between them, suspicious each side for itself that any second or even worse third party could only operate to reduce the budget since judicial analysis rather than *ex parte* argument might sway decision.

The February 21 action of the Council with all of its effective support to major functions of education and research, both as to opportunity and quality, did recognize the possibilities of some economies to be achieved in each of the segmental budgets. At the January 6 Council meeting without formal action various Council members had voiced both the possibilities of some cuts even as there was strong argument against any reduction of essential functions, all of this well reported in the press.

Fourthly, by the time of the February 21 meeting the Governor's initial budget had been sent to the Legislature, and the fact that there was in it practically no variation from the budgetary approaches first "tentatively" proposed on January 3 to State College and University representatives caused Council members, all of them, private and public representatives alike, to sense that the crisis the state faced might be far more than financial and that genuine threats to the availability and quality of public higher education existed.

This reaction had behind it also the dismissal on January 21, 1967 of Dr. Clark Kerr from the presidency of the University of California. For a number of Council members it was believed the dismissal of President Kerr was not wholly related to the results of the election or to positive action by the new Governor, and was even related partly to the decidedly unyielding attitude of President Kerr as to budgetary reductions, with some Regents repelled by the bleak outlook of four more similar budget years. Nevertheless, an alertness regarding the essential principles of the Master Plan as to educational policies was evident among all members and in all segments. The dedication of the Coordinating Council not to everything public higher education might have done or might propose but to its fundamental importance in the economy and society of California was demonstrated.

There are other aspects of the impact of the new Republican administration on California higher education, which in fairness should be considered.

Governor Reagan on February 28, 1967 manifested some confidence in the Coordinating Council in a request to it to undertake an analysis of various feasible alternative methods of providing financial assistance to students if tuition were to be charged at the University of California and the State Colleges. As president of the Council, I accepted this responsibility at once, and this action although criticized by some Council members who stated the president of the Council was not the Council and hence should not have taken on such a study without full Council approval, was confirmed by indirection at the March 28, 1967 meeting when the first phase of the staff report on that subject was received and after review forwarded to the Governor.

Again in late July, 1967, the Governor requested of the Coordinating Council a study of alternative methods of financing public higher education beyond the sources already used in California, this study to review all sources of support used in other states of the Union.

In early August, shortly after a conference among myself,

99

Director Willard B. Spalding and Keith Sexton of the Coordinating Council staff, and Governor Reagan and two members of his staff, a request from the Governor's office was made of me to canvass Council members as to a possible favorable vote on the principle of tuition at the August meeting of the Council. When the likelihood appeared of an unfavorable vote, and anticipating action of this subject at a prospective Regents' meeting, very strong pressure was exerted from the Governor's office to assure no action at the August Council meeting; and as a result a motion to reaffirm the principle of free tuition was laid on the table.

The meetings in September and October, 1967 were less than fully assuring as to cooperation with the Governor or his staff. After the Coordinating Council staff report on alternative feasible methods of providing student financial assistance was filed with the Council, preparatory to later Council report to the Governor, there was considerable debate both over the substance and wording of the report and over whether or no the report as revised or supplemented in accordance with Council instructions should be transmitted to the Governor at that time or much later after considerable revision. The Governor had specifically asked for the report as soon as possible and without Council recommendations as to a policy choice. The debate therefore should have been not at all on members' own conceptions of right policy but wholly upon the conceivable variety of possible coverage of student expenses where need existed under varied circumstances, the probable cost of higher education to the student and also to the state of one plan or another, as well as upon other related questions of feasibility. Furthermore, the Council earlier in March and at the July meeting had agreed to an inclusive approach in said review of possible plans and not solely tied to the possibility of tuition being charged in public higher education. Also, in late July, Governor Reagan had announced without waiting for the Council's report his own combined tuition and student loan and grant program.

The way it all worked out in the Council was not serene. Newer members of the Coordinating Council of recent gubernatorial appointment were apparently united in a desire to reduce the range of coverage and variety of plans for student financial assistance, as well as to rewrite certain portions. Friction was evident. Considerable changes in text were made, but the principal argument developed over transmittal to the Governor. All new appointees voted along with the three Regents of the University not to transmit; the vote, however, was 8-6 to transmit, and this was done.

Considering that I had been willing to continue as President of the Coordinating Council for 1967-68 in considerable measure because I had been assured it was Governor Reagan's request that I do so, my reactions to the experiences of the summer and fall of 1967 insofar as the independence of the Council, or a respect for its efforts by the Governor's office, were disheartening in character.

These misgivings on my part were not dispelled by the December, 1967 and February, 1968 meetings of the Council and specifically because of the positions taken in solidarity and the attitudes expressed by Governor Reagan's appointees. Never in the six years of Governor Brown's administration had there been any evidence of influence on the part of himself or his staff regarding the possible votes of public members on any issue. Indeed, at no time did the public members ever meet in caucus to determine in advance a position to be taken. The issue in last analysis boils down to the degree to which one accepts the viewpoint that public higher education should be free from politically partisan influence, a principle clearly written in law but not wholly observed in recent years.

Nevertheless, other members of the Republican administration and Republican members of the Legislature assured me and other Council members of their varying divergences in attitude and substance from some of the positions in regard to higher education (and the resultant image) taken initially and later by Governor Reagan.

Governor Reagan's initial budget for 1967-68 was filed on January 31, 1967. Although initially declared by his administration to be a 10 percent cut of the State Colleges' and the University budgets it was in fact larger in each case. Later it was modified upward for each segment. Both as a result of foregoing a required tuition for 1967-68 and in the magnitudes recommended, the Governor evinced a change of mind as detail in a later chapter on actual budget preparation will manifest. With the new figures submitted there was a greater possibility that two basic principles of the Master Plan, namely, availability of opportunity for qualified students and high quality of both segmental programs, could be embraced at least to a minimum degree. Hence, the Master Plan ideas were in part being recognized.

In my judgment the Governor in his speeches through the

101

spring, summer, and fall of 1967 showed some softening in his attitude towards public higher education, providing some basis of belief that he was less deserving of the charges of anti-intellectualism against him made as a result of some of his campaign utterances and some statements made in defense of his own administration's budget plans in early 1967. On this score, however, there is still much to be done before the general public view will be reassured as to Governor Reagan's attitude towards public higher education as such and not simply towards its less responsible elements.

In general, there continues to be some uncertainty as to the attitude of Governor Reagan and his administration toward both higher education in general and the Coordinating Council in particular.

The new appointments the Governor has made to Council membership are of high public status and repute. What the influence of his appointments to the Council will be on the work, influence, and image of the Council remains to be seen. At this moment my reaction is a decidedly mixed one.

The legally established functions for the Coordinating Council as an advisory body have been given in an earlier chapter. Mention has also been made of its distinctly administrative responsibilities as regards federal programs assigned.

In addition, a number of other tasks have been assigned and have received or are continuing to receive staff and Council study, as directed by the Master Plan, or by the Council itself:

(1) Continuing studies of admissions and retention policies of all institutions, and of the flow of students into all segments of higher education in California.

(2) Continuing review and counsel regarding the quasi-independent California Scholarship and Loan Commission activities, and of various aspects of provision of financial aid to students.

(3) Continuing study of space utilization by the public segments' institutions.

(4) Continuing studies of the relation of supply to demand in all professions and vocational fields covered by California's higher education system. Very thorough studies have been made on medical education needs, dentistry, nursing education, and engineering.

(5) Continuing studies of faculty demand and supply for all higher education in California and also of faculty salary levels

and fringe benefits in public segments, both clearly related thereto; such studies being based on data from specified institutions in other states and as available from national public and private sources.

(6) Continuing studies of the costs of instruction, noninstructional services, and auxiliary enterprises.

(7) Continuing studies of area needs for higher educational facilities.

Should the coordinating board or council be possessed of power, or should it be advisory only? Should it be statutory or in the Constitution? If possessed of too much power, it might easily in time become a single board, a superboard causing sublying segmental boards to lose status relatively and then some effectiveness. It is an error to assume that such a single board is necessarily the answer. The problems of coordination and adjustment often remain even after the single board has spoken.

The California Coordinating Council for Higher Education has six public members. There is the possibility that if the public members were larger in number and were to have clear control of action, the Coordinating Council might become a "superboard." At this juncture any further increase of the public members of the Council might tend to eclipse the status of either the Regents of the University of California or the Trustees of the State College system; a development which as of this time I would deplore.

The California Coordinating Council's success or failure in the last analysis depends upon the desire, patience, goodwill, and responsibility of all members of higher education from board members to administrators and faculty, as well as the concern of the members of the Legislature and the Governor. Its success or failure also depends on the effective operation of the Coordinating Council as an advisory coordinating not simply as a superboard control body. The Council itself must function as a body including its staff, continuing the frank acknowledgment of and encounter with the problems rapid change is posing, thus "coming to grips" with the situation boldly on a regular meeting basis*. This the Master Plan was credited with doing; this must be the spirit of the future.

*A study worthy of reference is "California's Coordinating Council for Higher Education" by James G. Paltridge, published (1966) by the Center for Research and Development in Higher Education, at the University of California, Berkeley, California.

The problems of governance of our so rapidly expanding universities and colleges will not be easily solved. The relation of an institution to the board of control of the segment of which a part will be no less perplexing and vexing as will be the relationships of that segment to other segments of public higher education in some degree of cooperation or coordination, as well as to the Legislature and the Governor. An internal struggle for authority and power is not new. Nor is a struggle between state agencies and constitutional authorities a new phenomenon. Only the predominant tolerating spirit of free Americans and concern for the highest purposes can cause machinery to function for the common good.

9

THE COUNCIL IN BUDGET REVIEW OF LEVEL OF
SUPPORT OF HIGHER EDUCATION

THE DONAHOE ACT OF 1960 in Section 22703 gave to the Coordinating Council for Higher Education among other functions a "review of the annual budget and capital outlay requests of the University and the State College system, and presentation of comments on the general level of support sought." This function was as were the other functions listed in the Act "advisory to the governing boards of the institutions of public higher education and to appropriate state officials." The language of the Master Plan Survey was almost identical.

From the beginning of the work of the Coordinating Council, the question has been debated as to what the clauses quoted were intended to mean for the Coordinating Council with reference to the budget process from the presentation of its budget request by the board of each senior segment to the Governor and the State Department of Finance for the review thereof by that department, then the Governor's budget presentation to the Legislature to final passage and signature by the Governor of the budget of expenditures, with the possibility of amendment by the Executive or the Legislature at various stages in the total procedure.

I do have some memory of what transpired in the discussions of the Master Plan team.

Due to the constitutional status of the University Regents and the practice of a single line item in the Governor's budget calling for an appropriation of x million dollars for the University, the University representatives were unwilling to approve any budgetary power or authority for the Coordinating Council which would by statute appear to supersede the authority and power already possessed by the Regents. Specifically, opposition was voiced to any fiscal participation for an agency lying between the Regents and the Governor, and also particularly to any detailed review of the elements of the University budget.

Yet the necessity of some review was present as a practical political and governmental problem particularly if the State College Trustees were to be subject to review; and if the State College Trustees were to be made a constitutional public trust like unto the Board of Regents as the Master Plan recommended, then obviously some check of some kind was necessary to give any meaning at all in fiscal affairs to the Coordinating Council. Furthermore, at the drafting of the Master Plan it was not foreseen that the Coordinating Council would have any public members for whatever significance the inclusion of public members may represent.

The result in the Master Plan was a "political" compromise, to be found in the wording "comments on the level of support sought." As with many political compromises the result is known in its meaning only after the fact, and as a result of later interpretations. From the first, in the Coordinating Council the meaning of "level of support" raised the possibility of comparison of budget requests with something else, and the question was, with what?

The logical consideration of private finance would be to look first of all to probable income. In public finance this is less likely to be true, because the current runs two ways. In 1967 the Governor's approach to the total problem of budget was based upon a fiscal emergency and ability to pay and upon an initial stated determination to introduce no new taxes or as few as possible so as to maintain so much as possible the *status quo* and also to achieve economy. In other times there was a greater willingness to let the general fund income grow through new sources of taxation or through expanded revenues from growing population or growing economy or otherwise. The capacity to pay should at all times be a factor for a responsible society to judge as to what it can do. In 1967 the Governor's final budget called for increased expenditures and also revenue sufficient to cover the expenditures budget.

Another consideration in level of support could be historical review of major items. Sometimes the Coordinating Council has insufficiently realized that the interrelationships between and among items in the budget do change historically, and although

106

some per capita figure might utterly obscure this fact, there is no really solid basis for assumption that the same per capita or proportionate ratio with reference to the problem necessarily continues to obtain. For example, the composition of student enrollment has never been analyzed as a factor in budgetary consideration insofar as any Council deliberations may have been concerned, particularly with reference to different campuses or at different times. Yet the changing mix of both the University and the State Colleges may have rendered some of the earlier work-load ratios less tenable. Furthermore, with certain policies adopted generally with reference to the lower division, it would have been possible to apply the factor of finance to aid the achievement of decline in the lower division proportion.

The bases upon which work-load requirements have been calculated have been taken for granted for too long a time. From the standpoint of budgetary review this is an indefensible position for a supervisory or advisory or coordinating body to find itself in. Past procedures have simply been frozen and projected forward without regard, so it would seem, as to whether or not the situations once obtaining now obtain. Furthermore, decisions about new and improved programs without the total background of what the budgetary requests might represent, judgments upon individual items without the conspectus of the whole picture, are completely illogical. To act and recommend with reference to specific programs before one knows what the total volume of expenditures and the total relationship to state finance might be is hardly defensible.

Level of support may mean also consideration in reference to major budget categories such as salaries, libraries, laboratories, custodial care, property maintenance, faculty-student ratios, and a whole host of such factors.

Then, too, the level of support may have to do with both intrastate and interstate comparisons, with private institutions and by categories or by per capita costs, or with reference to other public segments in California or elsewhere.

Level of support may deal with what other states yield in support of various types of public higher education. Such information kept to date and developed on comparable statistical bases can be valuable to observe the position of California among the fifty states.

In addition, level of support may bear a significant meaning with reference to the future insofar as it may be readily projected, and also with reference to the degree to which pay-as-you-go as a principle of capital outlay coverage may be adopted as policy, or not included at all.

This does not fully cover the possible comparisons in general level of support, but at least it is suggestive.

Some of these items, as the members of the Master Plan Survey team will probably recall, were items of full debate in 1959, and the phraseology in the Donahoe Act, as well as in the Master Plan itself, derived from an unwillingness to have any very specific comparisons made. One had to settle for the wording that is in the Master Plan document as well as the Donahoe Act in order to get something that would be significant for the future.

I held tenaciously to the principle of review of general level of support even though I wanted the plan to involve more than that, because in my judgment when a Council or an officer has no voice with reference to the dollars, finance, and budget control, the tendency is to have no significant voice at all. Efforts have been made since 1960 by Council members and some staff personnel to reduce the level of Council participation in the whole matter of budgetary review. Call it economic determinism if one wishes, the day the Council gives up any significant voice with reference to budgetary matters, its stature will have gone down greatly, and its possibility of being effective in other items will have been considerably reduced.

Since 1960, there has always been year by year the problem of timing, of developing schedules of appropriate review. University and State College representatives have sometimes regarded Coordinating Council review of budgets as a sort of "fifth wheel," i.e., unnecessary, and have not hesitated to say so. So also have some Council and segmental staff personnel. The statement has been made that budgets for higher education should not necessarily be subjected to possible additional reduction because of Council review and comments in contrast to most other state departmental budgets. This seems unrealistic in the light of the extent of the claims of public higher education segments for financial support. Reduction at times may be necessary to keep the segments in balance, because it is a human tendency to ask for more than one thinks one can get; and somebody has to review requests. The Department of Finance and the Legislative Analyst do make reviews, but the theory behind the Coordinating Council was that if reviews could be made first or last by persons in the educational world, a kind of self-policing might be looked for.

108

Some writers have claimed that this would never occur, because there would be a trading off within the two senior segments. The statement that "no other state-supported activity is treated in this way" doesn't impress me. The real question is whether or not there is a necessity for it. This review is necessary for balance in educational judgment. No one should be ashamed to be party to some reduction of requests if in careful informed judgment the reduction seems justified.

The Council's advice to governing boards, to the Governor, and the Legislature should proceed apace paralleling what is happening in the segments. Should the boards be advised before they adopt budgets? The answer is yes on items that may be continuing items of study or with reference to any aspect of the total sequential budgetary process if in the judgment of the Council this is desired. Should the boards be advised after their budgets have been adopted? Again the answer is yes if on items appropriate to Council consideration. In that way full budgetary review may be clinched.

The Council should advise the Department of Finance after receipt of data from the segments, but this can be in steps or stages. It does not have to be all at once. The Council should not advise the Legislature until after the Governor's budget has been submitted. The Council should assume that the statutory provision of its being an advisory board, advisory to the Governor and to the Legislature, should not preclude it from developing advice on any aspect of the level of budgetary support while the Governor's budget is in process of preparation, and before final action by the Legislature.

This does carry with it real problems of procedure and of staffing, and care should be taken not to develop an absolutely unworkable procedure.

Sometimes overall comparisons may be somewhat old as to their absolute comparability; data cannot be accurate up to yesterday; but it is probably true all others who deal with the same figures face the same problem. This same comment can apply to the problem of discovering the level of support which should prevail for higher education. Everyone else deals with cost categories, enrollment, and other units, that are oftentimes not uniformly classified or defined, but even inexact approaches may be useful. The Council could have a double stance: such and such are approved now; this and that should be done as soon as possible. These roles may combine realism and idealism.

109

In his review of the 1965-66 budget year, the Legislative Analyst, Alan Post, wrote as follows in reference to the Coordinating Council's record:

> "As regards the three main statutory functions, the Council has a mixed record of accomplishment. It has contributed very little through its annual review of University and state college budget requests, largely because of a failure to adopt a viewpoint which is significantly broader than that of any one of the segments."

In general, Mr. Post was right in his analysis of the Council's effectiveness for the first five years of its work, but his comment was applicable to a period in which the number of public members was three only, not six as is now the case. Public members represent the general public and not any segment of higher education and are appointed for specified terms by the Governor and confirmed by the Senate. As time passes, the effectiveness of the public members should increase and the Council's stance become more broadly representative.

Until 1965, I served as chairman of the Finance Committee of the Coordinating Council for Higher Education. The first budget review was in the fall of 1961 to deal with the budgets for 1962-63. During that period of four years neither the Committee nor the Council as a whole was satisfied with its role, and from this considerable discussion ensued. Hence, in September, 1966 the Council voted to "re-examine the various techniques and procedures and general approaches which have been tried in conducting this annual review, as well as others which might be used, etc."

A brief review of the actual behavior of the Coordinating Council would be helpful.

From 1961 to 1967 two differing budget review roles had been followed by the Council. The first general procedure, through 1964, involved three Council reports, annually one in August, one in November, and one in the following February. This arrangement proved to be faulty, because already in June or July the Governor's tentative allocations to governing boards had been made; yet insufficient time was available for the preliminary budget estimates of the State Colleges and the University of California to be received, processed, and analytically reported.

110

The second report was in November, but again the time element precluded significant action.

My own comment in November, 1964 to the effect that the Committee on Finance and the Council were being confronted with decisions already made, consideration by Committee and Council occurring too late in the budgetary process, implied that accordingly emphasis and process should be changed. I also could not help noticing that no Regent or Trustee member had been present at the Finance Committee's meeting, they being represented by staff as deputies and that this in itself indicated the importance they placed upon the then existing extent of review.

The February report had some value by way of review of what had transpired and provided opportunity for critical comment on the Governor's budget as filed with the Legislature and for restating positions already taken by the Council.

In the first general procedure through 1964, there had been regularly scheduled a review of maintenance of continuing program proposals, and also a review of new and improved programs proposals. Unfortunately, the meaning of the terms "new and improved" differed considerably between the State Colleges and the University of California, as based on long-standing budgetary definitions and procedures. Hence, or so it appeared to me, the tighter budgetary controls historically bearing against the Colleges caused them to suffer more seriously than the University for "new and improved programs."

A fundamental weakness in the above procedure, apart from the timing factor, was that the Council never had the perspective for item judgment provided either by the total budgetary requests of segments or the probable state finances available as based on both political and economic considerations. Hence, the Council's staff's comment is pertinent, "From the standpoint of other budget review agencies, therefore, the Council's review was considered to be perfunctory in nature and the Council's advice was largely disregarded."

The second budget review role of the Council was adopted in June, 1965. The August report was eliminated, the November report moved forward to September, and the Council's attention was directed to "in-depth analysis and evaluation of the more significant programs and program changes." In addition, the concept of a relative scarcity of financial resources available to higher education was introduced, and the February report was

111

planned to indicate points at which the Governor's budget failed to reflect Council advice on the level of support.

In this procedure maintenance of continuing programs, that is, the work-load budget increases, were simply compared with enrollment growth rates, and of course, the maintenance of continuing programs represented the major share of the total budget requests of each segment. In effect, this whole area of budgetary review was to be left untouched. This was largely so because of the confidence held in the historic dependability of the analyses of both the Department of Finance and the Legislative Analyst. It also reflected a growing awareness by the Council that in the past, as a staff report stated, Council comments "had the greatest impact when based upon special studies of major program and educational policy issues."

During 1966-67 as indicated, the Coordinating Council gave considerable thought to its responsibility in budget review, with a staff report summarizing individual Council members' and staff views presented at the May, 1967 meeting of the Council entitled "The Budget Review Role of the Coordinating Council for Higher Education" (Report No. 67-10, May 23, 1967). Although a wide variety of opinion had been expressed individually, the Council at that May meeting united in adopting unanimously a resolution on budget review which declared that while "there is no evidence that the annual budget reports of the Coordinating Council for Higher Education have contributed materially to the objective of improving the quality of budgetary decision-making in state government," nevertheless where it has "contributed effectively to the quality of decision-making in budgeting for public higher education" it has been "through its role in conducting special in-depth studies of program and fiscal policy issues," and therefore the Council expressed its support for long-range budget planning and for reporting on program accountability. These were envisaged as "new roles" for the Council.

Particularly significant are these new approaches, because in 1966 was instituted, by Governor Brown and his Director of Finance, Hale Champion, a Programming and Budgeting system, which in essence calls for a program plan over several years. The State Colleges and the University were urged to exercise every effort to integrate their financial planning with this new program. For the time being, in the judgment of the Council the latter should adopt an interim role as set forth in the staff report referred to above and meanwhile seek more adequate information on "program inputs, costs, and performance."

The newly adopted procedure for the Council was in general accord with the viewpoints expressed by the Legislative Analyst in his comments on the Governor's budget for 1967-68. Mr. Post recommended that the Council not attempt to continue the roles it had embraced but rather redirect its efforts to long-range budget planning, programming and performance review and engage in special studies in such important areas as organized research, health education, student services, and library resources to develop comprehensive statements of program requirements against which annual budget judgments could be projected. Also he suggested that in annual budget reviews the Council comments might yield "priorities in relation to other new and continuing programs" which might cause the Council's review to serve as a "cutting edge."

The efforts of the Coordinating Council in budgetary review have not been without some collateral values. The apparently ineffective voice of one year may become the effective voice of the next. There has developed greater awareness among all members of the budgetary problems of the several segments. The record of acceptance from 1961 to 1967 by the Governor and by the Legislature of Council recommendations related to the state's funds while not easily subject to generalization and not readily the basis for a book, in my judgment reflected increasing confidence in the Council and its staff. And no better proofs of this are to be found than the tendency until 1965 or 1966 for various segments to seek Council support when in trouble. In 1967 in the budget crisis of a new administration no help was asked for in the early stages, as another chapter will describe, and this may have reflected a similar concern about the strength of the Council.

Nearly all of the preceding discussion of budgetary review has been concerned with the State Colleges and the University of California, with no mention of the junior colleges, and this has been intentionally so. From the inception of the Coordinating Council's work the level of support from the state for the junior colleges has been an elusive topic, one on which it seemed impossible for the Council to take action of any major significance related to the magnitude of the junior college problem. The Master Plan had made several recommendations looking to increased support from the state for the junior colleges, but princi-

113

pally that the proportion of total current support paid to the junior colleges should increase from the approximately 30 percent in effect in 1959 to approximately 45 percent to be achieved not later than 1975, and that state construction funds through grants or loans or both should be distributed to junior colleges on a continuing program for capital outlay purposes as determined by growth. Both of these financial factors were related to the anticipated increases in junior college enrollments as a result of the Master Plan's other provisions and the anticipated natural growth in number.

In several years, indeed almost continuously, the Coordinating Council recommended larger junior college support but often without avail. Specifically, in the 1964-65 budget an increase of state support percentage to 35 percent was recommended, but no comparable legislative action ensured.

In 1966-67 the Coordinating Council and its staff deliberated at length on the financing problems of the junior colleges in both current operations and capital outlay. In March, 1967 by unanimous vote the Council adopted a series of recommendations on current support of the junior colleges which in its details is more technical than need be outlined here but which was regarded as an important forward step; and at an earlier meeting complete agreement had been achieved on state participation in junior college capital outlay financing. While the final decisions on new junior college financial programs have not been made, it is broadly believed the Council's role has been a constructive one. These problems will be treated at greater length in a later chapter.

The State Colleges from the creation of the Board of Trustees faced a less than ideal situation as to fiscal authority and responsibility. Since this matter clearly fell in the general field of "budgetary review," or if not there then under "orderly development," the Coordinating Council advised repeatedly (1963, 1964, and 1965) concerning the need to provide full recognition of the fiscal responsibility and authority of the Trustees of the California State Colleges. In the Master Plan's recommendations a status of fiscal autonomy comparable to that possessed by the University of California would have been a natural attribute of constitutional status for the new board of trustees. With only statutory status accorded, insufficient authority and responsibility characterized budgetary and financial control with a rigid "line item" approach to appropriated funds, there being practically no change from previous practices. Flexibility or logical transfer of funds to

114

similar or related functions was impossible for the Chancellor or the Trustees or the president of a particular State College. The Council finally asked its director to initiate conferences to assist in achieving for the State Colleges fiscal authority and responsibility to the degree reviewed in its meetings.

In 1965 by a Senate concurrent resolution the Joint Legislative Budget Committee was directed to study the subject of "fiscal and budgetary restrictive controls" in the State Colleges. After numerous conferences the Joint Legislative Budget Committee reported its findings and recommendations through a report prepared by the Legislative Analyst, Mr. Alan Post. The Coordinating Council endorsed the recommendation as made by this report, and also endorsed additional proposals. The authority granted to transfer funds among and between categories "within appropriate major budgetary functions," to allocate funds for preliminary capital outlay planning, and to make temporary changes in personnel positions and classifications, was of some aid to the Colleges. Authority to approve contracts involving $10,000 or less and the administration of certain funds on a revolving basis were to be studied to provide assurance to the Legislature that the State Colleges had the capacity to exercise wise judgment in educational and management decisions. The Coordinating Council has continued its concern for adequate authority for the State Colleges' Trustees to carry forward effective management of a large and complex educational system, but thus far the changes made do not really get to the heart of the problem.

Under the long-range fiscal and financial planning for the state introduced in 1966 and further supported by the Reagan administration, multi-year budgets will come forward for review. The Coordinating Council was requested in 1967 by an Assembly resolution to submit a report by November, 1968 concerning the development of multi-year budgeting and the integration of University and State College financial planning with the Programming and Budgeting system of the state's Department of Finance.

What the ultimate role of the Coordinating Council in budgetary review may be remains indefinite, but recent developments suggest a voice of value on a wide range of specific items of importance to the total process of budget making.

10

THE STRUGGLE OVER BUDGET 1967-68

NO MATTER HOW KEENLY the sense of crisis may have impended in 1959 when the Master Plan was a required task, it cannot be compared to the overwhelming mood of crisis in higher education starting with the administration of Governor Ronald Reagan on January 2, 1967. The political campaign from the June, 1966 primary decisions down to the November elections and the atmosphere after Governor Reagan's victory in the months of November and December, 1966 had caused to exist rightly or wrongly among many in public higher education not only a feeling of confusion, uncertainty, and widespread concern but also one of despair; yet all of this was but the prelude to the storm.

On January 3, 1967, Governor Reagan's Director of Finance, Gordon P. Smith, proposed "tentatively" to State College and University representatives a 10 percent cut in their budgets and also the charging of tuition to students, $400 at the University and $200 at the State Colleges. The extent of the involvement of the state's General Fund was to be reduced to the net figures resulting from these and other moves so that initially the General Fund commitment for the State Colleges was proposed to be $168,400,000 without reduction for tuitions recommended to be charged, against the initial request of $213,000,000, and similarly for the University of California approximately $238,000,000 against the $264,000,000 Department of Finance budget and the $278,000,000 initial Regents' budget submitted. The 10 percent cut referred to was to be imposed not on initial budget requests but on these institutional budgets as modified downward heavily by the Department of Finance. Such departmental reductions were not unusual historically, but the degree of such cuts for the

116

1967-68 budgets was heavy-handed. Initial reactions were that these procedures would cause the percentage reductions from budget requests to exceed 10 percent very considerably, and that higher education might be the object of higher percentage cuts than other departments. The $238,000,000 University figure was less than the $240,000,000 budget for 1966-67. The State College figure was less than the $176,000,000 budget for 1966-67.

In his Inaugural message on January 5, the Governor devoted considerable emphasis to the state's fiscal affairs, which were described as in a severe financial crisis. He indicated "the cost of California's government is too high," that the Director of Finance and he would "turn to additional sources of revenue only if it becomes clear that economies alone cannot balance the budget," that "we will put our fiscal house in order," and that "we are going to squeeze and cut and trim until we reduce the cost of government ... and it will involve every department of government." Although initial conversations with the University of California and State College officials had been held, the Governor did not mention the intended 10 percent cut and tuition charges planned.

On January 6, the Coordinating Council for Higher Education met in Los Angeles. Neither its president nor its director had been consulted by the Governor or the Director of Finance, although all previous Council actions on new and improved programs and a number of other items had been transmitted to the new Governor. The fact that the Council's services had been offered to the new administration has been shown in an earlier chapter. Comment at the Council table indicated only minimal support for tuition charges, although my own favorable position was indicated. Opposition to heavy budget cuts was clearly evident.

My own comment as president of the Coordinating Council and in the Council meeting ran about as follows: "As an economist I doubt if there has ever been a budget in the history of man that did not have some fat or water in it to be squeezed out. The Governor knows this, you know it practically, and I know it. Distinctions within budgets as to the more important and the less important elements are necessary. The last possible thing to be cut is that of the teaching process itself. Cut everywhere else first but leave the investment in human capital untouched. This is the most important investment at any time. Education takes time, and every day lost in the life of a young man or woman not

117

properly taught in a sense is lost forever, it cannot be regained. Also, all qualified students should be cared for in both senior systems." I also suggested areas where, if a crisis did exist, whose existence or magnitude I believed myself unable to assess fairly, budgets could be trimmed, such as in public relations, student recruiting, plant care and maintenance, landscaping, and in general the noninstructional items, with the principle of postponement into another year or two for approved and ultimately necessary items to be adopted.

On the matter of tuition my comment was in effect: "I am in favor, and have been for years as older members of the Council know, of a modest or moderate tuition but only under these two circumstances as the records of the Coordinating Council's Committee on Finance will show: (1) that provision be made for financial aid for poorer students so that educational opportunity is not disturbed and (2) that the tuition receipts not go into the General Fund directly to relieve the state of other costs of government, such as better meals or whatever at San Quentin penitentiary, but be used inside each segment for aid to needy students, improved faculty salaries, or strengthening library development or equipment, or even in capital outlay to come nearer to the 'pay-as-you-go' principle."

All during January, 1967 the press was full of comments from President Kerr (at least until his dismissal on January 21), Chancellor Glenn S. Dumke, and various presidents for the State Colleges, University campus chancellors, student leaders, self-appointed faculty spokesmen, party politicians and legislators of both parties, the Lieutenant Governor Robert H. Finch, the Director of Finance, and the Governor, about deficits, financial crisis, emergency behavior, budgets, cuts, tuition, and freezes on both faculty hiring and student admissions or marked reductions in each. Indeed on nearly every conceivable item there was so much uncertainty expressed that the whole state was in a fog about higher education. Probably public higher education was in the gravest crisis it had ever faced, the repercussions of which might last for a long time.

As to tuition, the Speaker of the Assembly, Jesse M. Unruh, also chairman of the 1965-created Joint Legislative Committee on Higher Education, on January 11, 1967 urged a two-year study of Governor Reagan's tuition plans, declaring the issue one of major magnitude, asking the Governor to hold off so that the proposal could receive "a full and fair hearing in depth." This proposal was

118

warmly received in the two senior segments of public higher education, and by some portions of the public if for no other reason than to provide a cooling-off period of relief from tensions and time to think things through.

Much of this public debate in January, 1967 was pointless except to affect public opinion, because it was not known exactly what the Governor would in fact submit to the Legislature on January 31, as required by law, as the budget for 1967-68. Of course, many apparently thought his mind could be changed. It was later changed but not then.

For myself, I kept silent until the Governor's budget had been filed and was available for review, and then on February 9 I was publicly quoted in comment. I had waited to see if Governor Reagan would in fact on his own motion or in response to my letters seek the advice of the Coordinating Council or of myself as its president.

Several aspects of the January and early February debates in the public forum were, however, not without usefulness. One was to point to the possible upward influence on junior college enrollments if a tuitional plan were adopted without adequate financial aid for needy students in the University or State Colleges. If not, it was alleged many of these students would transfer. Another was that if this happened it would add to the burden of taxes on property, not reduce it, since junior colleges rest primarily on district taxes; and Governor Reagan was pledged to property tax relief.

Another result was to force clear-cut statements from the Governor's office or from other officials that of course adequate financial aid was planned from the start for the needy to accompany any tuition program, a point which if made at the start had certainly never got through to the press or the public. Another was that there would be a distinct difference in the impacts on enrollments everywhere depending on the amount of tuition charged. Another was a greater public awareness of the extent to which fees already were being charged in the State Colleges and the University as well as how all these compared with other states in combined tuition and fees charged.

Some rather exaggerated statements were made by very responsible persons in each of the corners of this financial struggle. In the January arguments with emotions running high, both State College and University representatives often overplayed their hands, seemed incapable of recognizing that a popular election

119

had been held, there was a new governor, the Legislature was newly composed, and that the new governor however much disliked in certain academic quarters because of campaign statements was due at least the respect which should surround his office. Also, as to "emergency" psychology, one sensed practically none of the willingness or capacity for adjustment which immediately would have been imperative and taken for granted if the country were at war.

An example of exaggeration was the widespread talk that if the reductions indicated took place, there would be a great exodus from the staffs of the University and the State Colleges. This continued through weeks and months. In its own report as of July, 1967, however, there were only 165 resignations in the entire University to take jobs elsewhere. I never believed there would be an exodus.

While recognizing the emotions of persons in public higher education, one of these exaggerations also was Governor Reagan's reported press conference statement earlier in the month that tuition fees would be justified to help prevent a threatened $473,000,000 deficit in the state's General Fund for the next year, and with no reported reference to the necessary concern for financial aid to poor students, while at this same press conference, as quoted by Ray Zeman in the *Los Angeles Times*, he stated that his administration is not considering reducing higher education spending—"We are not cutting the budget," but rather, "we are seeking the money from new sources," adding that "nothing would be done to curtail the quality of education." This was clearly exaggeration if "not cutting" meant only approximately as much available including possible tuitional receipts as in the previous year and with inadequate calculation of increased work load. Yet in his Inaugural he had said, "Of course, the overall cost of government must go up to provide necessary services for these newcomers," referring to the "phenomenal growth" of population. But the then existing proposals of Gordon P. Smith, his Director of Finance, were in fact cuts, including the proposed tuition income, any way one read the figures.

For one who is not a novice in educational administration, such statements gave the impression of double talk and hence lowered Governor Reagan's image even among some of his own close supporters who talked to me and whose intelligence was offended. Actually, on January 12, the Reagan administration placed a freeze on all new hiring for state offices. Either this included higher education or it didn't, but the practical results were that it did and that in itself was "cutting" and an intervention in quality maintenance.

Then on this same day, January 12, after conferring with a committee of the Regents of the University of California, again according to Ray Zeman in the *Los Angeles Times*, "Reagan emerged to announce his administration has no intention of hurting academic standards," and the *Times* quoted the Governor as saying, "Tuition will be theirs to use and do with as they see fit. Tuition can be imposed only by the Regents. It cannot be imposed by me or the Legislature." Asked if he might force the Regents to institute tuition by cutting their budget extremely low, Governor Reagan is quoted as replying, "Yes, you could force this on them by slamming the door and saying 'This is all you are going to get.' I'd rather not do that. This is not the atmosphere we want to get."

Questioned about limiting enrollments to save money, Reagan was quoted as saying, "I'd hate very much to see that." Yet apart from the kind of relatively small budget savings I have earlier suggested if adopted segmentally, the only conclusion was that enrollment reduction was inevitable.

Governor Reagan seemed to be saying that in this particular budget crisis University and State College professors, instructors, and assistants should be teaching heavier loads of work and numbers of students in class sizes, thus appealing to a popular viewpoint that college teachers do not work very hard anyway, an attitude based on ignorance of what professors do, are expected to do, and of the nature of higher education. Unlike any other professional group in the state's employ as well as the students inevitably involved, the professors appeared to be used thus as whipping boys. What lay behind all this has been the subject of much debate. Furthermore, the suspicion was deep in all higher education circles, both public and private, partly based on other public statements about the University and higher education, that the emergency in finance was being used for long-range purposes; or stated differently and knowing legislators' tendencies also not to increase very much budgets which are submitted, once reduced to new "temporary" bases these would be used as the frame for future budget calculations.

To me the net intelligible derivative of all of this represented in a budget crisis a very special penalty on higher education, a position from which Governor Reagan was forced by a combination of circumstances later to retreat, for which shift he deserves credit.

On the side of higher education to me it appeared also many were not recognizing adequately that neither the University nor the State Colleges had a right to conceive of themselves as untouchable by the constituted authorities of the people they are called upon to serve.

If University and State College leaders had intentions voluntarily of achieving whatever economies might be embraced, neither the magnitudes intended nor the areas where such economies might be effected got through to the general public. Little emphasis on the "give" in crisis, on how far if at all economies were achievable ever got through. The result was to create the impression that President Kerr's feet were set in concrete and Chancellor Dumke's in close proximity. Each kept holding out for all that had been requested, apparently believing no other stance representative or acceptable to their constituencies, and looking to later legislative support.

In review, to continue perspective, for 1967-68 the State Colleges had requested $213,000,000 and this had been cut tentatively to $168,400,000; the University had requested $278,000,000 and this had been cut to $238,000,000. Each of these was below the actual final 1966-67 budget with tuitional receipts if any to apply against these figures, and not added to them. Within the Regents of the University were some who advocated a middle position seeking to negotiate a budget of state support to the University of $255,000,000. Similarly, some of the State College Trustees sought to negotiate a budget of $191,000,000. And in each instance, tuition for 1967-68 was not to be imposed. This sort of struggle within segments, and with the Reagan administration, continued for months until the Legislature finally acted.

In the public comments made by myself on February 9 and 11, 1967, the failure of the Governor's budget adequately to support the Master Plan's principles regarding available opportunity for youth and maintaining quality in higher education was pointed out. I also hazarded estimated necessary budgets to establish minimal continuance of those principles, stating that the University would require at least $250,000,000 and probably a few million more, and if it wished to spend more, to apply reserve or private funds under its administration. (This was before the Regents actually voted from their reserve funds accumulated from overhead payments on federal contracts a total of nearly

122

$21,000,000 to aid the state's financial crisis.) For the State Colleges I indicated a necessary minimum of $190,000,000.

My criticism of the Governor's budget was welcomed by both segments; my temerity in suggesting figures was criticized as inappropriate for the president of the Council; yet my comments were made also as a person, as a member of the Council entitled to an opinion, and in the light of my history as chairman of the Master Plan team in 1959. It has often occurred that persons engaged in controversies welcome strength of argument to their own side but sometimes challenge the right to speak regarding arguments not so strong for their own sides.

At the February 21, 1967 meeting of the Coordinating Council in approaching the subject of budget review, I as president opened the discussion as follows:

> As the Council considers its staff's comments about the level of support for public higher education proposed in the Governor's budget, we enter a field which has become charged with emotions almost beyond memory in state financial matters, a field which has appeared in recent weeks characterized more by controversial allegations than by clarification of issues.
>
> I believe the Council can speak calmly and firmly both for maintaining the quality and the opportunity of public higher education of which California has long been proud, and also for careful prudence in the expenditure of public funds. Let us not here embrace the tendency in controversies to set up extreme positions for their effect on opinion. Let us here search for and hold on to the bases of assuring that our desires and hopes for the future of our youth may be realized, as one of the major and abiding considerations of policy in a responsible yet dynamic society.
>
> Two major conclusions result from the staff's study of segmental requests and of the Governor's budget. First, the segments have requested more than the minimum required to maintain quality and opportunity as we have believed in these aspects or attributes in public higher education. Secondly, the Governor's budget proposes less than the minimum required to maintain quality and opportunity as we have heretofore endorsed them.
>
> The present edition of the Governor's budget does not

indicate where proposed reductions will fall; thus the present staff report does not compare segmental requests and budget proposals in detail. A later staff report may provide these comparisons and suggest specific Council recommendations.

The staff report mentioned above presented that day was an excellent document in review of basic principles in financing public higher education, attempting to place the state's support of higher education in perspective regarding the overall economic situation facing the state government in taxable income, tax revenues, the revenue deficit, general budget reduction policies, and the record of the state General Fund operating support of public higher education, together with a comparison of California's state and local tax burden and California's state and local tax effort in public higher education with other selected states. In addition, basic and corollary principles were set forth by which to judge the adequacy of the Governor's budget proposals for higher education. Also, these principles were applied preliminarily to the Governor's budget.

There were three principles:

(1) Continue to enroll all qualified students who wish to attend in 1967-68 and beyond.

(2) Existing quality of higher education will be maintained during 1967-68.

(3) Improvements in the quality of higher education will be made to the extent that funds are available after the first two principles are satisfied.

These were interpreted to mean that there should be maintained a competitive average faculty compensation, the existing average instructional load per faculty member, existing level faculty support and library development.

As to research and public service functions, all ongoing projects and activities supported in whole or in part from state funds should be maintained at existing levels but no new projects begun during 1967-68. Furthermore, supporting services, program development should be sustained, and all 1967-68 proposed capital outlay projects justifiable by the accepted plant utilization standards or needed to care for anticipated student enrollment should be funded.

124

This report also brought out that there was some evidence the quality of faculty at the University and State Colleges (on certain measurements) had declined in recent years, while the junior colleges were maintaining the existent quality.

On February 21, 1967, Dr. Willard Spalding and I conferred with Governor Reagan to present to him in person and orally to explain the Coordinating Council's position regarding the 1967-68 budget, the part the Council had played in formulating totals, and the principles or criteria of judgment which had just that day been accepted by the Council as the bases upon which the current budget should be evaluated.

Upon this occasion after this presentation, the Governor asked my personal opinion about desirable tuition amounts and uses and about the necessary financial aid to students to accompany the charging of tuition. From this and Dr. Spalding's comments about needed information not accumulated stemmed the Governor's request to the Council mentioned in an earlier chapter, to carry forward a study in cooperation with both the State Colleges and the University bearing on the extent of necessary provision for student aid, looking to the budget year 1968-69 if tuition were voted.

Before the Legislature really got down to careful consideration of the higher education segmental budgets, it had become clear that tuition for the 1967-68 budget was not going to be voted by the University of California Regents. It was also clear that a manifest injustice would occur were tuition to be voted by the Legislature for the State Colleges. The Coordinating Council voted unanimously against tuition for 1967-68 after the Regents had postponed action until after the 1967-68 budget cycle would be closed.

With no tuition receipts for the 1967-68 budget year a likelihood, Governor Reagan at the close of February, 1967 added to the budgets of the two systems a total of $38,000,000, and then approximately $35,000,000 more on various items. It had become recognized that the Governor's initial budget declared by him to be a 10 percent cut of the University and the State Colleges budget requested was actually a much higher percentage. In all of these adjustments the Governor at least for the situation confronted had evinced some change of mind.

With the budget increases which it appeared he intended to approve, there was a greater possibility two basic principles of the Master Plan would be at least minimally embraced, namely, availability of opportunity for qualified students and high quality of the programs of both senior segments.

As passed by the Legislature, the budget for the State Colleges totaled $191,049,015, but as finally blue-penciled and signed by Governor Reagan, the total was $187,660,580, representing $3,388,435 of gubernatorial cuts.

The legislature voted for the University a budget from the General Fund of $257,100,000 which the Governor cut to $251,500,000, but this figure really included the $20,800,000 item voted earlier by the Regents from special regental reserve funds as a one-year contribution to state finance. In effect, the Governor cut out of the Legislature's $257,100,000 University budget $5,964,243 of legislatively approved items.

These reductions for both systems brought final budgets at about the points at which he had said he would approve, although some accusations of bad faith were made.

Also, Governor Reagan reduced the faculty salaries increases to 5 percent only for both senior systems, which had been voted by the Legislature at 6.5 percent for the University academic personnel and 8.5 percent for the State College faculties. Both of these actions by the Legislature followed exactly the recommendations of the Coordinating Council for Higher Education. Furthermore, the Coordinating Council had recommended and the Legislature had approved an assured 5 percent increase for the budget year 1969-70, but Governor Reagan vetoed this also.

The Governor's position in reduction of salary increases was exactly opposite to the recommendation of the Legislative Analyst, Mr. A. Alan Post, whose report on the budget pointed out that the Legislature had recognized "the importance that a strong salary structure has for the maintenance of the quality of California's educational institutions in today's market for academic personnel," and quoted the Senate Finance Committee's report in 1965 describing salary increases for the State Colleges as "the primary means of strengthening their educational program." Mr. Post stated further that he endorsed the increases recommended by the Coordinating Council for Higher Education because "salary parity is mandatory if California is to continue to develop and maintain the system of public higher education to which it has been committed under the 1960 Master Plan."

At the time in January to March, 1967, as well as thereafter, my own view of the budget cuts by Governor Reagan and his embrace of less than full coverage on Council-approved budgets for the State Colleges and the University was that these cuts would prove to be temporary. The overwhelming need of these segments for adequate financing of essential functions and not frills would be manifest, and when thoroughly analyzed and reviewed I believed would be convincing. In another year when the financial crisis emanating from Governor Brown's administration and the Legislature's earlier failures to vote adequate fiscal balance would no longer be an excuse, budgets would mount again for thoroughly justifiable reasons, and indeed might go considerably higher than at first conceived or apparent.

Hardly can the operating budgets avoid rising at about 10 percent a year based simply on increased work load as well as overcoming any lags developed in past and current years without evaluation of the qualitative meaning of the items just mentioned. In addition there is the construction budget to get facilities ready for the years that are coming, whose reduction now may mean larger maintenance or earlier replacement and whose postponement may mean excessive costs for temporary facilities. From 1960 to 1968 both the State Colleges and the University have depended largely on bond issues. There have been three, and the total has been over $750,000,000. Often mentioned but seldom embraced, the ideal would be to arrive at a point where all capital outlays could be met on the pay-as-you-go principle.

There is no escape from meeting the costs of higher education within the principles California has embraced. Higher education must be available for all qualified and interested persons on terms that keep society democratic and opportunity open for all. The costs to achieve this goal are and will be such that a broad sharing of responsibility is necessary. This is one reason for support of the principle of a partial bearing of the costs of public higher education by the students and their parents who are able to do so through a well-developed program of tuitional payments and financial aids to balance such payments where family and individual economic well-being show that hardship worthy of public note would ensue. This is the question of tuition in at least the State Colleges and the University of California which is the subject of the next chapter.

11

TUITION IN THE STATE COLLEGES
AND THE UNIVERSITY

THE IDEA of charging tuition* at low, moderate, or high levels to California residents attending the University of California or one of the California State Colleges is not a new one and has been debated in governmental agencies and citizen groups for many years. Some of my comments relating to public higher educational finance and the costs of public higher education related to tuition are found in an earlier chapter. Support for tuition has not been wholly politically partisan even though with the Reagan administration determined upon its introduction it has been generally assumed that all Republicans favor tuition and all Democrats oppose it. While polarity of thought in these directions on this topic is evident, no simple generalization is acceptable.

On March 3, 1965, the *Los Angeles Times* in an editorial on "Financing Higher Education" asked the question, "Would it be unreasonable to charge a nominal tuition for those students able to pay for it?"

In September, 1965, at Governor Brown's Conference on Education held in Los Angeles, in the discussion section on finance, mine was the voice which spoke up for tuitions in the State Colleges and the University of California; but what is not known is that I was specifically asked by one of the Governor's secretaries presumably speaking for him to make this presentation in order that all viewpoints might be aired. Of course, the likelihood

*The Master Plan differentiated between "tuition" and "fees" in these words: "tuition" is defined as student charges for teaching expense, whereas "fees" are for charges to students for services not directly related to instruction, such as health, counseling other than related to the student's educational program, placement services, housing, recreation, and the like.

that I would have spoken on the subject of higher educational finance without mentioning tuition is small. Other speakers on this same program and who found my position unacceptable were Chancellor Glenn S. Dumke of the California State Colleges and President Clark Kerr of the University of California.

The Master Plan of 1959-60 embraced the tuition-free principle for state residents but only after much argument in the Survey team and only after its chairman (myself) clearly saw no yielding would occur and he would be almost alone in his vote.

Hence, a compromise was negotiated related to fees. The chairman of the Master Plan Survey team was not willing to have the whole host of services to students apart from teaching, which services had been growing in number and extent in recent decades in every college and university in the land, and were still growing everywhere, become charged against taxpayer revenues.

According to the Master Plan, a fee structure was to be devised to collect sufficient revenues to cover auxiliary services, that is, such operating costs as those for laboratory breakage, health services, intercollegiate athletics, student activities, and "other services incidental to, but not directly related to, instruction." Furthermore, "the operation of all such ancillary services as housing, feeding, and parking" were to be "self-supporting." It was expressly stated that "taxpayers' money should not be used to subsidize, openly or covertly, the operation of such services." This required consideration of which portions of amortization and interest payments on housing and feeding structures would be properly chargeable to operating expense. It also required that the cost of operation of such services as feeding, housing, and parking periodically should be recomputed and fees set accordingly. All of this was a marked advance on previous practice in which considerable portions of these costs were borne by the state.

As these fees of various kinds have been imposed or increased in amount since 1960, there have been protests by students and faculty on nearly every campus. Hence, protests against tuition in 1967 and 1968, and other increases of student payments, may be evaluated against this background. My support for abandonment of the tuition-free principle has this memory of behavior in public higher education in California. Furthermore, these services will continue to grow, and fees may have to rise as a result.

In reference to the fees referred to above, it took a bit of doing to get both the University and the State Colleges to be willing to apply the Master Plan principles really to eliminate the effects of inflation by establishing the real dollar equivalent of long-established relatively fixed fees and also to get an accounting developed which would calculate the effect on fees of the various state grants earlier made towards the costs of various services so that in fact the fees charged would contain no taxpayers' money so as to subsidize such services.

Tuition was considered by the Coordinating Council or its Committee on Finance on several occasions from 1961 to 1967. In its first year, to constitute a frame of reference for its activities, the Coordinating Council had adopted all the major principles and suggested directives for its own work found in the Master Plan document over and beyond the Donahoe Act, thus initially placing itself on record in favor of the tuition-free principle. Later, and upon two occasions the question of possible tuition was presented to the Committee on Finance of the Council. From this no serious review by the Council itself as a whole ever really developed until 1967, because the committee chairman who was known to favor tuition was blocked in trying to bring it to the Council agenda by a negative committee vote, the State Colleges and the University representatives indicating they would report back when they had studied the issues more thoroughly. Since neither segment initiated any such study, this constituted a deliberate action to avoid if possible a discussion of the subject. Later, the Council staff requested permission to study the subject, and a Council document on the tuition-free principle was prepared and issued, but not until July, 1967 was permission granted to the staff itself to study and recommend on the principle of tuition or on the uses to which tuitional receipts if received should be applied.

Charging tuition at a public institution of higher education may result from any one or more social, political, or economic considerations or reasons.

In the first place, there is history. In some public institutions in this country and elsewhere there has often been a tuition requirement in some amount from the student. In California, except in the early life of the University of California and in certain periods in the State Colleges, as well as in the junior colleges, there has been the tradition of tuition-free public higher education. Also, in California there is among private institutions the case of the earlier tuition-free years of Stanford University when its available resources and its endowments yielded sufficient sums to make

130

possible adoption of a tuition-free policy. Furthermore, in Texas, Rice University has been another private university institution which has had a history of no tuitional payment by students. However, most private, or independent, institutions have been tuitional throughout most of their history, and many public institutions have been nontuitional until recent years in most states. Most other states have come to grips with the issue long before California, principally due to rising costs.

In the second place, there has been financial emergency bringing about situations in various states where tuitions have been imposed for short or long periods to aid a state or municipality in weathering an economic storm.

Thirdly, there has been and is the imposition of a tuition of whatever amount as a continuing fiscal policy of a state or municipality. Today, tuitions of varying magnitude are charged by public universities and colleges in nearly all states of the Union. A very large percentage of the nation's state colleges and universities in fact raised tuition or fees for the year 1967-1968.

There has been and is also, as mentioned above, the imposition of fees to cover various services which the college or university renders the student, which fees in some instances may be devices to avoid the use of the word "tuition." This is a good way of expressing the California situation. Such fees, however, do provide revenue in whole or in part to cover the expense of such special services, and in certain states or institutions such services are paid in part or in whole out of the tuition as charged. Thus, distinctions without major difference can and do exist.

If fees as well as tuitional payments are combined showing cost to the student, there is probably no state which does not charge students in public institutions something; or at most only one or two states are exceptions.

Tuition in public colleges or universities has been urged by economists, politicians, or others on grounds of social reform, to aid in changing attitudes or relationships, on disciplinary grounds such as to prevent malingering, for sumptuary reasons such as to discourage "consumption" of one type of higher education in favor of another, and also because of a belief in various economic principles historically related to public finance.

In the literature of public finance, payment of some kind by the consumer for the public services rendered by government, i.e., for water, gas, electricity, transportation, public housing, medical care, even schools, has been urged as a means of causing the person benefiting to bear in some small or larger measure the cost of the benefit enjoyed. Rarely, even in socialistic countries, are all these services rendered completely gratuitously.

However, in all candor, schools, colleges and universities have generally been treated separately as public services under this doctrine of payment as a result of benefit since some writers have balanced that aspect with the social benefit derived from education in skills of a physical, mental, social, or moral nature or significance for which no monetary value equivalents have seemed calculable.

Nevertheless, more frequently in this regard there has been a distinction made on the one hand between the type of education which everyone in a democracy should have for its best functioning and those higher levels of education whose acquisition constitutes for the individual a substantial asset of intellectual capital, an investment from which, if he does not allow his mind and all his skills to atrophy, he as well as society and the economy will benefit financially in his lifetime far beyond the amount invested.

The line of demarcation between these two types or levels of educational advantage and achievement, that is, between general knowledge and special competence, was once thought, many decades ago, to be at the completion of the elementary school. Later this level advanced in general acceptability in this country to the completion of high school, i.e., the twelfth grade or age seventeen or eighteen. More recently and to a growing degree in the last fifty years, and especially in California, that level has advanced in the minds of some through the fourteenth grade, i.e., the junior college or the lower division of the undergraduate college or university where characteristically except for vocational, technical, or terminal course work the emphasis has been on a type of general or liberal education with only a minimal emphasis on specialization.

Now, with specialized knowledge so dominant everywhere, with its emphasis on competence and the acquisition of all kinds of specific skills, and with generally demonstrable concomitant financial advantage, and with the costs of higher education mounting so unprecedently, it is being argued that the individual or his parents should bear now or later, while studying or after earning, some portion of the cost to society of the education which provides such advantages.

Schools, the common or public schools including the high schools, have characteristically been free of tuition in American practice for a very long time. In California, the junior colleges were established as tuition-free extensions upward of the high school, and they have become collegiate equivalents for college and university programs as well as for the multifarious range of programs of a technical, vocational, and terminal nature. Whether or not the junior colleges should be exempt from a tuition charge of some amount, presumably much less, if tuition is adopted for the State Colleges and the University is one of the major moot points of the near future.

Forty years ago in a conference at UCLA while teaching economics there, I voiced a belief in the establishment of progressively larger tuitions in the University of California commencing with the junior year, and continuing through the graduate and professional programs based on the doctrine of benefit as well as later ability to repay. My voice was not well received. Since then I have seen little reason to change my mind on this stance as one element in a general approach to educational finance.

However, no policy could possibly be more unpopular today with university faculties with their strong involvement in graduate work or higher professionalized study and research. The universities, and in some instances the colleges, have changed decidedly in their educational interests and objectives in these decades. Today the universities for graduate work "bid for the bodies," compete vigorously to acquire the brightest, most promising minds, and even pay them to attend through research or teaching assistantships, fellowships, or instructorships, or fellowship grants with no duties at all except pursuit of the degree or study course involved. Hence, the application rigorously as a policy to tuition of the doctrine of benefit would constitute nothing less than an academic revolution. Accordingly, compromise practices prevail everywhere where tuition is charged by a public university or college. Indeed, some if not many university and college faculty in California have openly opposed tuitions for non-California residents lest graduate enrollments would decline; but we have succeeded in achieving a tuition of some respectability for out-of-state students, and this is now a firm policy. In this aspect, however, considerably beyond what is probably general public knowledge, the University has been allowed to waive such non-California resident tuitions for selected students to a considerable percentage, and possibly this happens also in the State Colleges to some degree.

While personally believing in a differential tuition in public higher education above the fourteenth grade reflecting the increasing intellectual capital benefit to the individual, I am willing to forego major differentiations to achieve an important present policy goal, namely, the establishment of a moderate, modest tuition which taken together with the incidental fee for the University or the set fees for the State Colleges would establish a total rate of charges approximating the average of such charges in comparable public institutions of higher education in the United States. At this moment such a total for the State Colleges would be about $350 per academic year and for the University about $500.

In general, the opposition to tuition lays great stress on the burden on the disadvantaged persons in contemporary society. However, today as against decades ago when neither nation or populace was affluent we already have (1) the California State Scholarships; (2) the newly enacted California State Graduate Fellowships program; (3) the whole miscellany of loan funds from federal, state, or private sources; (4) some opportunities in work-study programs; (5) the various private or foundation aid or scholarship programs; and other current programs. Nevertheless, public agencies and public policy must continue to be alert to the effect of tuition and all other college or university attendance costs on persons from low income status. So often is reference made to the problems of minorities that it might appear that these are the only elements involved. This is wrong, but to write this should not be interpreted as lack of concern for the special minority problems.

With the imposition of tuition, some further financial aid program for the truly needy is imperative. These are estimated to constitute from 20 percent to 30 percent of the University or State Colleges' student groups, depending on the amount charged and on the definition of "needy."

It is hard to understand unless it be political why University and State College administrations have opposed so vigorously a tuition from the 65 percent to 80 percent of their student body who are able even though in varying degrees to pay. The families from which these young people come, or the young people themselves, seem fully able to buy even if by installment credit, their cars, television sets, gasoline and oil and a whole host of items considered more necessary than education. In part these other items are made possible because youth have not been required to pay any tuition and hence are being educated in substantial degree at the expense of other citizens. Then, too, there are those students, generally but not wholly, from the more ample levels of income whose levels and manner of living and search for social recognition have in part been augmented by the tuition-free principle, by not having to consider in any degree the costs to the state of their education. Fraternities and sororities are made easier, some more luxurious and more exclusive because no tuition is charged. It is easier not to face costs, and to let the state bear the burden and the problem of finance. It takes courage particularly in a culture or society where so much of the "free public services" doctrine has been embraced to support a measure bound to be unpopular no matter how logical.

Genuine concern for the lesser privileged in family income background would dictate a tuition plan combined with a financial aid plan, the burden thus bearing primarily on those who are able to pay.

A combined tuitional plan and aid plan can cause "ability to pay" and "benefit" doctrines of public finance to be brought together effectively.

The word "tuition" has been like a red banner in front of a maddened bull. The term "fee" to which in time the faculties and students have become adjusted does not have such a connotation. However, note the inconsistency in suggesting increased "fees" but no requirement of "tuition." Yet some University campus chancellors and State College presidents and the Regents of the University have embraced such opportunism.

Attendance at the University of California or the State Colleges is not a right but a privilege or opportunity available only to those who meet the required standards for admission. Attendance at the presently no tuition, practically no fee junior colleges is open to all high school graduates and to many others principally adults not high school graduates considered educable by the junior college where application for admission is filed.

Imposition of a tuition at the State Colleges or the University might at first or for some time have some effect on enrollment transfers from the University or State Colleges to junior colleges, in part depending on the amount of tuition charged. One element of the Master Plan was a planned diversion from the State Colleges and the University campuses to the junior colleges to amount in 1975 to 50,000 lower division students who otherwise would have gone to the State Colleges and the University. Clearly such a policy was in the interests of economy for the state since the junior college segment is least costly to the state. This diversion was to be achieved by higher admission standards at the University and State Colleges and by percentage reductions of the lower division enrollments in relation to total undergraduates at these two segments so that the lower division would by 1975 be 40 percent. This percentage goal as noted earlier already is evident in the State Colleges but has not yet come into effect within the University's enrollment policies, because the University has been unwilling to achieve this ratio if it meant turning down the admittance of any qualified student. Tuition might aid this transfer or diversion policy. Admittedly, there is some evidence that such effect would be minimal if the general inelasticity of demand for higher education which in the past has seemingly prevailed continues to hold true, but there is no assurance that it will be so.

The Master Plan because of the diversion policy and as a matter of public policy recommended that the state contribute more heavily to junior college operating support than in the past and make state funds available to defray part of the capital cost of construction of junior college facilities. Thus far the state has been laggard on these financial support aspects, and the burden on local property taxes has not been lightened. Tuition at the other two public segments would possibly increase the state's responsibility in junior college finance even further. Sooner and not later the state's share of junior college finance will have to be enlarged. Will this mean the requiring of a tuition in the junior colleges?

It is already evident that a considerable body of junior college leadership holds such a fear. In early 1967 a number of junior college district boards passed resolutions against tuition in public higher education and filed these with the Coordinating Council for Higher Education. On January 14, 1967, also in prompt reaction to the suggestions of Governor Reagan for tuition in the other public segments, the Board of Directors of the California Junior College Association passed a resolution supporting what was labeled "the tuition-free philosophy of public education in California."

This resolution declared that "the California Master Plan represents the nation's first significant breakthrough toward realization of the American dream of full education for all, that "this master plan is founded on the fundamental philosophy of tuition-free public institutions," that "the public weal necessitates the maximum individual development of each citizen," that "the continuing growth, increased prosperity and general progress of California are . . . traceable to and dependent upon such an enlightened outlook," and that "abandonment of the tuition-free philosophy in the university and State college systems would certainly result in the abrogation of the master plan, thereby adversely affecting all segments of public higher education, but most particularly the junior colleges, which, although still languishing far below the level of State support promised in the master plan, would be called upon to bear the brunt of the sudden forced diversion of thousands of students unable to meet the tuition charges." This resolution also pleaded that the welfare of students, local property owners, and the State of California be "equally in mind" and declared "its unalterable opposition to any proposal for destroying" the tuition-free philosophy as "the cornerstone of public education."

Although that resolution represents a most sincerely held viewpoint even though flowery in praise of the Master Plan, this writer does not believe either that free tuition was "the cornerstone" or "the basic principle" of the Master Plan, nor is it fundamental to its other principles and relationships. In fact, the Master Plan in the matter of fees increased the expense to the student of all auxiliary and ancillary services, and will continue to do so as these services expand or their costs increase.

In the Coordinating Council's action on February 21, 1967 in rejecting tuition for the 1967-68 budget year in the State Colleges, language quite similar with reference to history and the Master Plan was initially introduced in the resolution, but reference to free tuition as the guiding principle of that plan was amended out, and the resolution as passed simply stated historical facts with which all could agree.

For many years, there has been question as to the ability and willingness of California citizens to bear the total costs of state and local government including their responsibilities for public higher education. The Master Plan Survey's study in 1959 of the State of California's ability to finance the higher education demands to be anticipated from 1960 to 1975 showed that adequate financing on established revenues was open to doubt. Prospective capital outlay, so heavily bearing on the state to care for new facilities, to house the projected increases in State College and University enrollments, it was believed, could not be borne by the General Fund any more than in the past. Special funds, reserves, and bond issues had characteristically been used in previous years, and continuance thereof was anticipated.

Competition for the use of the General Fund was foreseen by the Master Plan report, and this competition has not abated. While expenditures for education in all categories have grown beyond all previous estimates, so also have expenditures for social welfare, public health, and other purposes as the problems of dependency, delinquency, crime, and the needs of senior citizens among others, increased. Awareness of the continuing pressure upon the state's finances from public higher education prompted the Master Plan chairman to urge a tuition in 1959, but as stated that was set aside. In 1967 severe financial crises afflicted the state and many local governments. Under these circumstances with financial needs for all public higher education seemingly mounting faster in dollars than enrollments of students and with the dual burden of financing both capital and current needs, it has to me seemed not unreasonable to establish varying tuition rates for the State Colleges, the University, and even conceivably later, even though very, very much lower, even nominal, some fee for the junior colleges.

All of the foregoing has considered tuition from the standpoint of the state government, its finances, and what it may or may not be able or willing to do for its youth. The growth and development of students not only intellectually but also in character and as responsible citizens learning to carry in part at least the responsibilities of adulthood has also been urged as a goal. In part, the carrying by the state of the costs of education for young people well into their twenties in undergraduate education but especially for graduate education is but another example of the psychological prolongation of infancy, so much a malaise of contemporary society. Will tuition help on this problem, or has the disease run so far in its course that the requirement of sharing costs will render the situation unbearable?

If, on the other hand, one holds that no tuition should be charged because higher education should be regarded not from the standpoint of the individual's increase of intellectual capital and hence potentially of higher opportunity in income and wealth, but from the standpoint of all such education as a social good, as a strengthening of the economy, as development of technology, as cultural achievement, and as the basic fabric for defense and security in other than military terms, then another view may be in order. While all of these arguments may be true, they apply to all higher education whether of public or private sponsorship, and they are true only as students really seek an education. Hence, one might argue the state should be willing to move clear through to another approach or basis to state financial support of some sort for private institutions which make these same contributions to society, as well for the public colleges and universities.

This I am not advocating and for many reasons. My support of the dual system is of long standing and on record. In my judgment the State Scholarship program with free choice of institution is justified for the reasons just given, but probably represents the limits of state support even though indirect for private institutions under present conditions. However, gift support of private institutions depends in part upon the financial, i.e., tax, burden upon citizens generally. The burdens of public services should be spread widely. Tuition in public institutions is such a spreading of the burden, and only indirectly an assistance to private institutions. Tuitions in public institutions only indirectly will be of help to private institutions, and although some private institutions do favor public institutional tuitions, this is not a primary nor a satisfactory reason for advocating such public college and university tuitions.

One aspect of my views about tuition should be restated. That is that all tuitions received should not go directly into augmenting the state's General Fund subject to specific appropriations but be currently reserved for the use of the segment into which paid. While in the long run tuitional receipts will possibly or probably aid the General Fund, depending on budgets voted by the Legislature and if larger not vetoed by the Governor, students should be able always clearly to see their payments going for library and equipment, for faculty salaries, for scholarships and student aid, for a capital outlay pay-as-you-go fund, or for other objectives directly affecting their welfare. And as problems of emergency finance pass, these monies supplemented by appropriations conceivably could lead to larger total expenditures for higher education. Politically unwise would be a situation where students could argue that better meals were served at Chino or Folsom penitentiaries or the growing costs of the social welfare load were met at their expense.

Occasionally one hears the comment that there are too many students in colleges and universities anyway, and there should be a required tuition to keep some persons from attending. When this argument comes from a self-made man, one whose education was limited, this may be a belief that today's social policy should be based on his experience, which of course is untenable. It may be the argument of one who wishes not to have his financial position or security impaired by the taxes necessary to give all willing and qualified persons a chance. It may be the argument of those who want larger supplies of semi-skilled or skilled labor, who fear lest the supply of blue-collar types of workers will shrink relatively to the total supply so that pay checks will rise. It may be the argument of persons who have stereotyped all students into categories, or maybe only one category with all the traits of the least pleasing. No one of these arguments is very impressive.

The types of education beyond the high school are so varied, and the programs available in junior colleges, State Colleges, and the University of California so numerous, that no simple approach to the question of numbers of students can possibly be satisfactory.

Every student who is willing and able and who shows he can perform adequately in the program entered should be educated, or trained in the skills chosen. If it is desired to raise standards of admission, or of retention once admitted, or of probation if some failure occurs, or of the completion of a certificate program or degree, let such occur. But let not the test be dollars lest an academic and educational elite be built on economic and financial capacity rather than intellectual and moral abilities. This is the reason why every economic or financial barrier including tuition should be accompanied by adequate programs of scholarships for the able who have need, and grants of aid for those who are good enough to be admitted and in good standing but are genuinely needy, as well as loans for all who are allowed to continue their studies. These should always, in a democracy, be a part of the ethical conceptions of the frame of reference of higher education.

The general position on tuition which has been set forth above has been set forth orally before the Coordinating Council for Higher Education or to its Committee on Finance and hence is not a new position for the writer or the resultant of any recent change in the political environment of California. I hope it is a consistent one. In 1967 some comments from persons in the Reagan administration were not especially consistent. One cannot justify tuition as "imperative for one year to meet a fiscal emergency" and then in a matter of days justify it as part of a scheme of "social reform to increase the sense of student responsibility for their own education and welfare."

Because all segments realized that appropriate provision for financial assistance to students from low income families, or themselves in need, should be related to a decision on tuition, the University and the State Colleges initiated studies in the spring of 1967, and the Coordinating Council for Higher Education, at the request of Governor Reagan, carried forward a similar study in cooperation with them. In addition, the Coordinating Council on its own initiative, and with the full knowledge of Governor Reagan after a conference on July 21, 1967, carried forward a study of possible uses of receipts from such tuitions as might be voted by the University Regents and the Legislature.

With only disparaging comment of possible financial aid to needy students, in July, 1967 a campaign entitled Citizens for California Higher Education was launched by University and State College professors and sympathizers, led by Professor Charles Muscatine of the University of California, Berkeley campus, to organize opposition to tuition in either of the two senior systems.

It should be recalled that in January, 1967, the initial tuition proposal of Governor Reagan and of Gordon Smith, the Director of Finance, had been $200 a year for the State Colleges and $400 a year for the University; but this was stated as illustrative and not necessarily final. At other times, spokesmen of the Reagan administration suggested lower figures might be recommended. The exact amount of accompanying student financial aid to be provided was not made precise but was initially indicated as related to the newly-to-be-added factor of tuition.

On July 26, 1967, Governor Reagan made his program for tuition more precise, in an address in Los Angeles, but in doing so he gave his tuition proposal several new angles. His plan was labeled "Equal Education Plan." It called for a tuition of $250 a year in the University and $180 a year in the State Colleges. Four major objectives were stated : (1) "to achieve full educational opportunity for all qualified students in California, including those from the poorest families and from racial minorities—guaranteeing full opportunity in fact instead of opportunity in theory," (2) "to keep the University of California and the State Colleges fully competitive with the great private universities and colleges in attracting and retaining outstanding teachers," (3) to

141

provide a supplemental capital improvement fund for each campus of the University and each State College," and (4) "to eliminate existing inequities, so that low income families shall not pay a disproportionate share of the cost of educating students in comparison with upper-income families."

Governor Reagan stated that the total amounts received from tuition would be enough to provide generous grant-in-aid and loan funds for needy students. One-half of all the tuition receipts would be so used. Such loan or grant aid in his plan was to be in an amount as needed against the total cost to the student in not only tuition but also board, room, transportation, and other expenses. The loan program at minimum interest rates would utilize private, state, and federal funds.

According to the Governor, one-quarter of the total receipts of an estimated $26,000,000 for the University and $29,000,000 for the State Colleges could also well sustain 250 teaching chairs in the University and 300 in the State Colleges at salaries high enough and otherwise sufficiently attractive to obtain and retain "the finest teaching talent in the nation." In addition, one-quarter of the funds received would make available monies for campus capital improvements.

The Governor's student aid and loan plan, although declared tentative and subject to reconsideration, revealed his preference, once financial need were established by the individual, for an emphasis on loans in the earlier undergraduate years (first year, 75 percent loan, 25 percent grant; second year, 50 percent loan and 50 percent grant), and in the third year, 25 percent loan and 75 percent grant, with full grant of funds in the fourth year. His plan as issued recognized that "certain objections have been raised regarding the high amount of loan required during the first year." Hence, a possible alternative plan less likely to discourage "potential students from lower socio-economic and minority groups" reversed the above formula and placed "the emphasis on grants rather than loans." Such a plan would require an absolute-need category for "those particular cases which might be discouraged by the high loan during the first year of either graduate or undergraduate students." Under this alternative, there could be a full grant-in-aid the first year, 50 percent in grants and 50 percent in loans in the second year, 25 percent in loans and 75 percent in grants the third year, and full grants-in-aid the final year. Clearly this alternative was not the complete reverse of the first plan. It was a compromise with practicality. The clear reverse would have been 75 percent in loans and 25 percent in grants the third year and full loan and no grant in the fourth year, a scheme possibly likely to cause attrition and low retention, and hence failure to complete a degree program.

Governor Reagan's plan was opposed of course by those who were against tuition in public higher education at any time and in any form. The loan feature was opposed by the argument that heavy debt for the first year of 75 percent of a possible $1,600 to $1,800 if in residence, i.e., $1,200 to $1,350, would tend not to achieve equality of opportunity for the underprivileged. By the Governor's own admission "the major economic barrier to a college education is not tuition but, rather, the cost of more expensive items," and hence "relatively few students from low-income families or minorities actually are found on our University and State College campuses today."

The alternative plan was opposed by those who believed it wrong to give away such large initial individual amounts to persons not already sufficiently interested in attending the University or a State College to have made inquiry or who if college qualified and interested and already at a junior college should be by such a plan induced to transfer to more prestigious associations at the expense of the state. One also heard the argument, conceivably farfetched, that either the grant or the loan program for a person even though qualified to be a student but not really interested could become indirectly a family welfare project or an individual boondoggle.

Earlier in this chapter reference was made to the studies by the University of California, the State Colleges, and the Coordinating Council in 1967 on the amounts of student financial aid required. Initially, these studies were prompted by the proposal (or threat as seen by many) of tuition, and the intent at the beginning was to discover what student financial aid would be necessary equitably to offset such an added burden. However, after the University's Regents and administrations and staffs debated and discussed the issues, and similarly the State College Trustees, as well as finally the Coordinating Council, the problem of adequacy of student financial aid in California took on almost unbelievable proportions.

In one form or another, that is, grants, loans, or scholarships, and without a tuition or added fees or with such additional charges, and in higher education as a whole including the junior colleges and the private institutions as well as the State Colleges and the University where the tuition proposal had begun, the various studies brought forth every conceivable approach to what the State should do to help youth embrace higher education. The doctrine of equality of educational opportunity once conceived primarily in terms of the open college door for those qualified, able, and willing to attend was being expanded to include a positive effort to overcome as much as possible according to one plan or another the economic and financial incapacities of individuals and families. Emphasis turned to recruiting through student aid the largest possible qualified enrollments in higher education.

The Governor's plan gained attention but was only one plan, and it had been issued in late July, 1967, before the University's staff and contracted College Entrance Examination Board studies had been reviewed in August by the Regents or before the State College Trustees had detailed considerations or before the Coordinating Council's study which Governor Reagan specifically had asked for had been reported back in late August. No study or plan including the Governor's applied itself directly and solely to the question of what new aid of whatever kind would be needed simply to offset the one new factor of tuition at various levels of possible tuition and fees. Each tended to view the newly opened problem from the standpoint of the ideal arrangements regardless of cost or at least without sufficient consideration of opportunity costs which to the economist mean the alternative possible uses of the same funds, in this case to a very considerable degree according to most plans, the state's funds. One State College trustee pointed out most tellingly on one plan that it would provide "millions for mediocrity but not one cent for excellence" and indicated his view that it was folly for a state which was engaged in cutting essential higher education budget items and hence operating at less than excellence to put millions equivalent to budget cuts already made into student aid to spread opportunity for less than the best, indeed by increasing enrollments and not budgets to assure mediocrity.

Also, as before in the state's history each segment was quite fearful or at least concerned over the possible effects upon its own enrollments according to whether or not tuition were adopted and what particular scheme of financial assistance to students might ensue even if no tuition or added fees were imposed.

In August, 1967, the University's Regents voted down (14-7)

144

the adoption of tuition but voted to recommend an increase of fees, that is, a special student charge, appointing a special committee to work on the latter problem and report back. The State College Trustees voted against tuition. In the Coordinating Council a move to reaffirm endorsement of the tuition-free principle was successfully tabled by those who feared an affirmative vote might ensue. The Coordinating Council's study of possible alternative plans for student aid was forwarded to the Governor in October, 1967, without any particular plan being endorsed, but the Council did unmistakably endorse the continuance of the California State Scholarship Commission's program, described in an earlier chapter. The report to the Governor was entitled "Financial Assistance Programs for California College and University Students."

By January, 1968, the Regents' special committee to report back on the amount and uses of the special student charge voted by the Regents in August recommended an increase of fees by $156 a year. After his tuition proposal of July, 1967, for $250 in University tuition had been turned down by the Regents in August, Governor Reagan at once had proposed a new student "charge" of $200. The new charge of $156 was not accepted at once by the Regents, action being postponed until after the Governor's budget for 1968-69 had been submitted to the Legislature. The uses recommended by the special committee for the increased income were: additional student aid, improved counseling program, and relief for the University's regular budget for portions of the costs of deans of students and similar offices to cover services to students.

Speaker Jesse Unruh immediately labeled the recommended fee as a concession to the Governor, "a hypocritical bow of obedience" to the Reagan administration, and further was reported as declaring that the committee's report "proves once again that the Board of Regents is incapable of maintaining genuine independence from outside political influence."

The *Los Angeles Times,* a most powerful factor in public opinion, editorialized on January 18, 1968 against both the newly recommended charge and the Governor's $250 tuition proposal, thus apparently substantially reversing the editorial position this paper had taken in March, 1965 as quoted early in this chapter. The January, 1968 editorial stated the Regents have "no choice but to resist tuition under any label," stating that "to compromise with principle now could affect public higher education in California for years to come." Most of the officers of the Times Mirror Company, the publisher of the *Times,* and most of the editors of the paper are my personal friends; yet I must differ with their reasoning. It is one thing to be opposed to two specific tuition or student charge proposals and quite another to support the tuition-free principle on the grounds that "once the no-tuition principle is breached, no effective limitation on the amount of the charge will be possible again." This latter argument reflects no trust in the future composition of the Regents or any future governor or legislature, or for that matter the electorate itself. It is a denial of any confidence in the capacity for restraint or of respect for public higher education on the part of the people of the State of California in the future, a kind of insult to the understanding of all those whom all public higher education in last analysis must acknowledge as sovereign. What will this paper or those who have vocalized this viewpoint hold as opinion if and when through changing composition of the Board of Regents, or of the attitude towards total available finance for the University and the State Colleges of the Governor, the Legislature, or the electorate, or of changed economic conditions in years to come, a tuition or added charges are embraced? The argument for or against tuition or added charges should be based on other more substantive grounds than lack of confidence in the rationality and judgment of Constitutional officers as yet unknown.

In his July, 1967 presentation regarding tuition, Governor Reagan did not make any reference to tuition in the junior colleges. However, it had been presented to him as a recommendation from a member of his staff as follows: "A tuition of $100 will be charged at the junior colleges, providing both General Fund relief and property tax relief in its utilization." Counsel to his office at the time by me indirectly strongly urged against it or at least that a proposal of tuition in the junior colleges be postponed a long time, at least until after a victory for tuition in the University and the State Colleges had been achieved. Nevertheless, on October 16, 1967, Gordon P. Smith, the State Director of Finance, presumably speaking for the Reagan administration did publicly suggest the possibility of a junior college tuition. The intuitive junior college leaders' fears of early 1967 now appeared justified. Every portion of public higher education seemingly was to bring to the student an awareness of the public's expenditure on his behalf, and to require his participation in helping meet that cost. On October 24, 1967, however, according to Ray Zeman, in the *Los Angeles Times,* Governor Reagan stated that "the state never has considered imposition of tuition in the junior colleges." Governor Reagan said further, "I think Gordon was expressing a personal opinion," and "it's never been considered as part of our program at all."

In February, 1968 the Joint Legislative Committee on Higher Education, representing both houses of the Legislature and both parties, and chaired by Speaker Jesse Unruh, issued a summary of preliminary findings. With regard to tuition, after stating seven points considered, the statement read, ". . . , the Committee finds that under present circumstances the arguments offered for tuition are of insufficient relevance and merit to justify a departure from the state's historic policy regarding tuition. Accordingly, the Committee opposes the imposition of tuition for 1968-69 and any comparably large increase in student fees for the same purpose." The Committee expressed its belief that "the principal purpose of any decision to impose tuition or a comparable increase in other student charges must be to raise additional funds for the current support of public higher education, in addition to or in partial substitution for what would otherwise be available from the state's General Fund." It rejected tuition as a means to divert students from one system to another, to weed out the unmotivated, to aid private institutions, or to punish students for campus disorders. It also rejected tuition as a device to institute new or expanded expenditure programs such as student aid or faculty salaries. "The imposition of tuition may require additional student aid, but additional student aid is not dependent upon the imposition of tuition." (To the Joint Committee's majority opinion against tuition or increased fees there were three strong dissents.)

One of this committee's preliminary findings was that "the most persuasive argument for tuition is as a user charge"; however, if imposed, "it is important to provide for some system of deferred payment."

With clear perception the Committee observed that a large-scale student aid program coupled to tuition if effective in attracting or retaining large numbers of students not now attending or remaining in college "could result in a new increase rather than a decrease in support and capital outlay costs to the General Fund."

No early solution to all of the problems of student financial assistance, or even tuition as such (although apparently laid to rest in the University for the moment), may be expected. Inevita-

147

bly the issues discussed and the ideas released and now in the public domain will keep alive and moot the question of the appropriate degree of participation by the student or his family in meeting the state's cost of his education. Similarly, the adequacy of financial assistance to students will continue to receive even more extensive consideration, and from this crisis in finance may conceivably flow based on the decision later made very substantial influences on the enrollments, finances, and programs of all segments of higher education. This will occur because the practices of all segments public and private on many policies other than financial will be subjected again and possibly even more intensely to public scrutiny.

Causing higher education to be tuition free will not adequately solve one of the major problems of our times, namely, getting deeper into the educational streams able but poor youth of many varied backgrounds. The danger is by simply supporting the free-tuition principle we will do less than we should for those who really need much more. My view is and has been since the Eisenhower Committee experience and the data there set forth, that nothing less than special attention in counseling, in stimulating motivation to go on academically, in developing greater cultural awareness of potential opportunities will be of genuine effect. The problems are sociological and cultural as much as they are financial.

It remains my conviction that the costs of public higher education have already moved to levels, and will continue so to do, that will require a tuition from students; and especially so because of the continuing and unrelenting strain upon the state's finances for all the services the state provides. Since neither the Legislature nor the Executive has really come to grips with the problems of overall tax reform together with the built-in commitments of particular taxes, seemingly necessary expenditures annually mount beyond revenues. There is no alternative save greater user charges in higher education. This conviction for me is not new. It was foreseen at the time of the Master Plan but was not faced squarely then. It is being avoided and postponed now. The accompanying problem of adequate student aid should be faced first only in reference to the additional tuition or fees charged, and then only for students coming from distinctly low income groups. In a later chapter will be found further considerations regarding problems of finance.

12

RECENT AND EXISTING TENSIONS

THROUGHOUT 1965, 1966, and 1967 controversy over public higher education in California was at high levels of tension. Issues involved included almost every one brought forward in 1959 and in addition several others. These tensions were and still are both within higher education and outside higher education within the body politic.

Within each segment there has been some struggle between and among institutions, but the main struggles have been between and among segments themselves as major "corporate" entities vying for advantage, favor, and finance. At times these segments have sought or have found common ground. At other times, and much more characteristically, they have been vying vigorously for their own interests often with not much evidence to support the idea of a commonly respected profession, manifesting bitter animosity, charges, and counterclaims.

The tensions of recent years gather around items of major importance in addition to budgetary struggles, or faculty salaries and possible fringe benefits, or the financing of capital outlay, all of which have been in some degree in the forefront in the last several chapters.

There have been tension and struggle over new campuses for both the State Colleges and the University. During the 1963 session of the California Legislature, bills were introduced that would have created new institutions in five different areas of the state. However, on a number of bases of consideration, the Coordinating Council decided that no new institutions were needed at that time. This was clearly unpopular political advice, but nonetheless the Council was sustained by the Legislature. Such support was significant evidence of the confidence then enjoyed by the Council.

149

In the Council, differences were apparently amicably settled by early 1965 until, seemingly not content over decisions reached in the Coordinating Council, President Clark Kerr for the University launched with considerable publicity flair the University's Growth Plan over coming decades, a sort of new view which appeared to me a "trial by newspaper" of a sensitive problem and unnecessarily newly opened in this manner. On this, after considerable discussion in the Coordinating Council and in the public press, the result was a downward modification of important features of that Growth Plan to recognize possible wider ranges of projections of student enrollment. There was a review of campus enrollment ceilings and also of the rate of growth of new campuses, both the two or three recently developed campus plans for Irvine, Santa Cruz, and San Diego, and also for the two campuses for which a "definite ultimate need" had been earlier established in the Coordinating Council.

The new campuses of the University in 1967-68 had enrollments as follows: Irvine, 2,035 undergraduates and 450 graduate students for a total of 2,485 (its third year); San Diego, 1,870 undergraduates and 1,276 graduate students for a total of 3,146 (its fourth year as a general campus); Santa Cruz, 1,850 undergraduates and 75 graduate students for a total of 1,925 (its third year). Thus, at the end of eight years of planning and development these new or relatively new campuses had absorbed a total of 7,556 students in reference to the total need while other campuses grew in size also. The Riverside campus dating from the early 1950's had by 1967-68 only 3,100 undergraduates and 1,200 graduate students, for a total of 4,300, a growth less than hoped for and projected. The problem of developing new, or expanding old, campuses is evident in these data. It is not a speedy process.

Similarly, in the earlier debates, the State Colleges desired more new campuses than the facts as developed by the Coordinating Council staff seemed to warrant, and finally a campus in Kern County, together with possibly four others were indicated as to general areas under the concept of "definite ultimate necessity."

The Master Plan's recommendation of two new State Colleges at the earliest possible moment named one in the San Bernardino area and one in southwest Los Angeles County. Progress in development of these new colleges has been very slow, each a story of poor judgment or unpredictable frustrations. For

150

1968-69 the enrollment in these two institutions was estimated for only 1,820 (Dominguez Hills, 600; San Bernardino, 1,220).

The Colleges established by the Legislature in 1957 were four in number: Fullerton, with a present enrollment (for 1968-69) of 5,830; Hayward 5,530; Sonoma, 1,730; and Stanislaus, 1,090; a total for these four legislatively located colleges of 14,180. The Sonoma and Stanislaus colleges appear doomed to slow growth and to be unrepresentative of the needs of the State Colleges or their response to popular requirements.

Also, there has been tension over enrollment problems. The State Colleges were quite slow to move to full embrace of the Master Plan eligibility standard of the top one-third of high school graduates rather than the top 45 percent earlier in effect, thus irritating the University which had with considerable speed established their admission policies on the Master Plan's top one-eighth rather than the top one-sixth.

On the other side, once the State Colleges did embrace the "top one-third" rule, the effect on their lower division enrollments became evident, and the Colleges were fulfilling the Master Plan's 40 percent lower division, 60 percent upper division distribution of undergraduates which had been agreed to as the goal to be achieved by 1975 but which clearly could never be achieved then if not in effect gradually over many years. At the same time the University by following an historic policy of accepting all qualified applicants and hence not achieving the 40 percent - 60 percent by 1966 brought on themselves criticism within the Coordinating Council. Hardly can the University keep to its agreed acceptance in the Master Plan as to the undergraduate proportions unless it really does find a way of screening and eliminating some of the qualified freshman applicants.

The Coordinating Council in cooperation with segments involved made a study of the effectiveness of the devices and formulas used to apply the percentage eligibility brackets to high school students, found that they were in fact admitting higher percentages than intended, and recommended modifications of procedures which are being put into effect.

In regard to the junior colleges, whose problems, financing, functioning, and organization are elsewhere to be described, three major recent tensions have existed.

One was in reference to standards of academic probation. The Coordinating Council recommended to the State Board of Education procedures more restrictive and stiff in reference to students

151

who have not made good after two opportunities. Despite opposition from the junior colleges, the Coordinating Council stood firm. There should be even with all the open door opportunities to students which the junior colleges represent some limit to the availability of carrying academic work with less than satisfactory achievement year after year. For me this was not a new problem, because in the Master Plan studies a very wide range of academic retention policies was found to exist; one junior college leader then stated that in practicality he would never turn away anybody. In one junior college district a recent local bond issue was defeated partly because opponents cited illustrations of the number of students who had been registered in excess of six semesters thus creating even though perhaps falsely the impression that many students were malingerers. When there are scarce dollars and limited space, priorities must be established; but this is a hard doctrine for administrators whose financial advantage it is to have a large average daily attendance, the formula for A.D.A. being the basis for state payment to junior colleges.

Another major issue relating to junior college welfare concerned the flow of students beyond junior college into the State Colleges and the University, on which a thorough study was made by the Coordinating Council and on which final action has been postponed. The upward road to admission at the junior year must be clear and unblocked, or the Master Plan reliance on junior colleges would ultimately be inequitable to junior college students and therefore untenable as public policy. The cooperation manifest on this problem by the State Colleges and the University has been commendable.

The other major issue concerning junior colleges had to do with junior college governance, and principally with a Coordinating Council staff recommendation that a junior college board of governance or coordination be created by law to carry forward at least the powers and responsibilities which the State Board of Education already had, possibly to have further authority and to become the central voice or spokesman for the junior colleges in the state. At first strongly opposed by the majority of junior college leaders and representatives, a shift of opinion occurred, and the proposed board was recommended to the Legislature, receiving careful attention from the 1967 session. Further reference to this problem will be found in a later chapter, dealing with junior colleges.

Earlier discussions by State College personnel of the role of the

State Colleges, both before the Master Plan and after, referred to the growing sizes of particular campuses, their curriculum diversities and range, and what was considered by them the essentially university character of the State Colleges despite their nomenclature as "colleges." Several State College presidents as of 1959 desired the creation of the title "California State University" to describe the colleges. This was denied the colleges impliedly by the functional distribution in the Master Plan, as implemented by the Donahoe Act, but at no point was any reference made in the Master Plan or the Act specifically denying such a title.

Smoldering beneath the surface for a half decade, the campaign to effect a change of name became more clearly evident after 1965 both in statements of highly placed faculty personnel and the increasing indirect or direct reference to the issue by the Chancellor of the Colleges, Dr. Dumke. The report to the Academic Senate of the State Colleges filed as of August 1, 1966 by Professor Marc R. Tool of Sacramento State College under the title "The California State Colleges under the Master Plan" was prepared over a five- to six-months period under an apparently cooperative arrangement with the consent of the Chancellor but not necessarily carrying his endorsement on all that was written. From this report it is evident that a change of name was considered of fundamental importance and precedent to broadened functions including the Ph.D. degree to be available in the State Colleges, a resultant naively assumed as almost automatically sequential. In support of the ideas of this document, particularly the change of name, and certainly never critically vocal regarding it, has been almost every voice from the State Colleges quoted in the public press.

No overt move by Chancellor Dumke or by the State Colleges' Trustees to effect a change of name was ever made in the Coordinating Council. Rather resort was made to indirect methods, to active, vigorous support of the Vasconcellos Bill (A.B. 946 with 24 co-sponsors) introduced in the Assembly in the 1967 session, the origin of whose ideas may be surmised since their correspondence with the Tool report ideas was close. This Bill passed the Assembly; in the Senate was referred to interim study.

However, unmistakable support of the idea by the State College Trustee representatives on the Coordinating Council and by Chancellor Dumke was evident in their unanimous opposition in July, 1967 to a Council staff study proposed by Dr. Spalding, the Council's staff director, which would have examined within the

Council's prerogative to be concerned with "orderly development" of higher education, the several ideas and implications involved in the State Colleges' becoming a state university or universities but under the Trustees as constituted and not the Regents of the University of California.

My own view was that the Council had been by-passed possibly deliberately on this issue, the whole State College leadership hoping to confront the Council and the general public with a *fait accompli*. Clearly such a procedure carried with it an assumption that had the Bill not been delayed in the Senate but passed, Governor Reagan would have signed it. Such an assumption presumed the Governor could or would not understand the long-run expectations and anticipations of this legislative move, and if this view was held, was no compliment to the Governor.

The State College spokesmen said the chief effect of a name change would be to help the colleges in recruiting faculty members. To many non-State College Council personnel this seemed to reflect on the intelligence, awareness, or perception of the faculty personnel being recruited, that they would decide primarily on the basis of name, or it caused wonder as to the Colleges' presentations used in such recruiting.

Because State College representatives interpreted the Council staff move to study the name question in all its implications as a reflection on the Colleges and as an accusation of failure to abide by the Master Plan, the Council referred the whole question to committee review to consider broadening the study to include the relationships of all segments to the Master Plan; and it is engaged in that study in its broadest significance. However, a staff report on the implications of changing the name of the California State Colleges to the California State University containing several alternative proposals, and the staff's recommendation that the name not be changed at this time, was filed in March, 1968.

It will not surprise the reader, therefore, if it is stated that this struggle overshadows all others and continues to be the chief cause of strife between the State Colleges and the University of California. Already evident before the Master Plan in 1959, as described elsewhere, it has taken major form in the discontent of State College faculty personnel with the role assigned to them in the Master Plan and agreed to by their responsible leaders at the time. Also there has been very evident discontent over the financial support received, on which the most markedly vociferous

154

have been the representatives of the unions or professionally oriented bodies or groups organized outside the Academic Senate but of course seeking to control if possible the actual faculty organization of the State Colleges' system. In the minds of these faculty groups or their spokesmen, the lack of "adequate" financial support from the state, which means from the people, has been and is a direct derivative of the functions of the State Colleges as set forth in the Master Plan causing them in their view to be "second-class citizens" in comparison with the University of California.

The issues have revolved about (1) the University's clearly demarcated role of research not equally specified for the Colleges, (2) the University's primary and principal responsibility for doctoral degrees and the accompanying fact that the joint doctoral degree programs provided for in the Master Plan have been slow in coming to pass, (3) the relatively lower faculty salary scales than the University's and than hoped for by the State Colleges (even though these payrolls have been approved and financed by all the responsible bodies having advisory or decision-making authority), and (4) the heavier teaching loads as developed over many years within describable formulas and as allowable within the financial support provided by the state.

In the light of these viewpoints and threats, some of which endangered its present position, the University of California has tended to be on the defensive, and at times even earned the reputation of being more against State College desires, if not openly then covertly, than the situation demanded.

As to research the Master Plan called for the University being "the primary state-supported agency for research." This declaration did not preclude the possibility of some secondary role on state support for the State Colleges since the Master Plan declared that "faculty research, using facilities provided for and consistent with the primary function of the state colleges, is authorized." Regrettably in my judgment, the state has insufficiently supported the modest requests of the State Colleges for faculty research funds.

The doctoral degree, as discussed elsewhere, was made available on a joint basis with the University if it agreed in each instance, by specific authorization in the Master Plan, but except for this the plan definitely set forth that "the University shall have the sole authority in public higher education to award the doctoral degree in all fields of learning." It is interesting to note

155

that in 1959 the Joint Advisory Committee, composed of four representatives each of the junior colleges, the State Colleges, the University, and the private colleges and universities, had been unable to reach agreement on the most controversial issue which was then the proposal to permit the State Colleges to award the doctorate. But in the Master Plan agreement was reached, even though reluctantly on the part of the State Colleges, to allow the doctorate to remain where it had always been, in the University of California.

That agreement, however, was one element in an agreement which included many items. Several of these other items represented hopes of State College leadership and personnel such as a constitutional board, markedly increased faculty and staff salaries, funded faculty research as permitted, and other items which since that Master Plan agreement have not been supported by the Governor (Brown or Reagan) or the Legislature either as recommended or to the extent hoped for and anticipated. Such eventualities, of course, do not invalidate the initial arrangement, they do not cut the ground out from under the agreement, but they do emphasize the importance of a greater, a thoroughly adequate concern for an effective, efficient State College program capable of excelling in its assigned and accepted roles. They do help to explain the emotional and the psychological but perhaps nonrational aspects of behavior of some State College leadership.

Not a little leadership in the State Colleges seems to be possessed of illusions and delusions. An illusion is something that deceives by giving a false impression. A delusion is in itself a false belief or notion. Aggressive, vocal, organized faculty elements in the State Colleges, for which there are no opposite or matching elements of equal influence or activity in the University of California picture, have challenged the Master Plan's functional division, have made and issued interpretations of the Master Plan which represent distortions of the intentions of that plan as written and as generally accepted and understood at the time, or they represent demands for revision without clear expression of what specific revisions should occur, or they represent strictly self-serving demands without concomitant consideration of the impact on the state as a whole.

There is nothing in the Master Plan against more M.A. graduate students in State Colleges, nor for the presence of stimulating scholars. There is nothing in that plan against increased general levels of support for the State Colleges in library resources, faculty remuneration, sabbatical leaves, adequate secretarial and professional assistance, faculty professional travel or appropriate research, concerts, lectures, and arts programs, academic senates and system-wide administration, the lack or inadequacy of which are made to appear the fault of the Master Plan or the lack of university status or the Ph.D. degree curricula. The Master Plan is not to blame primarily for the attitudes over years of governors, legislators, and the general public as to the needed financial support of the State Colleges. Indeed, the Master Plan held the hope that with their own trustee board, chancellor, and state-wide administration free from the State Board of Education and its departmental customary procedures a new approach and rationale for the State Colleges might develop. There is nothing to stop that Board of Trustees, the Chancellor, the presidents and faculties from carrying their desires to the people in terms of a positive image of educational service built on the functions assigned rather than upon the negative image which somehow has developed out of emphasizing segmental contrasts and inferiority attitudes.

Authority to grant the doctorate is ardently and evidently desired by many State College faculty and administrative personnel. The Master Plan and the subsequent items placed in the Education Code are quite clear, and there is no way to construe the wording so as to allow the State Colleges to grant separate Ph.D. degrees. Clear-cut amendments would be called for if it were desired by the several constituted authorities to embrace this move. The Master Plan does not preclude later changes in functional differentiation and distribution, but it is manifest that such would be possible only through actions initially arrived at in the Coordinating Council for Higher Education, presumably reached after full review by the respective boards and other segmental representatives so as to avoid continuing battle at the expense of the taxpayers and people as a whole. In addition, such an action by the Coordinating Council would have to receive the approval as well as material support of the Governor and the Legislature; and if the issue were thoroughly joined, that is, if the affirmative vote were of narrow margin, it is not inconceivable that under referendum or initiative a popular vote on the issue might result. Such an eventuality would do no good to the general cause of higher education in the state. One cannot move about at random a fundamental factor in a complex situation without disturbing every relationship within that complex situation.

Since November, 1966, the Coordinating Council has been engaged in a study of "the quantitative and qualitative adequacy of the facilities and programs for advanced graduate study including the possibility of a doctoral degree with emphasis on excellence in teaching in higher education."

One of the State College faculty arguments is that "a significant increase of the graduate program to embrace the possibility of separate Ph.D.'s is desirable in order to strengthen the program for undergraduates." This idea has only limited applicability and as a generalization cannot be acceptable. If conceivably applicable it would be to upper division undergraduates primarily; otherwise logically all the junior colleges could argue they must have upper division academic work so as to strengthen their lower division academic transfer course programs. In some degree this has been heard before, but generally the junior colleges have accepted their role as lower division colleges, and the record of many of them in academic course teaching is very good.

Another faculty argument is that State College students are entitled to the stimulating intellectual atmosphere possible only by the presence of famous scholars and many graduate students which develop the university environment and "élan and a spirit of inquiry." Some even admit to academic mediocrity under present conditions.

Do the State College administrators, trustees, and other leaders believe that all eighteen colleges presently existing are now qualified to confer the doctorate even in limited areas as some apparently have advocated? But it may be argued, this is extreme, and it is not intended that all eighteen would be so qualified or designated. Then the query is, how many, and on what criteria, and who would finally decide, and how would the so-called sense of "second-class citizenship" of all the others be equated? Some colleges are small, and for a long time probably will be because wrongly located initially or because of the quality of leadership or faculty. Some State Colleges are strong, some are relatively weak. Some are now so large and so pressed for space that additional functions would require a substantial reconstruction of academic plan, physical plant, and of course financial requirements.

158

The cost of adding the Ph.D. to the programs of the obviously most strong State Colleges, Fresno, Long Beach, Los Angeles, Sacramento, San Diego, San Fernando Valley, San Francisco, and San Jose, even in all areas outside nuclear physics or similar extremely costly fields, has never been calculated. Neither the Chancellor nor any of his staff, nor any president, nor any of the trustees knows the magnitudes in need nor in cost of what is being talked about, and until some such concrete proposal is in hand any further public arguments for the general idea are something less than responsible leadership and administration.

The Legislative Analyst, Mr. Alan Post, in one of his comments on the budget for 1967-68 stated that programs at the State Colleges should be those which will "maximize their stated instructional objectives in the areas of liberal arts, sciences, and applied fields rather than merely permit them to expand into little universities attempting to duplicate areas reserved for the University of California."

The state's dollars are not unlimited. Such a costly venture without full justification will tend to start an academic war with the University alone, to say nothing of private universities; it will cause the State Colleges not so chosen to be on the edge and unhappy; it will bring further uncertainty to the already insufficiently state-supported junior colleges. And what about the private universities such as Stanford, University of Southern California, California Institute of Technology, the Claremont Graduate School and University Center, as leaders which have brought prestige to California? Will they make no protests and be happy?

The Chancellor and some State College presidents argue they can no longer staff the State Colleges whose major enrollments are undergraduate or including no more than the M.A. level of graduate work, because new faculty demand opportunity to teach advanced graduate students. The problem of recruitment as presently evident is thus being used as the argument to effect long-desired change.

There is something sadly wrong with this argument; indeed there are several things wrong. (1) The Chancellor's staff and the faculties ought to be able to calculate that the number of faculty who could work with "advanced students," by which are meant presumably predoctoral students, would be of necessity the smaller proportion of the faculties, not only immediately due to beginning doctoral candidates who would enroll but also for a long time if the Ph.D. degree were added. (2) If the number of faculty to be favored with Ph.D. teaching would be so few relatively, how then will those, the far larger proportion, who must teach undergraduates be motivated or inspired? Would there not be a new breed possessing so-called "second-class citizenship"? Does no one, no State College faculty, as a whole, really want to teach undergraduates? (3) Does the problem of recruitment bear no relationship to the California political environment of recent months and years? (4) Does the problem bear no relationship to the image of the State Colleges developed as a result of the actions in recent years of the State College faculty groups themselves? The problem of recruitment is not solely the lack of the Ph.D. Indeed, increase the uncertainties about what the State Colleges are all about, and the problem of recruitment will get worse not better.

The vocal State College faculties and administrators who have succumbed to self-pity and describe themselves as "second-class citizens" in academia have laid so much emphasis on the doctorate that there has been insufficient discussion of what more ideal conditions for professional achievement and growth and institutional excellence in the work of the State Colleges might represent. Faculty working conditions have not always been ideal, but are they not better than formerly, much better?

Faculty teaching loads in particular fields of teaching and in high enrollment courses may need to be reduced.

Faculty salaries should be increased especially if emphasis is given to merit rather than the automatic time served step-up process now used. The University has generally administered a percentage increase voted on the payroll according to standards of professional achievement long recognized and on which faculty counsel is obtained. This is one reason why in general the University's faculty receives more respect in the eyes of the public and in the academic world. The State Colleges have been more inclined to use time served as a guide to larger payroll rewards.

The State Colleges should have more faculty leave and research opportunities, but not to displace the University's priority in research. They should have an up-to-the-present functioning of sabbatical leaves, and better equipment in some departments and some colleges. Also, the use of building and construction funds could at times be distributed more nearly in accord with the total academic purposes of the institution.

160

At one State College I visited a few years ago I was impressed by the lavish investment in the gymnasium and physical education plant and noted the contrast with the less lavish science laboratories. Asking why this was true, I was told that community pressure upon legislative representatives from that area and upon the president and other administrators reflected the community popularity of athletic sports. The college's image was affected. For the needs of greater priority less money flowed. How characteristic this is only a broad survey would show; yet I recall in the years when the Coordinating Council's Committee on Finance reviewed in detail the capital outlay requests of the State Colleges and the University I would comment from time to time upon the amount of public funds going ostensibly into physical education as a subject matter academic field but actually strongly supporting the colleges' athletic interests, with the proportion of college construction money so directed being relatively larger than that of the University, and relatively too large in general to satisfy me.

In my judgment, the State College faculty groups which so often have criticized Chancellor Dumke and the Trustees for not defending adequately their interests have done a disservice to the Colleges and to themselves. The Colleges are not run for the faculties but for the students and for the people. The Trustees represent the people and deserve more cooperation than they have received from some organized faculty groups.

Also, in my judgment, above all, the State Colleges need to develop in their total public and professional relations a more positive support for their functions, abandoning the simple negativism which so often gets attention, seeking a supporting public image of their character. Excepting for a few relatively small because wrongly located Colleges, and a few which are relatively weak, the great majority of the State Colleges are strong, vigorous institutions of which California may well be proud. The pride of these Colleges in themselves needs fostering in a positive sense, rallying students, faculty, and local advisory boards into communities of intellectual power and influence and demanding in their own right for what they are the strong support of local journals of news and opinion.

The University of California since 1964 has been in the public eye not only in California but also throughout the world to a degree probably not matched by any other university in modern times. While Berkeley, understandably for older Californians, has been the focal center of the tensions causing such attention, the other campuses have not been exempted with the next largest, UCLA (24,000 students), leading from sheer weight of the student and faculty activities generated by such numbers. The whole field of internal student and faculty governance is not directly germane to the chief problems of this book, but suffice it to indicate that what happens in the meetings of the Coordinating Council for Higher Education, the Regents or the Trustees, is not unaffected by the impact of such developments and especially of events very much in the public eye.

Nor is all of this outside politics. The existence of the Joint Committee of Inquiry begun in 1965 and chaired by Speaker Jesse M. Unruh is one example of the influence of campus life on politics, and the debates and charges of the 1966 gubernatorial campaign are another. Some reported statements of Democratic legislators in 1965 when reviewed two years later read as if they might have been voiced at least in part by gubernatorial candidate Ronald Reagan (Republican). The University's travail of 1964-66 had unmistakable effects on the political popularity of both the State Colleges and the University and on the budgets achieved for 1967-68.

There are tensions within the University of California among its nine campuses that make the development of a sense of statewide institutional unity a difficult thing to foster. Local interests appeal. The divergences of one campus from the other, the diversities of program, teaching method, and type of faculty personnel, the total enrollment or rate of growth receive much attention in a day when the public relations officer feels keenly the need to establish the impression of distinctiveness in both public and professional minds. Except for the relatively uniform standards of admission, the public simply does not know what the other standards of the University are to assure a high quality educational program, and perhaps they cannot be fully explained.

The University needs to give more attention to its undergraduate education program and to explain its features to the public. There is a strong general public conception that the University professors teach little, have little concern for their undergraduate students, and spend much time on their own research so as to assure professional advancement, or spend time which belongs to the state on outside consulting, or research, or service other appointments, "moonlighting" and the like, for which lucrative fees are obtained. It will not be to the University's advantage to have no or only a few answers to these questions. And it is of little value in reference to the major campuses and the extent of the major problem to talk about the teaching programs and excellent teacher-student relations at Irvine, Santa Cruz, and San Diego where enrollments as yet are relatively small. These campuses are growing in size, and the general problems will be theirs soon, if not already on the way.

There has been some tension over the rate of growth of new educational, research, and service functions on the new University and State College campuses. This is in part the problem of numbers of students and when they will arrive, and in part the problem of the time and personnel involved in planning a new function which in the University's tradition is detailed and extensive, and in present State College practice comprehensive. It is also in part the problem of synchronizing the availability of space for the function with program, personnel, and student enrollment. And in all of this there is inevitably the influence of the personality and philosophy of the person chosen to head the program, school, or campus.

Logically, the University's president or the Colleges' chancellor should employ a campus chancellor or president, or approve a new school dean or program director only in terms of an educational policy already set forth and approved by the president and the Regents or by the chancellor and Trustees, choosing persons to fulfill program and policy expectations which have been already decided. Yet so often and to considerable degree, after it has been determined a campus, school, or program is needed, the responsibility of preparing the details of the philosophy, type of personnel to be sought, and steps in program development are sent down to the persons selected. Later, all of this comes back up the ladder for final decision and financing; yet in the meanwhile much change may have occurred, differences of final schemes as against initial planning become evident, costs have possibly or probably mounted and personal struggles inevitably ensue. Even the older well-established campuses are not immune to these problems of organization and planning. The excuse for what has occurred, some of which has been too greatly aired in the public press, is the desire to develop diversity or to avoid stultifying standardization or to allow for significant participation in decision making by those who will carry through a given responsibility. But in finality the central responsibility of Regents or Trustees must be maintained.

163

Perhaps it is too much to expect a central administration or responsible board to make basic policy decisions in the first instance which will be controlling. It has been said they are not or cannot be that wise.Yet some initial decisions are possible as to emphasis. It is not too much to expect that the kind of school desired be decided as in administration, engineering, law, or medicine, whether the emphasis shall be primarily towards one or another educational theory, and thus to avoid a public debate between the president, the campus chancellor, and the dean over, say, a new school of medicine's educational philosophy, programming over time, financing, and staffing.

Nor is it too much to decide centrally whether or no undergraduates are to get a decent break. The Regents and the President of the University and campus chancellors can do much more about this question than has been done, and I mean more than to make speeches or write books. Devolution of authority on this issue within the University wholly to faculty Senate committees will no longer suffice. If the University is so eager to have undergraduates, both lower division and upper division, in its enrollments and within Master Plan limitations, it must justify their presence by its policies and programs.

There appears to be a change developing across America, long overdue, which may manifest itself within the not distant future, to redirect attention to undergraduates. This is a revulsion from a research-dominated higher education and the present exaggerated emphasis on a particular type of scholarship or scholarly ability. Several major national studies inspired by associations, foundation and government agencies may yield an impact. The educational problems of higher education in America cannot be solved by running away from the education of youth. The role of limited supply relative to demand for faculty may change soon to a more balanced and relaxed economic situation. New, or for that matter, older concepts of scholarship and professional excellence may well restore the philosophical balance, and there will again be those whose depth is so great that they will rejoice in helping youth discover themselves and their potentials as well as the epistemological framework of a given area of knowledge.

A Berkeley professor in one of the social sciences said to me in Berkeley in 1965 that the troubles at Berkeley in 1964 and 1965 derived from the undergraduates who demanded attention as students whereas the Berkeley academic scene had always been developed on the doctrine of neglect, Berkeley historically draw-

164

ing undergraduate students strong enough to carry on their education by themselves. He regretted that the comfortable Berkeley had faded away. My prayer would be not for the return of trouble but for the return of the day of great teachers there whom undergraduates could come to know, respect, and hold in great affection. It is not impossible.

13

THE INDEPENDENT COLLEGES AND UNIVERSITIES

IN THE PREFACE to the Master Plan document in 1960 is the following statement: "The Master Plan Survey recognizes the great contribution private colleges and universities have made and will continue to make to the state. It has included these institutions in the recommended state-wide coordinating agency with the opportunity for an authentic voice bearing on policies directly affecting their welfare." To all the private institutions, especially the older nonpublic colleges and universities this heralded the dawn of a new day in California since for so long the segment which had carried so much of the burden of higher education in California had been in effect without voice in public councils.

Hence, under the Donahoe Act of 1960 the independent or private institutions of higher education in California possess statutorily a role of participation in decision making which some persons both inside and outside California find difficult to understand. In the view of some political scientists the position of representatives of private institutions on the Coordinating Council brings their voices and votes to bear upon issues of public higher education which it is argued are not strictly their business. Thus it is claimed they possess public power without public responsibility. In a sense this is a more legalistic point of view than it is a realistic and practical political one.

Already it has been pointed out that there were two persons identified with private higher education on the Master Plan survey team, one the chairman, and one appointed strictly as a "representative" of private institutions which the chairman was not.

In planning the personnel of the Coordinating Council at no

time was any doubt expressed seriously about the wisdom of equal segmental representation for the private institutions to be not simply observers but to sit with full powers of vote. There were at least five reasons in support of that representation.

One was the historical position of private higher education in California with academic strength and reputation possessed by several beyond the state on a national and world level. There had been written a record of development through private colleges and universities of the community's responsibility in higher education, and distinct contributions had been made before the State of California adequately awakened to its public responsibilities in higher education both as a result of population growth and economic development.

The second reason is that private institutions enjoy incorporation by charter from the state. They are today not really private but quasi-public corporations, and the very large majority of these so-called private institutions have been fulfilling public purposes, not private goals, as the federal government's policies in several areas of fund distribution have attested.

The third reason is that, except for certain interinstitutional rivalries better not detailed, there had been a considerable mutuality of respect and cooperation between and among public and private institutions, especially the stronger ones from each segment, to keep the standards of higher education in California high. Since 1946 an important agency to maintain standards was the Western College Association as it developed the processes of institutional accrediting. Both in the private and public segments admittedly there were institutions having considerably less adherence to acceptable high standards than was to be desired. Apart from the formal associations and relationships, as in so many phases of human life there was mutual goodwill and cooperation for certain ends and competition to advance one's own programs and approaches to problem solving.

The fourth major reason was political. The political weight of the private institutions was such that if this factor were overlooked there would be peril to progress. As to one item alone, namely, analysis of the educational background of the State Legislature showed a considerable identification with private colleges and universities, and although no simple conclusion could or should be reached from such a fact, the fact remained that at least a good hearing for private institutions would be assured.

The representation of private institutions on the Coordinating

Council since 1960 has been composed (but obviously not all at the same time) of one vice-provost and one vice-president of major universities, two presidents of Catholic universities, three presidents of independent liberal arts colleges, and one professor of an independent university. These persons have been: Robert J. Wert (Stanford University), Milton C. Kloetzel (the University of Southern California), the Very Reverend John F. X. Connolly (the University of San Francisco), the Very Reverend Charles S. Casassa (Loyola University), C. Easton Rothwell (Mills College), George C. S. Benson (Claremont Men's College), William C. Bark (Stanford University), and myself (until 1965 Occidental College).

The fifth reason was intensely down to earth, namely, the already demonstrated effectiveness of the private institutions in common action in support of the California State Scholarship program passed in 1955. At the time the scholarship program was being considered by the Legislature, it was openly or covertly opposed by a number of representatives of public higher education. However, the Legislature proved itself genuinely concerned about the case made by the private institutions, and this fact made an impression on public higher education leaders. Furthermore, as time passed, the choices by State Scholars of institutions to attend included so many public institutions that it was clear the private colleges and universities were not the sole beneficiaries.

The Master Plan recommended the expansion of the system of State Scholarships already in effect to include additional scholarships and to increase the maximum amount of each scholarship. The California State Scholarship program had provided a grant toward institutional tuition and fees with the individual recipient electing the college of his own choice, and had been of significant helpfulness to independent institutions, increasing their enrollments and thereby resulting in financial savings to the state. Since markedly expanded it has become a means of considerably strengthening the functions of private liberal arts colleges at all levels but particularly the stronger colleges and universities as well as among all types of operation in higher education.

The Master Plan had recommended that in addition to the State Scholarship program there be added a program of subsistence grants. Up to 1967 the Legislature had not approved. The 1967 Legislature approved such a measure introduced by Senator

Mervyn Dymally, but it was vetoed by Governor Reagan. Furthermore, there was recommended a program of graduate fellowships which up to 1966 had not received legislative support, but in 1966 was voted. In 1967, Governor Reagan's economy budget did not initially contain any provision for this statutorily established obligation, but an appropriation was finally voted and not eliminated by the Governor.

Prior to 1959 there was great concern existing within all higher education in California, both public and private, over the degree of competition between and among both public and private institutions for enrollments. Enrollments were looked upon as the basis of power as well as of finance. Hence, tension was increasing and there was the threat that the politics of higher education would exceed in attention and importance the procedures and achievements of higher education itself.

Aware of the growing concern among California private institutions of the possible encroachment of public institutions within their immediate areas of service, the Joint Staff for the Liaison Committee in preparing the study of "The Need for Additional Centers of Public Higher Education in California" developed a set of six principles around which the study was made. One of these, here pertinent, is stated:

> Extension of publicly supported institutions to the degree that the continued operation of private ones long in existence and seemingly serving the community well is jeopardized, *is not in the public interest.*

All of these principles were approved by the State Board of Education on November 9, 1956, and by the Regents of the University on November 15, 1956.

Very careful consideration was given to estimates by private institutions in the projections of possible future enrollments to be cared for, and these stated capacities were weighed carefully in the calculation of area needs and location of new public institutions so that these latter campuses would not be located "next door" to already established nonpublic colleges or universities and thus undermine their community relationships and in some degree supporting constituencies.

Therefore, under the Master Plan very careful analysis of the public institutional capacities and area needs was made. The Coordinating Council was made responsible for continuing studies of such utilization of facilities so that it might advise appropriately as suggestions are made for additional institutions to meet supposed area needs. Private liberal arts colleges have been considerably concerned that such analyses be made with great care.

The sense of assurance or reassurance as to public policy within both public and private sectors of higher education in California as a result of the abatement of the earlier markedly evident competitive concern has done much for the promotion of professional growth and development, of institutional attention to major tasks, and for the development of a high sense of cooperation within the academic profession in the state.

Important principles with reference to student fees and payments and tuition for nonresident students were recommended by the Master Plan and approved by the respective boards for the University and the State Colleges in 1959. The Coordinating Council is under instruction from the Legislature to make continuing analyses and to report on the application of these principles with reference to student fees and costs. This it has done. All of this has been of great concern to private higher education.

An important way in which the Master Plan in California was of meaning not only to public but also to private higher education is to be found in the many ways in which, while seeking to provide adequate educational opportunity, the whole program represented a concern for costs to the state, and this concern continues in the work of the Coordinating Council. All these developments have been constructive and many of them exemplary.

The Master Plan called for higher standards of admissions to the University and the State Colleges. The private institutions were admonished to raise not lower their standards. Similarly recommendations to all institutions on avoiding policies regarding retention of students which might undermine high standards were deemed desirable to lift the level of quality of all segments in higher education. The nonpublic institutions admittedly had then and have now quite varying standards, some quite high, others relatively low; yet in the years before the Master Plan many of the independent institutions had been admittedly and outspokenly concerned over some of the practices in admission and retention of students in certain public institutions, principally some State Colleges and some junior colleges but not exempting some University campuses in search of athletes.

170

Gains from the total Master Plan and its aftermath thus far evident, other than those implicit or already stated above, can be described. Except for the Master Plan Survey and its committees, the independent colleges and universities for the first time were recognized significantly in state-wide coordination with the opportunity of expressing in a governmental body an authentic voice representing their special character, bearing upon policies in higher education and which directly affect not only the state's welfare but also the welfare of independent institutions as they serve public purposes. Furthermore, the independent institutions have gained to whatever degree the whole situation has become stabilized.

Independent institutions do face everywhere difficult problems in their relationships with public institutions. The degree to which private institutions may enjoy tax exemption when their properties are used clearly for educational purposes in the public interest, or the extent to which their own dependence upon gifts as a prime source of both capital and current income may be respected and not subject to taxation or to undue competition, or the degree to which their own essential reliance upon tuitional payments may not be impaired but respected by all other institutions are important factors. The extent to which public institutions operate with an equitable and honorable eye to the capacity of students and their parents to bear a significant portion of the cost of benefits which they are receiving has some influence. The extent to which public bodies create benefits for public institutions not shared with independent institutions by forgetting that the cause of higher education embraces all segments of the total field may be of vital significance. Also, the applicability of particular taxes to private institutions which public institutions are not required to pay, or the general level of taxation and its effect on all individuals and industry are further examples of items private institutions must watch continuously.

Probably the items which provide greatest irritation to the private institutions are two unrelated items of finance: gift solicitations and no or low tuitions or fees. The continuing developing efforts of the public institutions to stimulate gifts on a large scale is no longer a surprise. It is a fact, even to the extent of organizing financial campaigns with staffs of public relations, publicity, and fund-raising personnel borne by the public budget and hence by the taxpayers. The appeal to the taxpayers or harassed executive and legislative branches of government may be that stimulating such gifts with tax money will reduce the costs of public institutions to the state; at least such may be hinted. In the budget crisis of 1967 re Budget 1967-68, it was openly suggested that both the University and the State Colleges might have to make special efforts to get gifts. Of course, it never proves to be true that gifts aid the budget problem solution, because the public institutions frankly look on gifts as the "something extra," the "plus factor" yielding some degree of excellence, and they never fail to request and press budgetwise for continuing the historic work-load support plus as many new or improved programs as seem possible.

Some gift solicitation by public institutions is logical and undeniably justifiable. Alumni who have received the benefits of higher education should contribute if able, and no one should prevent a donor if he so desires from selecting a public institution as the object of his benevolence. Then, too, many foundations and some corporations and certain federal government agencies seek to aid the development of new knowledge in areas of their especial interests.

But all these exceptions are of a different order from systematic and extensive campaigns for gifts from the general public. In California under President Clark Kerr and Chancellor Glenn Dumke reasonable statements of policy restraint have emerged as "working agreements," so to speak. However, there is continuing restlessness about the problem. The practices included and excluded are not clear, and probably the issues involved will receive broader public attention, including possibly Coordinating Council review. With the appointment of the new president of the University, Dr. Charles J. Hitch, new understandings may have to be reached.

The other irritation is the apparent determined opposition of the major leadership of all public institutions to tuitional payments by students of any amount. No private institution will make or break on this issue, but a narrowing of the range of costs to the student may have some benefit to private institutions. My own view is that this is a delusion, that tuition should be faced on the merits of the arguments in public finance and not on whether or no private institutions would benefit.

All of the issues and problems in the relationships of the private institutions to the public segments of higher education as well as to the various agencies of government have constituted the agenda of concern of the Association of Independent California Colleges and Universities organized in 1955. Year by year its activities and meetings have expanded, and today its work is considered essential to the welfare of the nonpublic sector. Its presidents successively have been R. J. Wig, onetime chairman of the Pomona College Board of Trustees; Dr. Robert J. Bernard, former president, the Claremont Graduate School and University Center, and Pitzer College trustee; Dr. Lee A. Du Bridge, president of the California Institute of Technology; Dr. Carl M. Franklin, vice-president for financial affairs, University of Southern California; and Dr. George H. Armacost, president of the University of Redlands. Also successively its executive director (or executive secretary in the earlier years) has been James E. Ludlam, attorney; Dr. Robert D. Fisher, onetime vice-president for financial affairs, University of Southern California; Fred F. McLain, former comptroller, Occidental College; Dr. Robert J. Bernard; and Dr. Morgan Odell, former assistant to the chancellor, California State Colleges, and Occidental College trustee.

When one casts the eye back to 1959, one may observe the threat of unrestrained competition for students among all public segments as the basis of recognition and support. It still exists but in defined channels. One could then observe the competition among localities for new campuses of both the University and the State Colleges and all of the dire political possibilities which such competition was bringing and might further bring with it. This became a more orderly process. However, when one recalls the fear that existed in each segment of public higher education and also quite broadly among the independent institutions in 1959, and the genuine sense of insecurity about the future, one may be grateful for the wisdom of present procedures for whatever value in social healing they may have.

To achieve a relaxation of the emotions, extreme tensions, unhealthy competitive aspects and elements of insecurity that once obtained has been in and of itself of prime importance for the commonwealth in its search for the harmony and goodwill in the midst of the appropriate continuing tension essential for progress.

Persons who by doctrinaire attachment are capable of seeing equality of opportunity only in public institutions, or a free society achieved only through public colleges and universities, often find difficulty in embracing public policies that do call in fact for programs whereby nonpublic institutions receive indirectly or directly partial assistance, forgetful that thereby substantial por-

173

tions of the burden of higher education may be transferred through such public scholarships and programs to parents, churches, corporations, and other agencies interested in sustaining private, independent higher education.

Independent higher education in the West functions in an atmosphere heavily dominated today by public institutions. Even though the private or independent institutions held a very large portion of the stage in many states in the West until just a few decades ago, the fact is that the tremendous growth of population and the increase in the strength of the economy and the demands of industry have brought it about inevitably that the rate of growth of public institutions must exceed the rate of growth of the independent institutions. In former years some strong exponents of independent higher education argued for increased support of independent education primarily on the ground that the then existing ratio between public and private enrollments would have to be maintained else the place of private or independent education would be sadly eclipsed. Today, there is far greater emphasis in most private institutions upon quality than quantity.

In California as elsewhere the problem of private institutional finance receives attention with comments increasingly in the context of coming doom, or questioned survival, or a suggested severe shaking down. Some aspects will be examined further in a later chapter. In my judgment, error is made in too easy generalizations and in assuming a homogeneity in the category of private institutions. Also, the real question for some time has been as it is now, not whether or no survival, but at what levels of effectiveness survival and continuity will occur.

It is not inconceivable that as in the past, independent liberal arts colleges if they (1) hold to their essential mission, (2) obtain the necessary financial support which does not come solely by wishing, (3) are not apologetic but are forthright and practical about being tuitional institutions while at the same time they possess an inclusive and representative program of financial assistance to students, (4) adhere to standards of admission that place them not one bit less than but in many instances higher than the average of specific public institutions or even the average of all higher educational institutions in the nation, (5) eliminate unnecessary and costly programs, and (6) maintain adequate managerial efficiency will continue to perform their tasks effectively. In so doing they may be of great service to California and American

174

society and achieve an influence in the public life of the state and nation that will be notable, commendable, and even inestimable.

Certain it is that in relative terms the private institutions in California have fared better than their counterparts in many other states; but this is no basis for complacency.

Certain also it is that at least one third or more of the nearly fifty private colleges and universities in California possess levels of achievement and consequent deserved reputation, national and even world wide, that have added great lustre to the reputation of all California higher education. The state would suffer grievously if these institutions should not be enabled to continue their steady forward progress; it would also suffer if the balance of private higher education were markedly weakened.

14

CONTINUING PROBLEMS OF THE CALIFORNIA
JUNIOR COLLEGES

IN THE STRUCTURE of higher education in California, the public junior colleges established by various types of local districts under provision of the Education Code until 1968 reported to the State Board of Education. Nevertheless, each junior college administration and faculty is responsible immediately to the board of trustees of the local district where established. There has been, however, a shared authority in that the State Board of Education has had the responsibility of general supervision to observe that the provisions of the Education Code relative to junior college operations are in effect.

This responsibility of the State Board of Education for the junior colleges was not comparable in extent, detail, or decision to the responsibility of the Board of Trustees for the State Colleges, nor was it anywhere near the authority possessed by the Regents of the University of California for the University and its campuses. Direct local district control of its junior college or colleges is a much hallowed tradition in California, but conditions have been changing.

In recent years there have been many voices purportedly speaking for the junior colleges, that is to say, district trustees, principals, presidents or superintendents, faculty organizations, members of the State Department of Education, members of the State Board of Education, and the State Superintendent of Public Instruction. In this situation the Coordinating Council for Higher Education has gradually assumed a greater responsibility toward the public junior colleges. The lack of a single voice on the major issues of junior college concern has been an important factor in causing the Coordinating Council to seek to achieve greater

176

coordination in the development of the junior colleges, and as a result a need was sensed for which in time a recommended solution was found. This need for single leadership in coordination of junior college interests results from several factors other than the interesting question of who speaks for the junior colleges.

One of these has been the increasing importance of the junior colleges in the fulfillment of California's aspirations in higher education. This has been evidenced not only in the acceptance of the Master Plan's recommendations calling for diversion to the junior colleges of lower division students, principally freshmen who otherwise might enroll in the State Colleges or the University of California, but also in the actual enrollment in junior colleges as experienced beyond what earlier had been anticipated, which enrollment in 1966 was over 487,458 students both full time and part time.

Another factor has been the continuing claim on state financial support and the concomitant desire for accountability and performance.

Another factor has been the problem of student transfer at the conclusion of the junior college educational program and the lack of a clear path in transfer for such qualified and capable talent into both the University and the State Colleges.

Still another factor has been the increasing awareness of legislators of the potential significance for their constituencies of the junior colleges there located. With eighty junior colleges in being or about to open, a person in politics would have to be somewhat impervious to normal political considerations not to be interested in the growth and development of the junior colleges (and of course of the State Colleges or the University campuses if any happen to be near at hand) located in his political district.

In addition, there has been in almost every topic considered by the Coordinating Council for Higher Education since 1960, even when seemingly concerned solely with State Colleges or University, some derivative significance for the junior colleges.

As a result, the Coordinating Council made several moves to aid a more inclusive understanding of junior college problems. One was a Council-sponsored seminar in 1964 to consider many aspects of junior college relationships and responsibilities to higher education. Another was to request of Dr. Leland L. Medsker and Dr. George W. Clark of the Center for Research and Development in Higher Education of the University of

California at Berkeley, to make a study of "State Level Governance of California Junior Colleges," and this report after a year's research was filed as of August, 1966. The Coordinating Council itself issued a report dated April, 1965 entitled "A Consideration of Issues Affecting California Public Junior Colleges."

In June, 1965 there had been issued from the California Junior College Association and the State Department of Education an "exploratory research and planning study" under the leadership of Dr. Basil H. Peterson entitled "Critical Problems and Needs of California Junior Colleges." Similarly, the State Department of Education published in August, 1966 "The Junior College Story." To this range of available thought regarding junior colleges should be added the Coordinating Council Staff study on "Financing California's Public Junior Colleges, Part I: Current Operations, and Part II: Capital Outlay" presented to the Council in November, 1966 and January, 1967. Obviously, the subject of junior college education was much to the fore.

One important conclusion of the Coordinating Council already referred to in a previous chapter was the recommendation of a new state board of governance for the junior colleges, to take over all duties and responsibilities regarding junior colleges as signed by law to the State Board of Education, and such other responsibilities in coordination between and among themselves as junior colleges as contemporary or later general agreement might assign. The 1967 Legislature through S.B. 669 introduced by Senator Walter Stiern provided for a board of fifteen members to carry forward the Council's recommendation which the Legislature approved and the Governor signed. Practically all major opposition to this move vanished. This was the "recommended solution" for the need so broadly sensed; the new board's title is "Board of Governors of the California Community Colleges."

On January 15, 1968, this new junior college Board of Governors came into existence by appointment of all fifteen members by Governor Reagan. According to the Stiern bill, seven of the members of this board had to be trustees of junior college districts, thus hopefully to assure some experience and awareness or developed competence as to junior college problems. This board will select a chancellor, develop a staff, and choose the representatives of the junior colleges on the Coordinating Council for Higher Education. It is too early to make any appraisal of the competence or program of this board. However, at the time of their appointment I knew personally and could identify as an educational leader only one individual.

Many junior college leaders were disappointed that so few were appointed, if any, of the recommendations made to the Governor's office of persons known to be possessed of outstanding knowledgeability and competence regarding California's junior colleges; or to put it differently, there is among the junior colleges regret that political interests apparently should have played so large a part in the choices made.

A second important conclusion was to recommend markedly increased support from the state for junior colleges both as to current operations and capital outlay. Since 1959 there had been the Master Plan recommendation of a gradual increase in the proportion of state support for junior college operation to reach 45 percent by 1975. However, at one point in the discussions serious consideration was given to a Coordinating Council staff recommendation to have the state accept a 100 percent responsibility for current operations in junior colleges. Support for this proposal derived from two opposite ends of the financial or political spectrum: one viewpoint distinctly favorable to increased state vs. local responsibility, another viewpoint, namely a taxpayers' association normally not so willing to see the state's financial responsibility increase, favorable since local district property taxes for junior colleges would be eliminated or at least in some instances markedly reduced. One net effect of this survey of junior colleges finances will be almost certainly an increase of state support. The Coordinating Council's recommendation was towards increased state support to current operations in the junior colleges, although the Council rejected the staff recommendation of 100 percent responsibility. The Legislature in 1967 did not act on the Council's advice.

Another resultant is almost certain to be a greater cooperation by the State Colleges and the University campuses in accepting for transfer into junior year or advanced standing eligible and qualified junior college students. Also, another resultant of these several studies has been to heighten respect for the widely varying curricula of the junior colleges.

In recent years, by no means a few, junior college districts have encountered opposition by the local citizenry to bond issues and proposed tax overrides to finance construction planned and additional operations beyond already established legal limits.

In financial support, several findings of the Council's staff studies are indicative that perhaps a too permissive approach has existed in many districts on which stiffening may come in order to increase the willingness of local citizens to vote necessary bonds for growth and tax overrides for enriched programs as well as increased state support. For example, fees for adults as defined taking courses in junior colleges are permitted by law. In 1964-65 only one-third of the junior colleges charged such fees. In a number of instances tuitional charges for out-of-state students were as much as 5 percent below current costs of instruction. Only one-seventh of the districts charged permissive health service and parking fees. The fee was then limited by law to ten dollars.

Furthermore, the variations in financial capacity of the junior college districts were quite marked, the wealthiest district measured by assessed valuation per average daily attendance being ten times the financial ability of the poorest district. Continued efforts in the direction of equalization of junior college educational opportunity through allocation of such state funds as are authorized seems indicated. Furthermore, some districts whose tax basis has been more than adequate, indeed generous, in the earlier years of growth may as population increases more rapidly than industrialization and the economic base of the district find themselves in troubled waters. Tax rates in the various districts vary considerably, from below 30 cents to 45 cents or more with the modal figure at or near 35 cents, this modal figure representing about one-half the districts.

In capital outlay financing by the state for the junior colleges some progress is evident. In 1961, for the first time the Legislature appropriated $5,000,000 for construction purposes; this was followed over a five-year period with $75,000,000. In 1966 the Legislature adopted a resolution declaring the program until that date was inadequate and asked the Coordinating Council to make a study of this matter to be reported back by January 31, 1967 (which is the study Part II on Capital Outlay referred to above).

The magnitude of the capital outlay needs for the state revealed by that study is shown by the estimate that expenditures for the period 1966-80, based on 1966 dollars will be $423,000,000, or an average annual cost of about $28,000,000. For the ten-year period through 1975-76, the estimated annual expenditures (1966 dollars) will amount to $24,700,000.

Among elements of inadequacy in the previous plan was a failure to coordinate state and federal programs of support as well as a failure to coordinate this program with other state programs of aid to education. Furthermore, other factors conditioning entitlement to aid were reliance on unrealistic estimates of need. The Council in January, 1967 approved without dissent a proposed new plan for state expenditures in support of junior college capital outlay, a program too detailed for description here. It did allow, however, for more explicit use of space and utilization standards, for more extensive state review and evaluation, for phased funding of approved projects, and for federal funds received by the district to be deducted from the specific project cost prior to the establishment of state funding.

The 1967 Legislature passed S.B. 691 introduced by Senator Walter Stiern which as approved by Governor Reagan established a new program for providing state funds to junior colleges for capital outlay purposes, as developed and recommended by the Coordinating Council. Also the 1967 Legislature passed S.B. 851, introduced by Senator Albert S. Rodda to place on the June, 1968 ballot a bond issue of $65,000,000 to be used for capital outlay purposes in the junior colleges. This measure also received Governor Reagan's signature.

The junior colleges are classified in higher education; yet historically they have been for certain legal and financial reasons classified under secondary education. The hour to make the distinction clear-cut, to make the break with all the attendant requirements of legal and financial changes, is not only here but it is long overdue.

The aura of secondary education hung heavily on and around junior colleges for decades. Partly this was because in earlier years so many principals, presidents, instructors, and counselors had moved up from high school. Partly it was because so many junior colleges were administered under the same conceptions of principal-teacher relationships characteristic of secondary and public schools. Partly the trouble lay in being geographically located upon the same campus or immediately adjacent to it, so that socially there was a commingling of students. Partly it was because some junior colleges were run (and some still are) by the same board of trustees, either of a unified school district or of a union high school district.

But all this is changing very rapidly. Separation and distinctiveness, and conception of role and task, are steadily being cast in collegiate terms as well as are the procedures of administration, faculty, and curriculum. All of this is heartening.

Nevertheless, remnants of the older order remain in the subconscious of many junior college persons. It is hard to shake off or transform the habits of thought which with little external challenge may have gone on for decades.

One recent experience may be revealing about junior college attitudes. At a state junior college association meeting where outstanding achievements of junior college graduates were being recognized, not one person on the program including both the officers of the association and the outside speakers referred to these students as young men and women. They were all just "kids"; yet one of the women honored was in her upper twenties and a mother. There is little hope of developing maturity for any college, junior or senior, which persists in referring to its students as if they were boys and girls. In all my over forty years of collegiate teaching and administration I never did it. The students of age seventeen and above are young men and women, or they ought to be, in attitude and behavior. They are capable of aiding the nation's defense. They are capable of human reproduction. They will not likely rise above the expectations their adult leaders manifest towards them. The tendency to refer to any youth, not yet twenty-one or even above, as "boys and girls" has never pleased me; it occurs in all collegiate circles to some extent, even in the lingo of students themselves who ought to move to a higher scale of self-appraisal. The junior colleges would be well advised to make every possible sharp distinction between themselves and high schools, even if to do so requires some exaggerated actions.

In the Master Plan discussions of 1959 various junior college spokesmen made representations that the lower division of undergraduate education should be eliminated at the University of California, with that institution therefore confined to all advanced work from the junior year on. This was not a new idea. It had been in the public domain of ideas for a number of years. The Master Plan team believed that a college or university performs its teaching function most effectively when it possesses within a given faculty the whole range of responsibility of presentation of a given subject in the liberal arts or in pre-professional training from the entering freshmen in collegiate status to the highest level which the institution embraces. This is the "no gap" doctrine, to attain continuous articulation in subject matter treatment. To achieve this need not require coverage of all students in either the University or the State Colleges who might wish to attend but only a significantly representative proportion of them, so the Master Plan argument runs.

It was also seriously proposed that similarly for the State Colleges the lower division be eliminated or if not from all of them, then of all new ones planned at that time. There was a fear that new State Colleges being planned would retard the growth of junior colleges geographically near at hand. There was precedent for this. It had been recognized for some time that, to the degree a State College were established with all four years available, existing junior colleges would or might receive less freshmen and sophomores. Also, new junior colleges in the area of such a new State College would not so likely be established. Since the junior college costs of operation bear at least from 65 to 80 percent against local property taxes, such preemption of the field by a State College constituted a shifting of the burden otherwise likely to be locally borne to the state; if successful, conceivably and probably to be reckoned to the political advantage of the legislators representing the area.

The Master Plan established a working rule that any new campus of either the State Colleges or the University should be established only at upper division levels unless junior college availability were adequate. This had the effect of encouraging, or as some would have said, forcing the formation of junior college districts in areas which had been laggard, content to pay to another junior college district the out-of-district fees levied on behalf of students resident in the nonembraced area. At the time, the junior colleges were apparently in support of this provision for their protection.

As to the senior systems, the Master Plan continued the lower division programs but under the percentage limitation and reduction plan described elsewhere.

The time came for reviewing in regard to the four 1957 legislatively authorized State Colleges as to the availability in the areas served of junior colleges. The junior colleges in general urged keeping these new colleges at upper division levels or above. The Coordinating Council after review voted to validate the beginning of lower division programs.

As the new State College and University campuses authorized by the Master Plan came nearer to scheduled opening, the Coordinating Council in each case made a study of the adequacy of junior college district coverage in the adjacent areas to advise as to whether such opening should be at the freshman or junior level.

At this time, strangely, a large number of junior college spokesmen changed their tune. Now, again, an attempt was made representing junior colleges to preclude the freshman and sophomore years in such new campuses on a precisely opposite basis, namely, if there were availability of a junior college education, and adequate junior college districts in existence and planned formation to cover the adjacent territory. This reflected a fear about the effect of new four-year campuses on existing junior colleges or on those in process of formation, a fear which statistically appeared to be wholly unwarranted. The Coordinating Council voted down this delaying action, and in each instance of new campus development in the four-year segments after area review validated beginning at the freshman year. There is really no reason for junior colleges to have doubts about their future so far as adequate enrollments are concerned.

What the situation will prove to be as future State Colleges and University campuses for which the Coordinating Council has advised the presence of a definite ultimate need come nearer to reality is of course uncertain, but the recommendation in each instance was made mindful of the factor of adequacy of junior college coverage, as well as the effect on existing junior colleges of new campus locations.

There should be concerted effort among all junior colleges on the development of the image of the junior colleges in the public and professional minds. Their administrators are no longer "somewhat more glorified school men" as one person described them some years ago. Their faculties have been developing in strength as to scholarship, professional relationships, and sense of inner institutional relationships. Their record of interest in good teaching is a good and enviable one. In many places their students of youthful years are developing in maturity and in concerns outside the colleges, relating themselves to state-wide and national student movements. Junior college leaders tell me there is still a long way to go to develop adequate external awareness, or the traditions of collegiate life. Yet it is evident from the records of achievement at higher levels of academic work of student transfers to the University and to the State Colleges that many of these junior colleges are doing a good job. Indeed, even the combined statistics of all of such transfers makes the whole junior

184

college story a good one. In 1959 the Master Plan Survey made a review of the junior colleges' academic policies as to grade requirements for the Associate of Arts diploma and as to retention, dismissal, and probation. A wide range was discovered varying from a junior college at the bottom which scarcely had any rigor and seemingly let anyone stay on to ones at the top with most approvable procedures. In my years at Occidental College we kept comparable records of the achievements of transfer students from particular junior colleges, which material was available only internally. The variation was marked, but as time passed the records became more comparable than in marked contrast. Much credit for these improvements should go to the junior colleges themselves in their program of self-policing in the Western Association of Schools and Colleges.

There is a future for the public junior colleges in California, not simply in the plans as laid nor yet in the yearning of those who wish to see them perform at their best, but also in the desires of many communities and hosts of parents and of students themselves. The state may in some degree thus far have failed the junior colleges; from now on, with the set of the sails now on the masts, the junior colleges must not fail the state.

The junior colleges with their roots in the local community now find themselves an element of major importance in the state's total higher educational effort and systematic plan with 80 percent of all lower division students enrolled in the state. It is inevitable that there shall continue to be raised, even with a new state-wide board for the junior colleges, the question of who should govern these public junior colleges. It is also inevitable that some tensions must arise, that at times the local interests will be clamant and at others the interest which by necessity the state takes in them shall be primary. Undoubtedly, the detailed questions of the precise meaning of governance under these conditions will be worked out in the give and take of particular issues. Historically, the State Board of Education never fully utilized its authority under law over the junior colleges. Hence, the new state-wide board will be watched to observe the role it essays.

15

EDUCATIONAL PROGRAMS IN CALIFORNIA'S MASTER PLAN AND COORDINATION: THE EFFECT ON THE LIBERAL ARTS; PROBLEMS OF PROFESSIONAL EDUCATION

THE INDEX to "A Master Plan for Higher Education in California, 1960-1975" contains no entry for "liberal arts" or "liberal education"; yet the whole program contains in its recommendations much of significance to the future of liberal arts education both in California and also, conceivably, elsewhere.

In writing about the responsibilities of the State Colleges, the following language is used in the Master Plan: "The state colleges shall have as their primary function the provision of instruction in the liberal arts and sciences and in professions and applied fields which require more than two years of collegiate education and teacher education, both for undergraduate students and graduate students through the master's degree." Note that this constituted legislatively a decided change in that theretofore the State Colleges had been considered to have teacher education as a primary function. In fact, the Education Code so defined their primary function. While teacher education was not eliminated, nevertheless, the placing of instruction in the liberal arts and sciences in a significantly prominent position in the list of functions was heralded favorably in the State Colleges, at least among some sections of many faculties, as a sort of educational philosophical victory. It had been well known for a number of years that the aspirations within the faculties of State Colleges, and shared by some of the presidents, had been toward a broader recognition of their functions in the fields of the liberal arts and sciences and not solely in the applied fields or in vocational or

186

preprofessional work as such or in teacher education. Prior to 1960 within a number of State College faculties there had been some tension among various segments of faculties as to what long-range institutional policy or dominant emphasis should embrace.

Indeed, one important weakness evident in the State College system prior to a decade ago or even prior to the creation of a separate board for the State Colleges was the tendency of administrators in the system from the center in Sacramento to the campuses themselves, to hold to a public school perspective, a rigid employer-employee attitude as between administration and faculty. This profoundly irritated the faculty in the liberal arts and sciences fields even if accepted in fact or by silence by those faculty members in the field of Education whose success in part lay in maintaining an atmosphere of common relationship and identity with public school administrators.

However, by 1959, the liberal arts and sciences faculty members clearly outnumbered the educationists and a new spirit of independent behavior was becoming evident. For example, to appeal over the campus heads of administration directly to the Sacramento offices of the Superintendent and the State Board of Education or to attempt to deal directly with legislators represented a distinct change in conceived status and relationships; and this had occurred.

In the early fifties Long Beach State College revealed a serious lack of communication and rapport between the president and a large segment of the faculty. Accusations of bad faith were made, the campus was aroused, and the public became widely informed. Superintendent Roy Simpson and the State Board of Education could not avoid making an investigation. I was a member of the investigating committee at Superintendent Simpson's request. I was astounded by the lack of perception and downright common sense of the president of the college who held rigorously to his authority and position. I was also amazed that some of the faculty behaved beyond the bounds of professional and gentlemanly courtesy. It was my belief the situation had been considerably brought to an untenable state through presidential inability to respect the faculty as appointees with status, not employees without status.

The Master Plan report also contained a recommendation that "the University shall provide instruction in the liberal arts and sciences, and in the professions including teacher education, and shall have exclusive jurisdiction over training for the professions of dentistry, law, medicine, veterinary medicine, and graduate architecture (but not solely limited to these)." Furthermore, the University was given the sole authority in public higher education to award the doctoral degrees in all fields of learning except that authority was given to agree with State Colleges to award joint doctoral degrees in selected fields. The declaration of the dedication of the University among other functions to the liberal arts and sciences was not a new thing, the outstanding position in scholarship and teaching of the University of California in the liberal arts and sciences both at undergraduate and graduate levels having long been recognized the world over. Thus far the areas within which the development of doctoral degrees on a joint basis between the University of California and specific State Colleges have developed have been in arts and sciences fields and not strictly speaking in the professional areas.

The Master Plan also defined the functions of the junior colleges, limiting them to instruction through but not beyond the fourteenth grade level and including but not limited to one or more of the following: (1) standard collegiate courses for transfer to higher institutions which would tend to be basically in the liberal arts and sciences and in general education, (2) vocational technical fields, and (3) general, or liberal arts courses. Here, too, among some faculties and some junior college spokesmen, but probably not the dominant voices, there was a rejoicing that considerable emphasis was placed upon the standard collegiate and liberal arts and sciences work of the junior colleges. Indeed, it was reasonably well known that among those students eligible initially for entrance to the University of California who attended junior colleges and who then transferred to the University of California, the academic record achieved at the University in work taken beyond the junior college was highly commendable in some of the University's colleges and for certain periods of time exceeded the academic average of the University's own lower division personnel moving into the upper division. Certainly these facts were strong support of junior college concern for the liberal arts and sciences.

The Master Plan recognized the growth in quality of the junior colleges. In anticipation of the possibility of future significant growth in the liberal arts and sciences work and transfer courses basic to university and college achievement, the Master Plan recommended, as referred to elsewhere, that there should be

188

developed over the period up to 1975, a diversion of students to the junior colleges so that by 1975 at least 50,000 students who, if historic trends were still in effect and if there were not an increased availability of junior college facilities to take care of them, would have gone to the University or the State Colleges. This meant that a gradual but not an inclusive diversion to the junior colleges would tend to go on for a period of years.

During the Master Plan discussions, there was considerable tension evident among the spokesmen for the various educational philosophies to be found in the various institutions and fields of higher education. This is one of the reasons why it was imperative, as indicated in an earlier chapter, and no solution could have been achieved without it, that a spelling out of the problems of differentiation of function and agreement for the future had to be achieved in 1959-60.

Private independent institutional representation on the Coordinating Council augurs well for the voice of the traditional liberal arts and sciences concepts being held in view in the considerations of the operations of public institutions. In fact, views expressed both in the Master Plan Survey team and in much public consideration subsequently, together with the thinking evident within the Coordinating Council, lead to the belief that no loss of strength for liberal education insofar as it may be achievable within public institutions, has occurred. Indeed, persons representing fields of vocational or preprofessional or professional training including the field of teacher education have remarked that the report gave insufficient treatment of these supposedly nonliberal fields of learning, and that there has been insufficient representation of all of these fields in the personnel of the Coordinating Council. Time only will yield the answer as to whether or no such criticism may be justified.

Not all junior college leaders were in favor of what was believed an apparent intent of the Master Plan in the items named vis-a-vis the junior colleges. Those whose devotion to the vocational and technical, i.e., the generally terminal programs, seemingly made these the primary functions of junior colleges and were fearful lest the diversion principle and transfer aspects would cause an increased emphasis on regular collegiate subjects in the arts and sciences by pressure of state finance, or of student choices leading to either the reduction in emphasis or elimination as time passed of vocational and applied work. One prominent junior college district trustee openly criticized the Master Plan from this angle of emphasis and opposed various features, declaring to me personally a suspicion of my own basic motivation due to my own long-time identification with liberal education.

Some justification for such views was forthcoming later in the voiced expressions of legislators or the Legislative Analyst or others that the state in increasing its support of junior colleges should take over the financing of the academic or liberal arts and sciences work and let the local property taxation pay for all else. This divisive view has in general been abandoned, and now the junior college is conceived as a total institution for all the functions provided for by law and approved for instruction by the local boards of trustees.

The Master Plan made no review of curriculum content. Strictly speaking, it was necessary for the Master Plan Survey team to accept the educational philosophy of each of the major systems of public higher education, except as some specific declaration on differentiation of function was called for as a basis of cooperation and harmony. Or to put it differently, no time or opportunity really was presented to the Master Plan Survey team to raise questions as to the degree to which the people of the state of California should be involved in one or another aspect of higher education.

The impact of this planning upon liberal education, the liberal arts and sciences, and the liberal arts college has always been a major interest. In my judgment the influences indicated are more than nominal, more than simply recognition of the function of the liberal arts and sciences as stated in law or in any *pro forma* statement of purpose and functions. The devotion of the systems of higher education in California to the liberal arts and sciences as content areas of higher education has been great, and through the developments since 1959 achievement of varying types of liberal education has been augmented.

Whether or no in the long run there will emerge a higher degree of truly liberal education will rest with the administrations and faculties within institutions and also with individuals in their devotion to the task, because liberal education is more than simply teaching the supposed content of liberal arts and sciences. Liberal education requires a certain spirit, not simply content. The liberal arts and sciences can be taught illiberally, and as former President Ray Lyman Wilbur of Stanford said decades ago, areas of learning not characteristically labeled liberal may become the vehicles of liberal education if they train in the

190

processes of thought and develop the kind of mind that historically has been conceived as the product of liberal education.

Three sets of conflicting tendencies are struggling today in professional education in nearly all fields.

One set of conflicts derives from the element of time. On the one hand there is the vastly expanded knowledge of all kinds which all to some degree of understanding must embrace or in fact master, all of which tends to lengthen the educational process. On the other hand is the pressure of society demanding skills and professional resources as soon as possible, pointing out society's needs and changing requirements, urging acceleration, urging elimination of unnecessary material, even demanding curriculum revision to eliminate what are called "frills" or "the traditional approaches," neither of which is ever defined but which are presumed to exist.

The professional spirit requires proper nurture: a respect for competence, a collective effort to assure such competence, identification of the able, self-respect and confidence in one's self as well as mutual confidence among those who practice a given art and have sustained a given discipline, the respect and confidence of society. Professional personnel must not worship in the cult of mediocrity. They will not let just anything get by without check. They will not join those who cheaply deride the expert, the man who knows how, and who knows why. They will not descend to maudlin sympathy for those who profess to know and do not, nor will they stand silent for long over ineptness or before ignorance. Professional persons have standards—of knowledge and skill, of trust, of mutual obligations within a scheme of ethics whose ultimate justification is not self-serving so much as it is broadly serving society and mankind.

The second set of conflicts centers around finance, the expense of expert professional education and training, the costs to the individual of the years of preparation, the cost to the state or to a private institution of the professional education and all its technical and equipment requirements. Every professional man knows, or he thinks he knows, what it has cost him financially to acquire the hallmarks of his profession. And as a member of the Coordinating Council for Higher Education, I have some idea of the millions of public funds which have gone and are going into professional education in California and elsewhere, the medical profession by no means the least costly. In the Coordinating Council, among other things, studies have been made of the requirements of the medical profession, nursing, hospitals allied to teaching, engineering, and a number of other fields, all of this in the effort to fulfill California's Master Plan for Higher Education of 1959-60. Professional education today includes much the larger portion of graduate education.

The third set of conflicts is cultural and moral. These derive from the nature of man, his knowledge and his culture, as well as from his relationships in modern society. Can a man become a true professional on technical knowledge alone? If not, how much of other things does he require? How much else must he know? And, the basic question, how much does he really know about the things he says he knows if he does not know about man and his present world or mind? This may appear to be a struggle between the two cultures, the scientific and the humanistic; and it is, although the dichotomy can be overstated. The humanistic traditions for centuries dominated education; in the last four to five decades the scientific emphasis clearly has been in the ascendancy. Balance is required between these two approaches to man and his world, a balance which must be struck repeatedly by institutions in curricula, by individuals in their personal lives, and by professionals in their practice.

Society demands manpower in the respective skills. Education, higher education, science, and all the fields of learning say, "You can't have it on a continuingly satisfactory basis unless such and such, unless *these things*, are done." And then institution by institution, state by state, profession by profession, the things necessary are spelled out, and placed in regulations; and sometimes these regulations ossify.

The problems of modern society are not solely technical; they are basically human. Yet because our knowledge and understanding of human nature itself, of human motivation and of characteristic human behavior whether as individuals, as professionals and as units of political or social action, is so limited we lean on the things we understand. We can understand and deal with technical, objectively observed elements of a given situation better than we can understand and deal with the uncertain, often vague and indeterminate variable and subjectively observable elements. So with human behavior, such as extreme hypertension, mental illness, drug addiction, or alcoholism, or in the problems of juvenile and adult delinquency, crime, poverty, and ready resort to violence in a society supposedly under guidance of reason or at least controlled emotion, we find ourselves paying a terrible price for the extreme specialization which our social pressures, our technology and culture, and our often too yielding educational situation have given us. That price is that with all our educational investment we have all too few persons who operate as professionals in a unified field of theory, experience, and practice.

We have all too few who try to integrate the disciplines closely related to human behavior in either their theory or their activity or their practice. We have all too few who even recognize there are problems. Even among the social scientists themselves we have possibly seen too much of model building, dominantly deductively formed, and we listen to assured policy declarations as derivatives that may reflect narrow, rather than inclusive, mental concepts, compartmentalized minds rather than behaviorally and philosophically instructed intellects, and occasionally an intellectual arrogance beyond all belief. As one writer has said, "assumptions about human nature underly every facet" of our lives. The important thing now is that we continually examine our assumptions to see how tenable they are. In doing so we should watch closely the behavioral psychologists who are doing so much to unify their field. And as this discipline comes to greater inner scientific unity there will be a profound effect upon all other social science fields and the major professions.

Several things should guide our thinking as we ponder the dilemmas of trying to develop adequate manpower in an age dominated by science and technology with expanding requirements where at the same time increasing numbers of youth vie for the opportunities of embracing an increasing variety of educational programs which will enhance, they hope or think, their earning capacities.

One of these is that few problems are simple; it is their internal and external complexity that makes them problems. Some may call this a struggle between the technical and the human approaches; but I am certain no one knows which angle is simple and which is internal and which external.

Another is that as the elements of a given problem can be segregated, defined and hence seemingly simplified, the present tendency is to run these elements into the computer. This procedure may delude us, and all too readily, because accompanying intangible and indefinable concepts can only with acknowledged difficulty move through computers.

Another is that the mass approach, which is one contemporary derivative of both technical fact or analysis and computer processing, combined with the collectivist or socialist approach to society which has had its run now for over one hundred years, is apt to destroy the essential genius of the individualistic culture in which so much of our thinking has been cast. This culture is still our dynamic factor upon which we rely to get things done throughout all society. Despite the growth of unions, and of government, and of social security programs, not one of these has supplanted or has provided the equivalent of the true moving force of persons who are greatly inspired, deeply devoted, and determined to see moral and social values which must be linked to individuals reasonably achieved in our confused society.

Observe some of the effects of modern technology on education. Education faces the prospect of being overwhelmed by massive concepts. We talk so readily about mass communications, mass opinions, mass appeal, and the mass mind. There are also mass production and mass consumption, and the effects of both on mass population. In my active career I taught and administered in relatively small institutions until in 1959 I was suddenly confronted with the task of wrestling with the problems of master planning of California's public higher education from 1960 to 1975. The magnitudes then and to come were staggering, the resultants then and now uncertain. The prospective doubling and tripling of the number of students within less than a generation in the several segments of California higher education of necessity caused a reexamination of the means of providing higher educational opportunity. There was a resort to economies and methods involving more selective admission to the University and the State Colleges, limits on instructional functions and ceilings on enrollments which have not been liked by hosts of educators and students. Yet, what was devised has not yielded economies sufficient to satisfy major portions of the electorate as the 1966 political campaign showed.

It is not that mass learning is necessarily in and of itself bad, or that from it no good only evil will flow. Some persons have grown stronger, become well-organized persons and well-developed minds under the doctrine of neglect and with only limited contact with professor or tutor. But for the mass of men this will not do, any more than the practice of medicine can escape the personal contact of physician and patient, or of the law of the contact of attorney and client. There is of necessity intellectual confrontation, personal inspiration, and the rigorous pursuit by

194

individual minds with stronger better ordered minds in the pursuit of a given discipline.

But all of this has a price. Just as the affluence, general prosperity and comfort we possess did not become fact unless in earlier years men labored and even sacrificed to achieve the scientific and technological base upon which our present culture is built, so now a similar view must be embraced by those for whom this age of technology and high specialization has yielded great rewards. We must help bear the cost of educating the youth for whom the knowledge and culture of the days that are coming become foundation stones.

Education should stress principles rather than merely acquiring skills, important as these are, the principles lying behind the techniques themselves. Otherwise there will be little increase in the power to analyze, reason—in short, to think.

Often change is in order so as to do better the same job that we are now doing. We need to keep asking ourselves what we are trying to accomplish. A kind of academic and professional radicalism is needed, not radicalism as irresponsible extremism, but radicalism in the etymological sense, having to do with roots, with fundamentals. Objectives are fundamental, and the question, what are we trying to accomplish, becomes more pressing as the information and knowledge explosion accelerates. We shall probably come to realize more and more that since it becomes less and less possible to cover subject matter completely, we should find ourselves interested more in methodology, analysis, concepts, relationships, and how we can come to know more than we do now. Striving to acquire new knowledge may be the key to understanding more fully the knowledge we have.

Relationship may turn out to be a key word in broadening and deepening education in the future. We may turn toward a type of general education at an advanced level, not to replace the major discipline but to supplement it and open it up. It may be, if we are professional radicals enough, that we will find ourselves interested in concept or idea courses, for example, a course called simply Professional Pattern, in which would be brought together, in a fresh and arresting relationship at the end of training, the sciences, psychology, and art. When one disengages himself from present routines and methods, one may see relationships and possibilities one did not realize existed. When we concentrate on objectives, we grasp the rationale for orderly and warranted change.

Any single profession or occupation should not be too narrowly conceived, since with the acceleration of technological progress the nature and content of many tasks and fields of endeavor are in a highly fluid state. Everywhere, in a sense, we are preparing for tasks that will not or may not exist when we have mastered the techniques of these tasks. Upon what shall we depend for our versatility if not the wealth of the educated, not merely the trained, mind? Versatility is not only a present basis of progress but an investment in economic security.

Skills themselves must be seen in broad terms. Skill has a narrow and also a broad meaning. There are skills purely mechanical and manipulative; but there are skills of judgment after analysis, of rendering data more meaningful, of organizing ideas clearly, concisely, cogently, and effectively. Also, there are the skills of insight, of imagination, of projection, of creative suggestion. Furthermore, there are the skills of controlling one's own emotions, or at least of channeling them into new paths, of guiding others, of organizing humans beings into meaningful relationships. And so one could go on recounting the mental, moral, and social skills that constitute the greatness of any profession at its best, and constitute when well and sufficiently exercised the cement of mutual confidence which holds society together.

The developing frontiers of knowledge are exciting. One can hardly keep abreast of the new developments in the biological and physical sciences or in the behavioral, psychological, and social sciences. Yet each administrator, professor, or scholar must make the effort in his own way. Higher education is of first importance for the whole economy. Of course, its doors must be open for qualified and responsible youth, but in addition where possible there should be opportunities for adults under expert guidance to advance themselves in their own professions and for which they pay the necessary cost. The breadth and diversity of higher education required is really very great, regardless of how financed.

I have spent most of my active life in the field of general and liberal education, as a teacher of economics and finance and as an administrator of a college of liberal arts and sciences. One of my continuing concerns has been that liberal education be relevant, practical in the best meaning of that word, and not merely utilitarian. The highest types of skills, the ones to which I have paid high tribute, may be the products of liberal education. So

196

may liberal educational elements be of excellent meaning for professional education. For me it is no problem at all to stress the importance of professional education today. Most advances in the professions will come as a result of the expansion of knowledge in the basic sciences dealing with nature and with man. These basic fields of study are the historic province of colleges and universities. The task of education in either a liberal or a professional sense deals in part with the most intangible and hidden elements of the mind and personality, for in all our education we must recognize we are dealing with whole personalities in actions, both minds and moral character. It is no problem at all for me to seek to advance professional education, because as time passes the increasing concern of the college professor for awareness, relevance, and meaning will draw him nearer to all the agencies and institutions where professionals function. Similarly, as time passes, the increasing concern of every profession for depth of meaning and for discovery of knowledge at new levels will draw him nearer to the university and the college. Divisive struggles once thought significant will assume lesser importance.

The late Dr. Albert Schweitzer said that a civilization or culture is essentially moral and ethical. This means that without this aspect a civilization becomes mere technology. For men in a free democratic state supposedly without the slave whip, motivation depends upon values, moral values; and most decisions, at least those of any importance, become value judgments and therefore moral, even though for various reasons so many dislike in this day and age to admit it.

The real questions are, what can we afford, but also, can we afford not to do our best? What in the end will satisfy us? Or, at what level of behavior dare we find satisfaction with what we have done and are doing?

16

A LOOK AHEAD IN THE PROBLEMS OF FINANCE

IT IS THE DUTY of the state through its government to support public institutions to the level of adequacy in fulfillment of the requirements of law or the expressed wishes of the people insofar as these may be known. Moreover, it is the duty of the Governor and the Legislature to determine adequacy of support at any one time, to declare what they consider satisfactory in fulfillment of law, of the expressed wishes of the people, and of their own view as leaders as to what is for the good of the whole fabric of society.

Both the executive and the legislative officers of state government should be held responsible by the people for the levels they choose to support. It is desirable for the citizenry to have agencies of their own to discover what these facts are and to communicate them back to the people. Regrettably there are more government watchers who represent relatively narrow special interests than there are who represent the broad interests of the people, because of the historic tendency to regard what is everybody's business, usually the most important things, as nobody's business. Any officer of government who resents citizen inquiry into the facts and also into the nature of his own action in either the executive or the legislative arm is not worthy to hold his office, and possibly should not be returned in the next election.

For California, adequacy of support to higher education, both public and private, from both public sources and private funds, is clearly higher than many states because of level of economy, level of per capita income, and level of expectation based both on wealth and historic conceptions of what is desired as well as the constitutional commitment which is the best evidence of the state's commitment to the support of public education. This

198

provision is found in Section XV of Article XIII of the State Constitution and was added in 1933 during the depths of the depression. It appears in these words:

> Out of the revenue from state taxes for which provision is made in this article, together with all other state revenues, there shall first be set apart the moneys to be applied by the state to the support of the public school system and the State University.

No state should turn its back on its own history of support to and development of all the finer elements of the culture and civilization of its heritage without doing so consciously. This applies to what the general public pays in taxes which go primarily to support public institutions as well as what alumni and interested corporations, foundations, and persons give. It also applies to what persons of modest, moderate, and large means as well as alumni, churches, corporations, and foundations give to private institutions.

In the modern world, with expanding enrollments, rising proportions of high school graduates and college age youth seeking admittance to higher education, rising faculty and staff salaries, new technology and accompanying equipment, expansion of available knowledge and all which that fact connotes for library needs, as well as for professional expertise, and the inevitable accompanying needs in research for the refinement of new knowledge all mean higher total expenditures. In addition, larger availability of scholarships, loans, and all forms of financial aid to needy students, to say nothing of rising building costs in an inflationary society which is neither at war nor at peace, make the resultant a continuity of high budgets for higher education.

In the matter of adequate finance for higher education, public or private, there really are two quite extreme positions from time to time voiced, neither of which is tenable. On the one hand is the viewpoint of extreme niggardliness, holding all expenditures down to the absolute minimum necessary to embrace the minimum functions of a college or a university as these may be described. Such a policy in provision of funds would inevitably carry with it acceptance of the fact that the goal embraced was not excellence, nor even mediocrity, but simply what the state or the institution could get by with. Such a point of view holds that there must always be some teachers available, no matter how weak and unscholarly and incapable, to be purchased at some price, and that there are some students who do not significantly care as to the quality of the instruction or library or other educational facilities available. Such a program is really negation of higher education and is the point of view of the noneducated or of the anti-intellectual.

At the other extreme is the point of view so often seemingly espoused by educators, namely, that nothing is good enough, that everything is needed, that nothing should be denied, that excellence demands a virtually unlimited supply of funds. Such a viewpoint is clearly unacceptable to any informed persons possessed of a knowledge of economic facts. In general, in political arguments the effort is made to place the opponent in one or another of the extreme positions characterized above.

All too frequently, political leaders do not understand the academic establishment and the reasons behind the continuing upward pressure of the academic world for financial support. Characteristically also, many educators do not understand why more funds are not available, and in general would tend not to establish any linkage at all between their own policies or their behavior or that of their students and the willingness of the people through their elected representatives or of the constituency of the private institution through the trustees to support what is being carried forward.

In any institution there is always the necessity not only over the long period of time but also in the short run to raise the question as to the practical limits of expenditures, and any administrator knows that it is absolutely necessary to establish certain priorities in claims upon available funds.

It is just such planning of laying over against all anticipated needs and desires and their respective costs with the funds likely to be available, together with some expression of the possible benefits to be derived from spending a dollar here as against spending a dollar there, which becomes imperative both for the state and for individual institutions.

California's electorate and its officers of state government must decide whether or not they want public higher education to carry forward its important tasks at levels that are good, very good, or actually superior to other states. Much is said about excellence. Excellence means to excel, to be better than others. Clearly, within the state as a whole not every institution can excel every other, only some can excel others; but it could be a goal of policy for California institutions to strive to excel all other states. There is no present requirement of law that this be true, but there is a natural inner tendency of our culture to strive to excel, and from this comes one of the driving motivations of progress of all kinds. Actually, there are no absolute objective criteria by which levels of achievement or of quality in higher education may be assessed; yet some lines along which to move and to observe are definable. This is not the place to spell all of this out in detail.

The real question is, can California afford not to be very good in fulfillment of the several functions of higher education, both public and private, and to strive to excel? My view is, quite apart from the regrettable considerations of emergency finance, California cannot afford not to support higher education at the highest possible levels.

In September, 1965, speaking at Governor Brown's Conference on Education, I made the statement relative to Budget 1965-66 that the levels of public higher education were not then being adequately supported. That statement would also, in my judgment, apply to Governor Brown's Budget 1966-67.

As to private higher education also, not sufficient support in gifts had been received, although several institutions had markedly improved their records of support from gifts.

Also, in neither Budget 1965-66 nor Budget 1966-67 had Governor Brown or the Legislature supported the State Scholarship and Fellowship programs so as to allow opportunity for maximum use of private institutional facilities.

Governor Reagan's Budget for 1967-68, already discussed, which developed within the pressures of emergency finance, did not adequately support public higher education. Thus for several years there has been built up a considerable lag if excellence was the goal within each segment.

The California State Colleges sought for 1968-69 a total state appropriation of $249,600,000, a total of $35,000,000 more than was asked for 1967-68 and $60,000,000 more than finally approved for budget year 1967-68. The State Colleges anticipated an enrollment of 156,940 full-time equivalent students in 1968-69.

The University of California sought for 1968-69 a total increase over the 1967-68 budget year support of $68,000,000, not only for expanded work load anticipated but to restore partially the austerity reductions made in the 1967-68 budget year and to replace the $20,800,000 of Regents' Funds applied in 1967-68 to the State General Fund. The University's filed request was $311,000,000.

The University anticipated an enrollment for 1968-69 of 103,000 students, actually a full-time equivalent of 96,601 students.

The total state budget of $5,699,536,000 was up over $629,000,000 over the finally approved 1967-68 budget of $5,070,016,000.

As presented to the Legislature on February 5, 1968, Governor Reagan's budget for 1968-69 included for the State Colleges a budget of $224,300,000, which was a cut of over $25,000,000 from the requested amount but $35,000,000 above the approved budget for 1967-68.

Similarly for the University the Governor's budget was a total of $280,000,000, an increase of $37,000,000 from the 1967-68 General Fund allocation but still a total of $31,000,000 below the requested amount.

Both the above segmental budgets are exclusive of faculty salary increases.

Clearly, neither President Charles J. Hitch of the University of California nor Chancellor Glenn S. Dumke of the State Colleges was satisfied. The 1967-68 financial emergency budgets were used as the base in calculating 1968-69 recommendations, as it had been predicted would happen. Crisis and austerity were now the continuing servants of economy. Various reductions in work-load support which in 1967-68 were regarded and talked about freely as one-year cuts were not restored. The existing level of support of 1967-68 was in effect to be continued under Governor Reagan's policy.

Some items passed over are indeed regrettable. One was a $2,500,000 item long approved by the Coordinating Council to enable the State Colleges to reduce the backlog of 2,500 sabbatical leaves to which faculty members have developed a recognizable claim but which has not been reduced effectively because of insufficient funding over several years. Another was a proposal of $300,000 for special faculty research leaves in the State Colleges. It could have been cut in amount, but it was cut out. The other items of growing importance finally cut out were $200,000 for moving expenses for new State College faculty members and $87,000 to pay expenses of interviews with prospective faculty members; both of these are related to the recruiting problem referred to in an earlier chapter. In addition, the long-run view was sacrificed to the short-run view by the postponement of conversion of the State Colleges to year-round operation on the quarter system on the plan which had been projected.

Similarly, for the University an important principle underlying the Governor's cuts is postponement. This means that various programs planned and approved by the Regents and the Coordinating Council at both undergraduate and graduate levels will be deferred a year or more; such actions tend to affect the newer campuses at Irvine, Santa Cruz, and San Diego but also will have a broad effect. In the case of library development, the Regents' request for funding library growth on the several campuses was cut 50 percent. Here again the long-run view is sacrificed to the short-run situation.

In both segments there is considerable deferral of equipment installations and repairs, maintenance of grounds and buildings involved in the actual amounts allowed in the Governor's budget.

In addition to the standard budgets, the Governor proposed a faculty salary increase for the University of 5 percent and for the State Colleges of 7.5 percent. The Coordinating Council at its December 6, 1967 meeting had recommended a 5.5 percent increase for the University faculty and a 10 percent increase for the State College faculties which the data of comparison institutions in other states showed to be necessary to maintain a competitive level. Even that action was strongly protested by the State Colleges whose Trustees had in October, 1967 proposed for the State Colleges' faculties an average salary increase of 16.85 percent and in addition an increase of 3.3 percent of the faculty salary total in fringe benefits.

For myself at the time of the Trustees' action I regarded the 16.85 percent faculty salary increase as extreme, due for extensive debate, and impolitic. These items alone if adopted would have increased the State Colleges' budget for 1968-69 by $33,000,000 and thus tended to jeopardize the reliability and necessity of all other requests. For the year 1967-68, for the normal academic year, representative top salaries for State College faculty were: professors, $17,016; associate professors, $13,332; and assistant professors, $10,548. For these ranks University of California top salaries were higher. The reader for himself can calculate the effect of the 10 percent increase recommended by the Coordinating Council and the 7.5 percent increase in Governor Reagan's budget.

By mid-1968 the position of Governor Reagan regarding the relative importance of public higher education will have become history. The Legislature will have acted and if increases are voted, he will have decided whether to veto. Budget 1968-69 is the critical year. This was my personal message to the Governor stated in his office in late July, 1967. Governor Reagan in a letter to Chancellor Dumke of the State Colleges, dated September 7, 1967, wrote, "Many worthwhile items were reduced or removed from the 1967-68 budget simply because of the financial crisis in which we found the State of California upon taking office. It is not, and never would be, my intention to damage the excellent State College System that exists." Similar statements have been made regarding the University. However, during the fall word came to me that the total increase of Budget 1968-69 would be, indeed must be I was told, limited to a percentage increase much less than the estimated work-load percentage increase alone in all public higher education systems. I was not therefore unduly surprised to see the final budget figures submitted for these two segments. Not adequately covering basic work load as increased due to larger enrollments is faulty public finance.

At the February, 1968 meeting of the Coordinating Council, there was presented a staff report analyzing the Governor's 1968-69 Budget against both previous Council actions and the work load as reflected in the anticipated "mix" of graduate and undergraduate enrollment for both the University and the State Colleges. On this analysis, which I supported heartily, the budget of the University would have to be increased $13,500,000 to $293,500,000, and the State Colleges' budget increased $5,500,000 to $229,800,000. For me these amounts were needed to meet the requirements of the Master Plan, even though in each instance they were less than each segment was declaring to be necessary.

What happens in Budget 1968-69 to all aspects of higher education will tell the story as to what the State of California really thinks about higher education, the price it is willing to pay for high quality and broadening opportunity in its colleges and universities. It will also show clearly the kind of values its leaders really embrace and seek to foster.

Discussion of the disputes in 1967 over Budget 1967-68, tuition, and the status of higher education in the counsels both of the Reagan Administration and the Legislature left uncovered one interesting aspect. At the close of 1966 and in early 1967 confusion over interpreting the mind of the electorate was a complicating factor. At the same November, 1966 election when Ronald Reagan was elected Governor after a campaign which involved much debate and comment on the problems of higher education and on the necessity of economy in state government, the voters had approved Proposition Number 2 on the ballot which called for a $230,000,000 bond issue for capital outlay needs in higher education specifically labeled for the University of California and the State Colleges. (From this bond issue the junior colleges had been specifically eliminated by their own choice.) These funds were to be divided nearly equally for the two senior systems.

President Clark Kerr at the time heralded this voter approval as meaning that "the people of California have once again confirmed long-standing commitment to public higher education." The real issues for the future are whether this is true, and if so, to what extent, and as paid for by whom.

That bond issue's proceeds were to be used to meet construction, equipment, and site acquisition costs for the two segments until exhausted but with a probable duration and availability for two or three years, together with federal funds which may be available by using these state funds in whole or in part for matching purposes.

The capital as well as current needs of California public higher education as well as of all state responsibilities have been a matter of public concern for many years as the implications of the rate of population growth have been carried through to calculate total financial burdens for the state to be anticipated over a period of years. Of course subject to redefinition, reapproval, and recalculation, the magnitudes of any one calculation never become less, only greater, to account for too conservative estimates of population growth or the effects of inflation and the changing pattern of factor costs upon the total costs of construction, or the enlarged conceptions of the needs of all state agencies as well as of the three segments of public higher education.

In 1964, the Legislature declared its "intent to reduce the need for future bond proposals by establishing a method of financing capital outlay needs that relies far less on borrowing, and that is equitable to both present and future taxpayers, and that produces a maximum of necessary construction at a minimum cost." The Legislature further declared its intent ". . . to establish a specific program calling for major emphasis on pay-as-you-go financing." These were noble and brave words, but neither Governor Brown or the 1965, 1966, or 1967 Legislatures acted upon this expressed intent. Actually, considering the total of financial claims on the State of California, possibly they couldn't. This hope of pay-as-you-go lingers. Most thoughtful persons wish it could be true.

Somehow, the notion seldom seems embraceable, and least of all to those whose need for space and equipment is as of now.

Governor Reagan in mid-1967 stated that the $230,000,000 bond issue voted in 1966 should be the last one, and if this is truly adopted as policy, it means inevitably an added annual expenditure of many millions of dollars for capital outlay for construction and equipment. However, Governor Reagan's budget for 1968-69 cut on capital outlay items severely. The capital outlay items requested for 1968-69 by the University totaled $80,000,000, this figure being below what the Regents really believed necessary. Governor Reagan recommended only $44,800,000. Also, for the State Colleges, the building fund items requested totaled $108,000,000, while the Governor recommended only $45,500,000.

Through the summer and fall of 1967 the problem of the anticipated magnitude of capital outlay requirements hung over the planning of new budgets. Attempts were made quietly but unsuccessfully to obtain sufficient leadership support for another bond issue for $100,000,000 to $200,000,000 to cover nonbudgetable needs for one or two years for these two senior segments. Since a junior college bond issue for $65,000,000 had been scheduled already as mentioned in an earlier chapter, for the June, 1968 ballot, another bond issue might be defeated and the success of the junior college issue endangered unfairly. It should not be a matter of great surprise, however, if by legislative action the issue is forced either for the fall of 1968 or the earliest feasible date.

No one appropriately can take exception to a search for economy in public finance. This applies to higher education even though some college and university administrators in their more emotional moments have equated economy, i.e., almost any cutback from requests, as an evidence of a lack of belief in the value or importance of higher education, if not in fact proof of anti-intellectualism.

Also, on the other hand, no one can morally justify or today intelligently embrace for higher education a policy of parsimony, whose dictionary meaning is stinginess. At least such a policy cannot be respected if at the same time speeches about the greatness of California's University and State Colleges and the importance of higher education are being voiced as representing the best interests of the whole people. If higher education and learning are being espoused, then the advocate of a policy of parsimony cannot be supported.

Governor Reagan does not impress me as being an anti-intellectual. He is, as I see him, too intelligent to be simply anti-education. Apparently, however, he does not fully understand what contribution the state's higher education system has made to the prosperity of this state, nor does he understand the degree to which the people value its opportunities. Even as a politician in which he has excelled he undervalues what contributions higher education can make to virtually every aspect of the state's economy and development. He should be giving it a major priority and taking pride in what he has provided to higher education for continuing its accomplishments.

Criticizing segments of higher education for failing to do more or to do better what they purport to do, while providing them with support for their tasks, is a better stance. This has been my own approach: clear adequacy of financial support and a continuing critical eye on quality of performance through constituted bodies of review and control.

There is always a legitimate basis for argument, on dollars and also on performance. My experience leads me to a belief that both the University and the State Colleges on some items have asked for too much, or have done too little with what they had. Similarly, my view is that on some items or on overall totals the executive and legislative arms of government have not given enough, or have not explained what reasons underlie their actions.

The University under President Kerr too early and too rapidly, but primarily to occupy the high ground and to close out State College competitive possibilities, embraced the doctrine that each campus, old and new, should be a general campus. This carried the possibility if not probability of too early overexpansionism and duplication. At least, in all probability it actually led to high initial costs of campus development. It has created also widely variant patterns of curriculum and internal organization from campus to campus. For example, it is yet to be proved that conceived as a general campus, Santa Cruz or San Diego will be able to make good the initial commitment that their internal essentially collegiate plan will not prove more costly per student, at the various levels of undergraduate, graduate, and professional instruction, than in the rest of the University.

The Coordinating Council as well as the executive and legislative departments are now substantially bound by this general campus interpretation of the Master Plan's functional arrangements. Now no other plan seems embraceable; but the rate of growth of new functions at the several campuses may be restrained until enrollment demands elsewhere require larger faculties and facilities. An example of the potential cost of tendencies to rapid growth is found in the request by one chancellor of a new campus for one hundred new faculty posts for a particular budget year which the state-wide administration reduced to forty-two. It may well be asked, Which figure represented what was both adequate and necessary for that year?

The administrators of the State Colleges have found it difficult to avoid satisfying the tendency of each State College to want many programs that other State Colleges possess. Of course, there are specializations and areas of no or limited duplication; nevertheless, proliferation of programs and courses may be observed. The practical appeals of community service are evident. The Coordinating Council may be relied upon to reduce unnecessary duplication to a minimum.

Such continuing review of academic and campus plans has been a function of the Coordinating Council. It has been done with care. Academic plans have been submitted to the Coordinating Council since 1961, and annually reviewed. These academic plans are closely related to the physical development of a campus, that is, the availability of space. Long-range planning, details, and adequacy of "lead time" have been debated. All have had careful scrutiny from other possibly related educational interests represented in the Coordinating Council. Most elements of the grandiose have been steeped out by this boiling process. The Governor's budget for 1968-69 does not properly give financial support to the steady embrace of these academic plans of the University and the State Colleges which the Council has approved so as to be ready for the youth already born and in secondary or elementary schools who confidently expect a place will be ready for them in the next ten years. The plans submitted to the Coordinating Council in February, 1968 deserve the most careful scrutiny by the people's representatives. By and large, without accepting every detail, they deserve support.

The exponents of increased institutional autonomy have yet to come up with some plan more viable than the centralized administration and policy planning of the Regents, the Trustees, and the Coordinating Council. Broad and inclusive aspirations for departmental, functional, or institutional growth or development in numbers or quality are to be commended. They should not and need not be restrained from drawing their plans or formulating their dreams. Any administrator should welcome persons of ambitions, ideas, visions, yielding new plans for improvement in contrast to those individuals content to let run-of-the-mill operations continue year by year. Of necessity, however, and in this day an imperative necessity, is the need of priorities in claims to limited resources. (Even if resources are doubled they are still limited.) Hence, the need for planning, programming, and budgeting with care.

This is a forceful argument against undue decentralization or autonomy and in continuing support for responsible Regents and Trustees and Governors who scrutinize carefully what comes up from the operating units and strive to achieve an onward movement yielding pride to a cultured and civilized society. Continuing justification and explanation to the people of the state by the boards and agencies as the people's representatives of what they are doing and why they are doing what they do, and how they are exercising maximum economy in the use of the people's money towards great ends that transcend their own individual self-interests, is becoming an increasing responsibility for leadership in higher education.

For me, there are orders of priority in all budgets, capital outlay or current. For me, youth is in clear priority over age, and education at all levels over many other things. For me, wisdom is to build the future and do only what seems reasonable to overcome failures of the past. For me, wisdom suggests that one distinguish normal behavior from the abnormal, and place two dollars or more on the normal as against one dollar or less on the delinquent, defective, necessarily detentive, dependent persons except for those below responsible age, and the "dehydrated" oldsters.

Yet the tendency of all too many politicians, of those who possess the power, is to turn the whole process around, and to do everything possible for all the abnormal elements and force the normal and promising elements of the economy and society to bear the burden, and even to force what is done for those who are in youthful years and are also needy to be financed by repayable obligations. Those who really need a hand to prove themselves for the future deserve better treatment if they are intellectually able and do perform satisfactorily.

Our public higher educational institutions should accept the principle of tuition combined with adequate and genuine grants of financial aid for those really unable to pay the tuition, before they seek to rely more fully on gifts from those not affiliated with their institutions, or before they expand their present dependence on the federal government. Those who come from above the minimum levels of family or personal income but who for the moment lack funds should have available loan funds on the "go now, pay later" principle, reasonably applied.

It is by now no news that California has been and is in a great crisis in higher education, although as the previous chapters have shown, there is nothing new about all this. It is only in the last decade that we have admitted crisis; it is only in the last year or two that its meaning in finance and control have come directly home to the general public. How the state emerges from this crisis will depend greatly upon the depth of perception of what is involved, of how significantly the whole technologically based economy of California relates to all higher education in California and its output in knowledge, persons, and processes of action.

The crisis in California's finance of higher education is not solely due to higher education or the forces operating within it. It is due also to the extent of other burdens against the state's finances voted by an electorate or embraced by the people's representatives who find temporizing remedies more appealing than the processes of prevention in so many problem areas, or who are putting other things ahead of education.

One cannot separate, unless he is ignorant, the long-run welfare of California from the work of the University of California, Stanford University, California Institute of Technology, the University of Southern California, the California State Colleges, the Claremont Colleges, Occidental, and the many other private colleges, as well as the junior colleges. The galaxy of institutional scholarly brilliance of California is the envy of many states. Sad it is that so many Californians are seemingly so unaware of the degree to which industry, business, and finance are interlocked with these academic communities in their front and back yards.

Also there is insufficient belief in the degree to which the freedom prized in the marketplace is related, as warp is to woof, to the freedom necessary for learning, teaching, and new knowledge in "the groves of academe." Industry's health, the state's economy, the nation's well-being, and the quality of the universities and colleges are inextricably bound together. Quality means more than buildings, more than courses, and even more than persons. At its best, higher education demands an atmosphere of unfettered imagination, unrestricted exploration, and opportunity to discuss all issues without fear.

As has been noted throughout this book, public higher education and the private colleges and universities are intimately bound up with each other's welfare. What is done in public higher education inevitably affects the welfare of the private institutions. With charters from the state and with the necessary elements of policy they must pursue, the private or independent institutions are serving a public purpose. Although in earlier decades it was tenable that public higher education should embrace only those activities and programs which private higher education could not develop or sustain adequately, a doctrine derivative of earlier views of the interrelationships of the public and the private economies, this view can no longer be the primary guide in public policy. Nevertheless, the doctrine should not be forgotten, and the private aspects of higher education should never be lost to view. However, for leaders of public higher education it is very easy so to do while at the same time making beautifully worded speeches about private higher education that sometimes have little significant content in action.

The extremely opposite position from that of earlier decades is to accept public higher education as the normative posture of the state, the economy, and society, and simply to tolerate with a minimum of adjustment the private sector of higher education; tolerate it indeed so long as the public segments of higher education in no degree suffer from such adjustments. That this has become the viewpoint of whole segments of the academic profession in public higher education, few would now have the temerity to deny. Yet if this extreme position were followed to logical conclusions, the burden on the state of the 20 percent of all higher education enrollments now in private institutions would cause the state's total bill for both current operations and capital outlay to be at the minimum 20 to 25 percent higher than it now is and will be, but in all likelihood very much higher.

The irony of it is that a careful observer might note that some of the most ardent exponents in public higher education of the advancement of public segments at whatever costs were themselves educated in private institutions, and with the subvention of considerable scholarship, other financial aid, the benefit of incalculable benevolence, and the strength of then existing private institutional influence for their personal advantage.

There is no simple solution to this nexus of relationships.

211

Extreme positions will ultimately be repudiated. Indeed, in some instances they already have been. The value of the private voice in public counsels is thus underscored so long as it does not become solely self-serving.

In the problems of financing higher education California does not stand alone. This is a major issue facing the nation and currently is receiving major attention in every collegiate association, every church-related group of colleges and universities, in major journals, in the major philanthropic foundations, and in the privately-sponsored Council for Financial Aid to Education headquartered in New York.

The Carnegie Corporation of New York with the former University of California president and present Berkeley professor Dr. Clark Kerr as chairman is sponsoring a special study group on this topic. In earlier years under similar sponsorship there was the Commission on Financing Higher Education of which Dr. John Millett was chief of staff. There is no lack of literature on this important question either on a national or a state-by-state basis, with some of the best work done by Professor Seymour E. Harris, Dexter M. Keezer, and John D. Millett.

Everywhere and in every institution, and in both public and private segments, educators keep asking where the money is coming from for both construction costs and for operating expenses in the light of the rising costs. Building costs, rapidly expanding enrollments, and rising faculty and staff salaries to mention nothing as to the changing external expectations of the modern college or university in research and public service, or the changing internal relationships and conceptions regarding student counseling, experimental teaching methods, health and other services, and faculty relationships to students, all mean a continuity of high budgets for higher education, a cost structure which somehow must be met with appropriate adjustments internally or adequate financing externally.

A search for new sources of income for both public and private higher education is taking place. This is because of the pressures described as well as the inability, or at least in the light of all present claims to earnings and other income the unwillingness, of the people to pay through taxes for the benefit of others, or of many who are able to do so to give of their substance.

In the case of private higher education since tuitions are already high and the upper limits are being reached, there is an increasing reliance upon gifts for current operations and also a doubled search for capital funds. It is quite evident that the private institutions which now have the best reputations and generally the better educational programs and faculty personnel are those with the larger endowments which because of strength are also capable of charging the higher tuitions; but this is sustained also by the strong demand for admittance. These institutions can command strong faculty and superior administration. However, now even with the strongest, costs seem to be rising at a rate higher than income from normal sources, thus bringing increased reliance on gifts for current operations and upon undesignated funds. All of this has caused increased appeals for gifts to those historically affiliated with these private institutions and to potential new donors, with a steadily broader use by institutions and individuals of methods of giving with tax-reducing or tax-avoiding advantages once reserved primarily for the well informed and persons thoroughly sophisticated financially. Hence, a sort of democratization of the privilege of tax counseling and estate planning has been going on.

These conditions have also brought about an increased willingness of private institutions not only to borrow from the federal government at low interest rates and with long amortization plans, but also to accept federal grants for facilities, equipment, research, scientific, and other departmental development where once such assistance was spurned on ideological and politically partisan grounds.

Public higher education is of necessity forced to seek out new sources of income not heretofore tapped such as (1) tuition for instruction even if accompanied by grants-in-aid to those not able to pay the charges, (2) fees and other charges for the public services once rendered gratuitously, (3) royalties on patents or the results of research to agricultural, commercial, or industrial advantage, even if all costs were borne by government, and (4) participations in research programs deemed of private advantage. This latter point may mean a partial reconstruction of how applied research is paid for. Governor Reagan has requested the Coordinating Council for Higher Education to make just such a study of the total possibilities in financing for the public higher education systems of California. A similar study for the University of California has been ordered by the Regents.

Possibly useful might be a select committee of distinguished citizens representing alone neither the Governor nor the Legislature, nor any single party, nor any single segment of higher

17

A LOOK AHEAD IN GOVERNANCE AND COORDINATION
OF CALIFORNIA HIGHER EDUCATION

WHAT DOES THE FUTURE HOLD in the interrelationships of functions, structure, and organization of California's public higher education? In an earlier chapter the situation in 1959-60 was described with the central importance of functions, structure, and organization emphasized. Since then the situation has changed; yet well may it be asked whether conditions have changed fundamentally and whether the need is present for a wholesale revamping of the Master Plan as some dissident voices declare.

In 1965-66 the Coordinating Council requested its staff in cooperation with staff personnel of the various segments to make a review and report on the Master Plan five years after its major recommendations had become operative under the statutes. That report was made to the Coordinating Council, with its analyses of the extent to which the recommendations of the Master Plan and the provisions of the Donahoe Act had become operative. In general to a very considerable degree it was found the Master Plan was being put into effect. Certain major exceptions due to the failure of the Legislature to accept all of the Master Plan recommendations have already been indicated in earlier chapters. The failures of each segment either to live up to the Plan's requirements or to transform operations to the Master Plan standards as speedily as intended have been noted and discussed, and at present work is moving forward in each segment effectively. Practically speaking, the Master Plan is in effect today.

However, in mid-1967 a feature article in an Oakland newspaper heralded the 1959-60 Master Plan as a failure, citing as proof the continued "rivalry for funds, prestige, and political favor" between the two senior segments of public higher education. This emphasis suggested that "success" could or would be represented as a condition of peaceful coexistence with no competition of any kind among the warring tribes. Such a view represents socially immature analysis because it causes silence and progress to be equated; yet more than one legislator in the years 1965 and 1966 voiced similar sentiments. No one should expect a complete absence of struggle.

In mid-1965 under the leadership of the Speaker of the Assembly, Jesse M. Unruh, a joint legislative inquiry into the status of higher education under the Master Plan was launched. At the time the memories of legislators were fresh regarding the 1964-1965 difficulties over the Free Speech Movement and other student organizations and activities at the University of California campus at Berkeley. From the speeches or comments made at the time by Speaker Unruh and Senator Hugh Burns and others it seemed clear that the frustrations of legislators in reference to the University and its authorities, particularly the independent constitutional status of the University, were prompting such legislative inquiry into the University's administration as the only way other than the budget in which the Legislature could have an influence. This inquiry was broadened to include all the University campuses, the State Colleges, the junior colleges, and the entire Master Plan. The Joint Committee on Higher Education emerged as the result of A.C.R. 156 in June, 1965. Nevertheless, at the time, Speaker Unruh stated he had never intended "to zero in on the Berkeley thing." Press reports, however, quite generally indicated faculty unrest at the State Colleges, financing problems, and Master Plan reevaluation along with student unrest as primary elements in the study. The Senate specifically balked at a full-fledged probe of the Berkeley student demonstrations.

In August, 1965 there was an official release regarding the establishment of this Joint Committee, in which it was stated that "an exhaustive, two-year study of California's university and state college problems was assured." It further stated quoting Speaker Unruh, "I would be less than candid if I said that the Berkeley riots had no effect upon the Legislature," but "the majority of the Legislature in both parties never entertained an intention to investigate the Berkeley affair by itself."

Speaker Unruh indicated deep legislative concern about "the future of higher education in this state" and the "mass decentralization of the state university as has been proposed to the Regents," and "a growing unrest among the faculty of the state colleges." In reference to the University at another time, Speaker Unruh referred to the Byrne Report of 1965 as proposing "an almost complete reallocation of the resources which the state has made available to the University of California." He also stated that it (the Byrne Report) "went to the heart of the issues facing higher education in this state."

Interested parties were invited to submit proposals for the format of the study. Many leading educators, probably over 250 persons, were invited to counsel by correspondence and in personal conference. The Coordinating Council in the fall of 1965 took action offering its full cooperation and assistance.

For myself, it was fully logical that the Master Plan, described by one newspaper as "so broad a blueprint," should be subjected to reexamination. The important question was and is what attitude would guide such a reexamination. During the months of relative quietude in the Joint Committee's actions there was considerable speculation over what course the investigation would pursue. Indeed, this sense of disquiet was present upon the occasion of the Joint Committee's first meeting with educators representing all segments and the Coordinating Council officers in August, 1966.

The Joint Committee was slow in getting started, partly because the membership on the Senate side was not appointed until many months after the Assembly's members were selected. The Honorable Jesse M. Unruh was chosen chairman of this Joint Committee, and the Honorable Donald L. Grunsky, from the Senate, became vice-chairman.

The Committee's activities in the first year of its existence, 1965-66, were extremely limited, which the Committee in 1967 explained "as one way of allowing topical excitement to subside and normal mechanisms of academic administration to be restored." An effort was made during that year to enlist the leadership of a distinguished educator either from within the state or from another state, apparently hoping to obtain a new, fresh, and unbiased approach. Failing the signing on of an educator of renown, the Joint Committee chose to employ as consultants and as directors of the studies to be made the firm of Alfred Baxter and Associates.

Reference was made to the August, 1966 meeting of educators with the Joint Committee. Present other than members of the Joint Committee were Superintendent of Public Instruction Max Rafferty, President Clark Kerr and Chairman of the Regents

Theodore Meyer for the University of California, Chancellor Glenn S. Dumke and Albert J. Ruffo, Trustee Chairman, for the State Colleges, Mr. Stuart White and several others for the junior colleges, Carl Franklin and Robert J. Bernard for the private institutions, Willard Spalding and myself from the Coordinating Council, and several others in attendance. In advance uncertain over what might transpire, over what this committee might set as its goals, the educators present were reassured by the expressions of desire to cooperate with higher education in the studies to be made, and by the disavowals of any intentions to go on a witch hunt. Lines of possible study were discussed even though tentatively, such as the relationships of all segments to the state's potential manpower needs, the appropriate balance among the several segments for the achievement of these long-range needs, and the problems of financing all segments including the degree to which the junior colleges should continue to be so largely dependent upon local district financing. Possibly the most critical question of all was alluded to but not discussed in any detail, namely, whether the forward view from 1966 rather than 1959 seemed to require any basic changes in organization and structure of control of public higher education, principally the State College system and the University of California.

My own memory of that meeting and the dinner gathering which followed includes several points made by the educators that bear making a matter of record. One was that the work of the Joint Committee must at all costs be divorced from current partisan political debates for the sake of the freedom and purity of higher educational processes. Another was that the opportunity presented to this Joint Committee was of great challenge to bring in an objective report of historic significance to the State of California and also by indirection to the whole nation.

In addition, it was pointed out that the contemplated study appeared to be the first in the long line of major studies of higher education in California (see Chapter III) which would be made by persons outside the higher level academic profession. Also it was stated that since no inquiry into the functioning of the legal or medical professions would for one moment be tolerable without seeking cooperation from the legal or medical leadership, so no inquiry without voice or participation from the leadership of the academic world could probably stand the test of time, or for that matter be acceptable *ab initio*. The world of higher education includes many elements (governing boards, administrators,

218

faculties, and students) which when they work together yield great and wonderful results, but when they engage in internal struggles or are induced to become concerned about the *loci* and *foci* of power inevitably create conditions which cause the students to suffer in their educational growth or society to suffer through the false direction of scholarly energy.

The Joint Committee's chairman Unruh stated he realized fully the risks involved in legislative study of academic institutions and of the necessity of separating academic institutions from day-to-day political conflicts. He also pointed out that the Master Plan (as I have indicated elsewhere was a necessity at the time) ignored the substance of higher education and that there was a hope this aspect could be related to the long-range manpower planning needed.

Earlier, in 1965 Speaker Unruh had stated that "the Donahoe Act (i.e., the Master Plan) did not begin to deal with the question of proper organization of the University of California," and as he continued in his statement of July 7, 1965, "the proof of this lies in the attempts" (i.e., the Master Plan) to create "a state college system with precisely the same sort of organizational structure and insulation from public pressures as the university now has, and has had for many years. More importantly, the Donahoe Act did not address itself to the delicate subject of the control of a university or college campus. . . . Who *does* control an institution of higher learning, the administration, the faculty, the students, or a combination of all three? I am concerned when high officials both within and without higher education become incensed over the efforts of the Legislature to find the answers to such a basic question."

These questions by Speaker Unruh were pertinent, thoroughly legitimate questions, and undoubtedly by a broad construction of the language of Assembly Concurrent Resolution No. 88 in 1959 could have been included had there been time. That Resolution called for "a Master Plan for the development, expansion, and integration of the facilities, curriculum, and standards of higher education. . . . to meet the needs of the State during the next ten years and thereafter." Items dealing with the internal administration and control of particular institutions could have been covered if time and energy as well as funds had been available. However, some sifting or screening had to take place. Furthermore, the representatives of the two senior systems were unsympathetic with any effort to preempt the authority of controlling boards regarding internal management. Hence, most of the Master Plan dealt with segmental responsibilities and relationships.

At the August, 1966 Joint Committee meeting I took occasion to comment to the Committee on the problems of governance of higher education, striving to contrast the extreme control of a totalitarian society and the extreme permissiveness of the historic private nondenominational college or university in terms comparable to those set forth in Chapter VI and elsewhere. My viewpoint expressed the necessity of finding answers outside extreme positions, and I acknowledged Speaker Unruh's publicly declared point that "the public and the taxpayers of this state have a strong stake in the solution to the basic question of the governance of the University." However, my view differed from his in that I have been, was then, and am now opposed to challenging in any degree the constitutional status of the University of California. In July of 1965 Speaker Unruh, however, referring to the constitution of the state drawn in 1879 and the form of governance and control for the University of California set forth therein, said, "To me, it is inconceivable that our educators and apparently our highest elected officials can believe that a nineteenth century organizational structure can meet the needs of the public in twentieth century California." He did not indicate why "it is inconceivable." Certainly age should not be a controlling factor, else what about the eighteenth century United States Constitution's "organizational structure"?

The issues in this problem as in so many others outlined in this book center around what is right; and with all the respect which I hold for legislators and governors and their responsibilities, I will not be party to creating instruments whereby they can control, beyond budgetary action, the public higher education of California. It is my profound hope that Speaker Unruh and all members of the Joint Committee, regardless of the forensics, really believe the same thing.

And I would go one step further, namely, establish constitutional status for the State Colleges also, but in so doing, I would urge their functions be set forth clearly and unmistakably.

On November 30, 1965 I wrote to Speaker Unruh in response to his request for the Joint Committee for counsel, among other things stating:

(1) Concern for the problems of the governance and responsi-

220

bility for performance of the various segments of public higher education is one of the first elements of responsibility.

(2) While I do not in any manner intend to imply that the Regents of the University should be changed as to status, it is appropriate for that body to report more frequently and systematically on its performance of its constitutional responsibility.

(3) The State College Board of Trustees also has a responsibility in this regard, conceivably greater than has thus far been recognized.

(4) The California State Board of Education should with reference to the junior colleges more clearly define from time to time the way in which its responsibilities have been discharged.

(5) The present controversy over year-round operations which has brought out the laggardness of the State Colleges indicates the importance within that system of understanding more fully and delineating more clearly the degree to which centralization shall occur.

(6) With reference to the Regents, the question of autonomy if not almost virtual independence of the several campuses of the University from the President, and conceivably to a great degree from the overarching supervision of the Regents, needs very carefully to be examined.

(7) Another concern should be greater budgetary control upon the part of the State College Board of Trustees, i.e., greater flexibility and authority if not autonomy in fiscal matters.

(8) The Legislative inquiry should avoid discussion of personalities or problems of educational policy or faculty organization or curriculum planning or many of the items that belong to the segmental authorities as already provided for by law.

(9) An important point has to do with possible bases of finance of higher education in this state. The Legislative inquiry could appropriately look into the question of fees and tuitions if any from students in the public segments of higher education, and along with this consider fully and appropriately not simply the present State Scholarship plan but also some form of grant-in-aid to persons of low family income or inadequate personal finances. This suggestion as to participation in financing upon the part of students brings into relationship all aspects of our present relationship to the federal government. Before the Legislative inquiry will have finished its work, it undoubtedly will have reviewed what the federal government is now doing vis-a-vis higher education.

What will result from the Joint Committee's inquiry at this writing is quite uncertain, but certain it is that as to funds and opportunity, the setting has been most advantageous. The Joint Committee has a budget of $350,000 and is enabled to continue through the 1969 session of the Legislature. Major issues have posed; let wise measures emanate from their labors. Personally I regretted to read in Speaker Unruh's release of August 11, 1967, in announcing two new Assembly appointees (one a Democrat, one a Republican) to the Joint Committee, the implication that of necessity the Master Plan required revision. His statement was, "I believe that quality representation on the joint committee is essential if we are to develop a meaningful revision of the Master Plan for Higher Education which will have a good chance of legislative passage."

A few things should not be forgotten at any time. One is that the Donahoe Act of 1960 (S.B. 33) passed the Senate initially 36 to 1, then was amended in the Assembly and in conference. As amended it passed the Assembly 70-0, and the Senate 28-8. Assemblyman Unruh did not vote against the Donahoe Act. That 1960 Assembly vote with no negative vote was something of a record.

Another item not to be forgotten is the very broad acceptance and approval of many Master Plan ideas by educators and public officials of other states and the general high reputation in other states of California's higher education system. The movement towards coordination in many different governmental forms and often with superboard tendencies or powers has taken hold. As of 1967, 38 states had some form of a coordinating board, but with varying responsibilities and powers. In 30 states the authority of the coordinating agency was managerial, and included other powers theoretically at least greater than the California Coordinating Council had. The states other than California in which the coordinating board was advisory rather than managerial were in that year Arkansas, Kentucky, Maryland, Michigan, Minnesota, and South Carolina. As for myself, since 1960 I have been invited to speak in the formulation of public policy or to serve as consultant on master planning or coordination in Colorado, Florida, Illinois, Maryland, Missouri, Texas, and Utah, but until 1965 I limited my participation to a few speeches only, and since 1965 have rejected all such requests.

Various organizational alternatives, not all equally acceptable, have been envisioned by the staffs of the Joint Committee and the Coordinating Council, as well as of Governor Reagan's task force survey on efficiency and cost control. The latter report although bearing a November, 1967 date on the working copy was not made public until February 7, 1968. This task force survey was composed of 250 business executives, professional persons, and management specialists. All of these various alternatives are now in the public domain for consideration and discussion.

One is a single large higher educational system with a single governing board. The Governor's task force recommendations, admittedly heavily influenced by conceptions of what would be necessary if the administrative structure of any large industrial company or institution were involved, by analogy recommended for more thorough study such a combined system to include the present University, State College, and junior college systems, the controlling board replacing rather than being superimposed on the present governing boards. Under such a plan in the case of the junior colleges the principle of local district control or even significant participation in control probably would be lost. On this ground alone it may be predicted, unless 100 percent state financing of junior colleges also were to ensue, the suggested scheme would fail of adequate political support.

Another proposal, not to be associated with the Governor's task force but on the back burner since Master Plan days is a single university system for both the State Colleges and the University of California with the possibility of two or more standards of admission, or only one which of course would be lower than the present University level.

The State Colleges' viewpoint today regarding a single constitutional board I believe would be (1) it must be new and not simply a transformation of the present Board of Regents, (2) there is comparability of representation, and (3) there is recognition in its constitutional mandate of the fact that the State Colleges are performing a major share (State College personnel would say the lion's share) of the teaching load in California public higher education. Or to put it differently, the State Colleges, and also the junior colleges if included, must not be an afterthought, and the new board must be committed to helping attain higher academic prestige and an overall achievement record for that system, or those systems, as well as for the University.

There is no doubt about the broad political issue. The University wants money, much more money than it has been getting, and so do the State Colleges, and so do the junior colleges, and there seems not to be enough tax money willingly levied by Legislature and Governor for all of them.

To absorb all the State Colleges, and also conceivably the junior colleges, under the existing Board of Regents constitutes a structural and legal problem of major magnitude. If the Legislature should vote to place by statute one or the other or both systems under the Board of Regents, then thereafter they could never be removed except by constitutional amendment and also, although the statutory transfer might spell out the terms of transfer and all manner of protections, once transferred and accepted, it is doubtful if such conditions would be binding. Candidly stated, without a constitutional amendment stipulating conditions and what these two systems might want as "guarantees," the so-called "guarantees" would not avail since under the constitution the Board of Regents probably cannot be forced to do anything it does not wish to do. Even voluntary commitments of the University's president or of a group of Regents may not assure no later reversal of action. Only representation and full participation would satisfy. This is the State College viewpoint as I understood it in 1959 and as I see it now.

Another alternative in organization is the transference to the University of California of all State Colleges of complex organization and large size with the remaining State Colleges committed to collegiate work only.

Any one of these proposals if effected conceivably would carry with it within such a new University structure a modification of the concept of a general campus as being of necessity the resultant in new institutions formed and developed. The Regents' decision on recommendation of President Kerr to make nearly all University campuses general campuses has been criticized as potentially an overextension of some programs and hence of unnecessary duplication. Considerable curriculum modifications might result from such a merger with the intent of eliminating duplications of low enrollment programs.

A variant of the last proposal is to associate all the State Colleges not transferred to the University with the junior colleges and to develop further State Colleges as needed around or in proximity to chosen junior colleges. Thus under this idea there would be only two systems: a university system and a collegiate system.

224

Another proposal is based on the idea of extreme decentralization with a board for each institution of public higher education. Such a structure could not function effectively without a very strong state agency of coordination functioning clearly and unmistakably beyond the advisory role.

One proposal considerably distressing to present leadership and boards in the three public segments is that the state be divided into four or five regions each with its own board and each having jurisdiction over the University, State College, and junior college campuses in its area. This proposal continues to receive the attention of the Joint Committee on Higher Education. Again, such a situation would possibly if not probably require some coordinating agency for the state as a whole. Otherwise, the jockeying for funds, programs, and political position would carry controls back to the Legislature. All legislators of necessity would bear important relationships to major decisions. This would constitute the most evident departure from historic traditions of seeking to separate the capitol from the campus. Understandably, legislators and executives do not enjoy the process of devolution of decision-making authority which the requirements of a technological civilization and complex political involvement of a modern state call for. However, successive legislatures and governors learn each for itself or himself the limits of their capacity informedly and intelligently to make decisions other than the essential ones required to maintain internal balance and progress. Of all the proposals, this conception of a geographical subdivision into regional units of a single system seems the least viable for the best interests of higher education.

It has been suggested that the Coordinating Council be converted gradually or at once into a superboard with more public members of a number more than equal to all educational and segmental representatives. Some observers believe this is the inevitable development of the tendency of both executive and legislative arms of government to look to the Council for authoritative disinterested factual material and counsel as a result of which its leadership will steadily emerge. Yet others believe there is little to show in the way of Council leadership. My own view is that the record is mixed, that such leadership as has developed has been in considerable degree the work of the staff; and further that weak gubernatorial appointees could cause the Council to be inconsequential.

A recommendation that the Coordinating Council's role should be increased, at least in the interim before a single system could be achieved, was one of the proposals of Governor Reagan's task force on efficiency and cost control already referred to.

The report stated, as quoted in the *Los Angeles Times,* that "the most significant improvements" in higher education it could suggest would be to give the Council authority "to prescribe and adjudicate" in areas of budgetary control, curriculum, coordination, admissions and transfers, course proliferation, utilization of facilities, new sites, programs, and long-range academic planning. Such an extensively increased role, obviously at the expense of authority in all the other segmental boards, was needed the report declared because "there is lack of sufficient coordination to prevent overlapping of roles, duplication of facilities and lack of specialization of campus and programs." While this indictment of the Coordinating Council is severe, the important thing is that it is recognized even though limitedly to fill a necessary function and capable of fulfilling a larger one. The task force criticizes the Council for some developments which have been beyond its control. In fact, the Council has been more than "a quiet, scholarly voice." The amazing thing is the role it has so far filled considering the very powerful parallel boards controlling the University and the State Colleges.

The staff of the Joint Committee on Higher Education in a 1966 prospectus listed as one possible alternative the conversion of the Coordinating Council into a contracting agency charged with "buying" educational capacity at the margin from public and private institutions, or from combinations of institutions. Similarly in the Joint Committee's staff memorandum of 1966 was mentioned another conceivable alternative: "a program of drastically increased support for students coupled with a reduced support for institutions. This approach would generate some of the aspects of an 'open market' in education."

Most of the alternative organizational proposals which have been suggested would very largely eliminate participation by the private institutions in decision making except those related to the Coordinating Council unless some amendment of its composition were to do so.

In reference to the private institutions, both the Joint Committee as well as the Constitution Revision Commission chaired by Judge Bruce Sumner must decide whether or no it would be wise to revise the California Constitution to make it permissive for the state to grant state funds for either current or capital purposes to private colleges and universities. This is not an easy one to decide. The inclusive policy of the federal government in making grants as well as loans to private institutions has had a distinct influence in those states where constitutional prohibitions have existed. Now, with the possibilities of contractual relationships emerging, the constitutional language used has an important relationship. My own view through many years has been negative, that is to say, against revision, against state funds going to private institutions. Now, in the present complexities such an outcome does not appear as threatening as once seemed true. A permissive clause seems now wise. Maintained should be all prohibitions against any use of state funds for sectarian purpose. The Legislature and Governor should have the power if deemed of public benefit to use state funds for grants to private institutions or for contractual relations, or for loans on terms established by law.

At all times the organizational alternative always exists of making no important change at all. This would mean carrying on with the three parallel board formula for the University, the State Colleges, and the junior colleges as now existing, with the Coordinating Council continuing in the advisory role it now has on state matters and in its administrative role on federal programs assigned, but with the role in state affairs strengthened.

The Coordinating Council's positive influence for good in the year-round quarter system decision in spite of State College stalling, in obtaining modification of the University of California growth plan in spite of President Kerr's opposition to change, in winning finally unanimous support in the Council for a new junior college board of governance in spite of the opposition of State Department of Education spokesmen and the Superintendent, Dr. Max Rafferty, together with the Legislature's and Governor Reagan's approval in 1967 of this junior college proposal in S.B. 669 introduced by Senator Walter Stiern, are all examples of the contemporary usefulness of the Coordinating Council.

In January, 1965 President Kerr was quoted in the *Los Angeles Times* as saying that the Coordinating Council "is becoming increasingly an administrative agency, not a coordinating agency," and said that his top staff had to prepare as fully for a Council meeting as for a meeting of the Regents. He was further quoted as saying, and I have heard him in Council meetings make a similar complaint, "We have just too many decision-making groups. The Council has become another layer of bureaucracy between us and the Legislature. Also, it has become a centralizing influence at the same time the University administration is decentralizing."

Some administrators at least appear to like a Council that will be weak. In that same article in the *Los Angeles Times* of January 10, 1965, Dr. Willard Spalding, the Council's director, was quoted as saying there was no doubt the Council would deal increasingly with controversial issues and that all the studies it has undertaken were its proper concern, the intent of the Legislature being to develop an arena where conflicting interests could be discussed. Dr. Spalding recognized "the danger of centralization in inappropriate areas always exists" but further declared, "The question you must constantly ask is where do you need centralization in order to assure individuality? Where centralization leads to conformity it is bad, but where it is necessary to protect individuality it certainly is desirable."

At that same time I declared the University and other segments should be cautious about criticizing the Council, because unless coordination as a process is followed with a reasonable degree of success it will be inevitable that pressures will build for a single board for all higher education that will take important powers from both the State College Trustees and the University Regents. As between chaos or a single board, I stated, "I think they would do well to try to make the Coordinating Council work." I hold the same viewpoint today.

And I believe further that the Coordinating Council must be given constitutional status with delineated functions and responsibilities, a position not likely to be supported by the University's Regents nor possibly by the State Colleges' Trustees.

Earlier in this book in several connections, reference has been made to the critical importance of gubernatorial appointments. The quality of an organization can be no better than the abilities, competences, and characters of the persons who compose it. This is especially applicable to the functioning of the various lay boards which constitute the responsible managerial structure of all higher education: the Board of Regents of the University, the Board of Trustees of the State Colleges, the Board of Governors of the Community Colleges, and the Coordinating Council for Higher Education. Do these boards each within itself have the capacities to develop adequate management? Can they achieve common action on major policies? Are there persons on these boards who have the capacity for leadership, and who also will make the effort to exercise leadership? Will their inability to come to grips as a group with major problems, even though leaving detail to staff, result finally in the virtual dominance of action by the several staffs? Are the boards in some instances too large for effective action?

There is a meaningful relationship between the character of gubernatorial appointments and the performance of individuals on a board. If the attitude or outlook of the individual is dependent, is one of waiting until he gets instructions from the Governor, then the significance of the lay board is weakened and its potential strength and independence vitiated. If the individual makes his decisions by purely politically partisan positions (or if not those of a whole party, then of a fraction thereof), it is equally destructive of the significance of a board.

Personally, I yearn to see appointments to such boards in higher education made as much if not more from the standpoint of the best interests of the segment of higher education involved, than simply as patronage to reward political support or to assure a block of votes on the board on a particular issue of policy. The Governors who chose as Regents persons of the stature of Philip L. Boyd, Edward W. Carter, Mrs. Norman Chandler, Mrs. Edward H. Heller, Samuel B. Mosher, Edwin W. Pauley, and Norton Simon chose persons of high community distinction, and although some political consideration may have been involved in each case, they chose persons whose devotion to the University and not to a political position was and has been of primary importance. So also on the State College Trustees, the entire composition of which in 1960 was appointed by Governor Brown, there are such outstanding persons in leadership as Donald M. Hart, Louis H. Heilbron, Charles Luckman, Theodore Meriam, Albert J. Ruffo, and Paul Spencer.

The problem in each of these boards as well as in the Coordinating Council is to develop leadership for the future. Indifference to this necessity will mean disaster. There is no point in giving greater authority to any board or council unless the personnel of said board or council is of a stature competent to match the responsibility.

In an earlier chapter the apparent demand for a new Master Plan emanating from State College faculty groups was indicated. In this chapter suggestions from legislators have been noted; and at times expressions of staff persons related to the Legislature's Joint Committee would imply a new Master Plan. Staff personnel of the Coordinating Council queried whether or not a new Master Plan should be prepared. In addition to Speaker Unruh's statements about University and State College governance, other reasons given to suggest need for a new Master Plan include: (1) the increasing federal government participation in financing higher education, (2) the increasing strength of the State Colleges in organization and enrollment, (3) the rising demands of faculty and of students for participation in decision making, (4) the failure of financial support to keep pace with rising enrollments and rising costs, (5) the increased consciousness of and conscience toward disadvantaged young people, primarily minority youth, on the part of both society and those in political responsibility, and (6) the rates of growth of California's problems in higher education beyond those projected in the Master Plan from 1960 to 1975.*

In my own view, there is not one new situation that cannot be accommodated within the existing patterns, procedures, and plans. Not one of the items cited above justified the creation of such a huge effort as writing a new Master Plan would entail. However, every item cited calls for continuing alert consideration of how the Master Plan may be made more effective, and how possibly if needed it could be improved in substantive arrangements or procedures. The procedural answer is to use the Coordinating Council as intended as a continuing master planning body. The Coordinating Council at its October meeting in 1967 took action to study further both present effectiveness and possible improvement in the Master Plan.

Apart from any personal views of mine here expressed, the issues involved in governance and coordination are of such overwhelming importance that far greater consultation and cooperation should occur on these issues than is taking place. Continuing consultation should take place during the coming year among the Joint Committee on Higher Education and its staff, the Constitution Revision Commission and its staff, the Governor and his staff, the Coordinating Council for Higher Education and its staff, and the boards and staffs of the several segments of higher education.

*Regretfully, the progress report to the Legislature from the Joint Committee on Higher Education, entitled *The Academic State*, which was issued to the press in late March, 1968, was not made available to Coordinating Council members in time for me to make direct comments on its observations on organization and governance.

18

ATTITUDES TOWARD HIGHER EDUCATION
FOR THE CONTINUING FUTURE

IN AN EARLY CHAPTER the point was made that there is broad concern about higher education among the people in both the whole nation and California. Today more people are involved in higher education. There are reasons. The sheer size of every function embraced is relevant. Furthermore, no single type of education beyond high school will satisfy. We all believe in educational pluralism. The stereotype in the early twentieth century of higher education as a small rural college, old Siwash, as an intimate, isolated collegiate community of president, faculty, and students is no longer applicable even though important collegiate programs of this type remain. The dominant types today are also the university or the large college of many functions and the junior college as well as the medium-sized college. Furthermore, higher education is increasing in public significance and influence. There is scarcely any field of human activity today in which one can speak informedly or intelligently without involving the resources of higher education.

There is a necessary variety of California higher education even as there is an essential diversity of society and economy. In this respect California is like the whole nation. California, however, not in contrast with the nation but in some aspects to a greater degree, in higher education has shown an extraordinary adaptability in developing concepts and forms of education, types of institutions, and programs of instruction suitable to the rapidly multiplying and diversifying needs of an expanding technology in service to the nation and the world as well as to the state. There have been also constantly rising economic expectations of the people, and expanding perceptions here as elsewhere that no capable persons of whatever background if able to carry college and university work successfully should be denied the opportunity of admission.

Certainly today, no less than in the past decade, a high responsibility bears upon the whole state to continue what it has so significantly begun. Considering the larger numbers of a growing population, there is a greater share of responsibility and a greater challenge than ever before. Also, life is becoming more complex with increased urbanization but also due to the advances in learning which have been brought about in whole or in part in the institutions of higher learning. California's colleges and universities, public and private, have directly or indirectly affected the culture, technology, and the life of every citizen in many ways.

From what has been written, if not from the personal experience of the reader, it is evident that higher education is very important business. My view is that no one familiar with economic development in this generation can gainsay that fact.

My view also may be expressed at the end as at the beginning, that educational progress in higher education is or should be our most important policy to achieve a product which will aid the state in carrying on at high levels, and conceivably higher levels of economic and social attainment. We need, and have, a well-developed educational system, private and public, through all levels and all types of institutions so as to present to youth the broadest possible opportunity for an education to each individual to the level of his ability and willingness to embrace with large opportunity developed for persons of economic levels that might not otherwise be drawn to higher education.

Our pluralistic educational system draws from the many streams of culture, ethnic, economic, religious, and social elements that have made modern California what is is. No system which does not recognize the varied aptitudes, skills, knowledges, and interests of such a diversified society can long endure. California's people are not moving towards a monistic or monolithic society.

The modern economic challenge in California is visible so markedly in the steadily increasing need for persons capable of filling just about every classification of occupations except that of unskilled labor. The effects of automation and technological change underscore the very dynamic character of the demands on California higher education.

232

Veritably, we are in the midst of an educational revolution in which the predominant emphasis is, or should be, on achieving competence equal to capacity. In my lifetime I have known other emphases to hold central educational or political concern: citizenship and civic participation, democratic living, the cultural heritage, collective and cooperative ideals, and equality in various forms. None of these ought to be rejected fully, nor is today, but today the individual is being recognized more fully. This involves planning for differing abilities and hence differentiation in educational programs. It also means variations in rewards if competence and competition are recognized. Hence, some social and economic inequality becomes acceptable, and it is being accepted. This represents renewal of an ancient concern for excellence which means not simply quality education but also superiority of some over others in the various aspects of learning and doing. Mediocrity will not suffice as a standard. No one in his right mind can accept it. This is indeed the academic revolution which is visible. Each should strive to achieve at his best, and this will mean that some shall excel.

As for higher education in particular, it is concerned more with those types of education that are intellectually demanding, which call for something more than personal physical skills of hand, voice, visage, or limb. Those possessing these latter skills have been receiving under fortunate circumstances a disproportionate share of the economy's fruits, the product of an affluent society concerned with ease and pleasure. Yet now a more rational view not only of California's problems but of the place of the United States in the world calls for greater economic reward for linguists and masters of languages, statisticians, mathematicians, economists, scientists, technologists, and philosophers.

Education has not yet fully conquered the problem that youth will face as adults not only to meet changed occupational requirements that themselves do not remain unchanged but also to meet responsibilities as citizens in a society that seemingly insists on transforming itself in so many ways so fast. I have no nostrum on how to achieve such later adaptability except that of the individual achieving at the highest level possible while in the formal educational processes and keeping the mind open thereafter. Our psychologists, biologists, and sociologists in recent years have suggested that yet higher level in individual achievement may be embraced by more of our people. We know we probably are not educating fully even those who appear to be at the height of achievement; certainly we are not educating all of those who have the top levels of ability.

There is no other way to improve the state, the nation, and the world than to educate our youth. The facts, ideas, ideals, disciplines, methods in knowing with which we surround them, and of course the lives they lead, will considerably determine what our future shall be. Hence, our objectives for the coming years of educational growth should be on these factors as much as on the campuses and buildings where they will study. In these factors, the outlooks, attitudes, abilities, and actions of our faculties and administrators are of profound importance. The context or environment of learning as well as the content or substance of the academic program is of great importance.

Will there be not only the requisite "discipline unto mastery" but also a spontaneity, freedom, and receptivity to new ideas? Will we manifest any interest in the creative impulses? Will we cultivate the processes of reason, or shall we, as so many in our society today embrace as a philosophy, appeal increasingly to emotion? Will we shrink from the expression of conviction which may derive from a conscience or inner moral outlook? And will we seek to know the bases of the convictions voiced, or will we stereotypedly label them and reject them? Will we learn to accept the present setting of institutions of government, the economy, and society in which our lives are inescapably cast without developing a self-defeating negativism which rejects all suggestions for change? Will we adopt the sophomoric view which assumes all the established institutions to be evil simply because they exist, or will we seek to understand their true nature, how they came to be, what essential ideas lie behind them, and how they can be improved? Will we cultivate an attitude of human sympathy or world view which, while not maudlin and while operating within present loyalties, does not lose sight of ultimate goals for all the world of mankind? Will we seek to possess, while yearning for the better life of whatever kind or form, an awareness of practicality, a search for immediately realizable goals, holding the mind to earth even while the spirit soars?

Because it has been argued by some persons of considerable wealth, business leadership, and social influence in the last year or two with considerable political impact that the emphasis on higher education in California has been exaggerated, I think it justified that I state my conviction about the appropriate concern of business, finance, and industry for the quality of higher education both private and public.

Business interest in the quality of education at all levels, and consequent motivation for the support of education through taxation or through gifts where appropriate by corporate standards and choices, is just good business as well as good citizenship, corporate and personal. Responsible business management today sees to it that those resources which are of first importance to the present and future progress of a business, or of business in general, are not allowed to weaken or deteriorate. Among these are educated manpower, new knowledge, maintenance or improvement of the economic, political, or social climate, and the development of humane, ethical, and moral character of persons to be employed. These are all, or have been, expected end products of higher education.

Not only business and industry but also government at all levels needs the best in educated manpower. As Goethe said in 1826, "There is nothing more frightful than ignorance in action."

Former President Clark Kerr, and now a professor of the University of California, Berkeley campus, in 1963 delivered at Harvard University certain lectures which became the basis for his book, *The Uses of the University*. Wholly apart from any pro and con argument over his dismissal in January, 1967, and wholly apart from any evaluation of his success as president of the University, certain of his ideas set forth in that book and elsewhere elaborated are worthy of keeping in mind now. I said this in May, 1967 at a convocation in his honor at the University of California, Davis campus, where I spoke of "Clark Kerr's influence on higher education in America." There I described him, wholly apart from what had transpired, as "a prophet not without honor in his own country and among his own people."

I stated in effect that in his book, already a classic, or in other papers, there are evidences of great insight, such as an awareness of the necessity of rethinking the significance and role of the huge university of gargantuan size and complexity, with numerous campuses, programs, and functions, that is to say, the idea of a multiversity whose final form or meaning is not known. Also, Dr. Kerr sensed the emergent problems of the federal relationships, and of what he called "the Federal grant university."

The problem of internal governance so freshly sensed since 1960 (and especially since 1964) involving students, faculty, the alumni, the immediate campus community, was one of his concerns in those lectures. It was discovered to involve quite more than any simple doctrine of the power of a legally constituted board of regents or trustees, and revealed were the multifarious tensions and the necessary discovery of accommodation of interests, principles, and ranges of responsibility whether or no ever before written out.

Dr. Kerr spoke and wrote about the regrettably losing status of undergraduates and their teaching in the modern major, complex university. He also stressed the inevitable and ever-changing involvement of the university or the college, or any "city of intellect" in the life of society, and with varying tensions, the process which though old is now very characteristic, and which is being continuously debated in new settings, namely, the place of the expert, the scholar, the teacher, even an intellectual elite, in a democratic environment not always hospitable to him or them or to new ideas. We would do well to think along with him in these matters even though he is no longer the leader of the University of California.

The significance of the conflicts and commonalties among and between all the natural sciences, the social sciences, the humanities, and the professions in reference to emphasis in curriculum, financial support and influence both within and without university or college walls has received much emphasis in recent literature, and will continue to influence the way in which the general public regards the college and university world.

Also, the degree to which the increasingly international flavor and import of higher education may be recognized will wield an influence on the extent to which a new or renewed community of learning and scholarship comes to pass, or at an opposite pole, all learning and scholarship are conceived of meaning and are devoted to exalting the conflicting concerns of national purposes.

The educational system by its very nature depends for its success on persons, i.e., upon presidents, professors, and pupils. The American tradition is one of a large degree of freedom and of independence for persons. Similarly this has been true for institutions. In the midst of controversies over finances, or structures, or functions, or programs, or any formalized presentation of the process, it is important not to forget that what takes place in fact rests on the attitudes and intentions of the persons who are involved. It is a common peril for those who hold power and develop the process to presume the plan will prevail if only enough power is put behind it. There are no panaceas, and all programs depend on persons. In the long run presidents and professors must persuade others that a plan or program is right. Dependence primarily on power whether by directives or by demonstrations will fail. Higher education is complex and multipersonal; and the answers to what is good and right for now will really not be known for many years.

Yet actions must take place, responsibility cannot be shirked, decisions must be made, and the ideal can seldom be embraced in the immediate future. One learns from engaging in the process of planning that it is impossible at any moment of time to satisfy everybody without state bankruptcy. Although as an economist I had known this for decades, it has been impressed on me indelibly in these recent years. There are limited resources to embrace unlimited desires.

Unless some persons become protectors of the public purse, concerned about costs and potential revenue and location of the burden of public finance, there will be little restraint on what is charged to that public purse. Seemingly, everything proposed is good, but somewhere, somehow priorities must be developed for right now. There are altogether too many persons elected to act as guardians of the public purse who conceive it their duty to vote for expenditures but not for revenues.

In every field of government, and higher education must be included, what is "demanded" as "absolutely essential" and "necessary if we are not to turn back the clock" generally runs some distance beyond what is immediately available, or what is later proved to be adequate for the period in question.

One may learn also from the process of planning and from political activity in the nonpartisan sense that quite often if not generally, if one follows the doctrine of consensus above all else, it is inevitable that there be a sacrifice of principle somewhere by someone. In the 1959 master planning program as described in an earlier chapter, the major approach was consensus or at least it was action without dissent. In the struggles in the Coordinating Council and in recent crises, the doctrine of consensus has been dominant but has not always been followed. At times there have been struggles of considerable emotional involvement. In the main, however, the strength of the Coordinating Council has lain in its devotion to principle. This was very clear in its position on the planning of new campuses where segmental and community pressures were very great. But the Council was advisory only, not finally administrative. It is those who hold power who achieve or do not achieve consensus. A person who is determined not to seek accommodation with a new situation of facts or of power determines in a sense in advance to accept the role of martyr.

However, some persons such as presidents, chancellors, regents, and trustees have greater responsibility in these matters than others, that is, than professors whose deepest joy it is to assure personal professional purity from any compromise of principle. As one long in higher education, as professor, dean, and president, I sense the varying requirements and attributes of the roles administrators are called upon to play which differ so much in their demands from those which professors must fulfill. Power does force compromise, at least until the possessors of power are changed.

In this book the reader has observed the extent of the recent educational challenges before higher education and especially confronting the people of California. There has been an ethos of public support of higher education. If this ethos does not change profoundly, and I predict it will not, governors and legislators who strive for stringently tightened fiscal policies affecting higher education denying opportunity and quality will not finally be supported.

Meeting the challenges of higher education will require that everyone face them honestly, not strive to run from them or to escape behind barriers of cliches. The only way to maintain and to go beyond the progress of the past is through the highest uses of trained intelligence, and this will call for using the institutional resources California now possesses, both public and private, through the wisest commitments of the community's resources that California is able to make.

This calls for plans, programs, principles, persons, professional and political leadership of the very best that can be discovered. The process is continuous. May the day never come when anyone may say, "Well, we don't have to worry about the colleges and universities of California any more."

Throughout this book the principle of equality of educational opportunity for all persons as interested and qualified for the levels of learning they individually would embrace has repeatedly been brought forward. In one expression or another, it is to be found in the Truman Report, the Eisenhower Committee Report, and other studies; in the various reports in California preceding the Master Plan and the Master Plan itself; in the actions of the University Regents, the State College Trustees, junior college boards and the State Board of Education, and in the recommendations of the Coordinating Council for Higher Education. It has not always meant the same thing to all persons. But it does reflect an underlying moral or ethical element in twentieth century culture. It is the view that if society and the economy are to be constructed on competitive individualism, if the rewards of production, profession, service, or labor are to vary according to the individual's abilities and skills as well as the forces of markets and opportunities, if inequality in results or rewards is inevitable, then opportunity to run the race of life should be as equal as possible in order that society's relationships might be as fair as possible. Furthermore, a democratic society dare not politically go along without equality of opportunity for self-improvement.

In American culture and society equality has many manifestations. There are the conceptions of equality at the bar of legal justice, equality in the exercise of the right of suffrage, equality in the right to stand for public office, equality in treatment for like skills in the hiring hall, equality for buyers and sellers in the marketplace, and equality of children in the public schools.

Citizens are not equal in physical or mental abilities and skills, nor are they equal in personal or moral character. However, the equality most critical if there is to be economic and social justice is that of equality of opportunity.

Opportunity may exist and be available but not be grasped. Students are not equal in motivation, aptitude, persistence, drive, and all the other traits that make for success as students. No matter what is done, some will drop out, some will malinger, some will fail to perform in fact or up to their capacity. These are familiar experiences to every teacher. However, the largest opportunity not for loafing but for achieving is what educators desire. No program can possibly equate all deterrents to equality of opportunity, nor remove all barriers or handicaps thereto, but at any one time society must do its best. And that best is through the arrangements for equality of educational opportunity. At the least, equality of entrance should exist for the successive levels of learning if the individual possesses the requisites for each such level; and possibly more should be done for persons not yet arrived at adulthood to make available on a minimal basis the financial resources needed by those who lack them to embrace if able and willing the fundamental steps in higher education.

This is the new equality, the new moral basis for the democratic and economic liberty which we have sought and should seek.

INDEX

California, University of, campuses: Berkeley, 22-23, 53, 60, 71-72, 76, 78, 84, 141, 162, 164-65, 177, 216, 235; Davis, 22, 53, 79, 235; Hastings College of Law, 53; Irvine, 53, 79, 150, 163, 203; Los Angeles, 22, 44, 45, 47, 53, 72, 79, 133, 162; Mount Lick Observatory, 53; Riverside, 22, 53, 79, 150; San Diego, 53, 79, 150, 163, 203, 207; San Francisco, 22, 53; Santa Barbara, 22, 53, 79; Santa Cruz, 45, 53, 79, 150, 163, 203, 207

California Civil Service Employees Association, 65

California Educational Commission (1899), 27

California Institute of Technology, 26, 159, 173, 210

California Junior College Association, 29, 41, 44, 136-37, 178

California State Assembly: Concurrent Resolution 88 (1959), 24, 28-29, 33, 45, 61, 219; Concurrent Resolution 156 (1965), 216; Bill 1765 (1967), 78; Bill 946 (1967), 153; Committee on Education, 42, 65-66, 94

California State Chamber of Commerce, 36

California State Colleges: tensions with University of California, 3, 24, 149-51, 154-56; competition for campuses, 5, 19, 29-30, 149-50, 173; Master Plan principle, 7, 83, 177, 186-88; enrollments, 8, 151; change of name to university, 20, 52, 153-55; history, 20-22; admission standards, 30, 77, 102, 170; governance, 49-55, 223-25, 228-29; doctoral work, 57, 59, 60, 77, 79-80, 153-60, 187-88; faculty research 57-58, 83, 155, 160, 202; bond issues, 83, 127, 138, 204-206; faculty salaries and recruitment, 102-103, 126, 155, 160, 203; level of support, 105-109, 114-15; fiscal authority, 114-15; Budget 1967-68, 101, 116-27; tuition, 128-48; Academic Senate, 153, 155; image, 161; gift solicitation, 171-72; elimination of lower division, 183; liberal arts, 186-87; Budget 1968-69, 201-204

California State Colleges, units: Chico, 53, 59, 63; Dominguez Hills, 150-51; Fresno, 46, 53, 58, 159; Fullerton, 53, 59, 63, 151; Hayward, 53, 59, 63, 151; Humboldt, 53, 59, 63; Kellogg-Voorhis, 53, 59; Long Beach, 53, 63, 159, 187; Los Angeles, 53, 58, 63, 159; Sacramento, 53, 63, 64, 67, 90, 153, 159; San Bernardino, 150-51; San Diego, 46, 52, 53, 58, 63, 159; San Fernando Valley, 53, 59, 63, 159; San Francisco, 41, 44, 52, 53, 58, 60, 63, 159; San Jose, 20-21, 53, 58, 63, 159; San Luis Obispo, 53, 59; Sonoma, 53, 59, 151; Stanislaus, 53, 59, 151

California State Graduate Fellowships program, 79, 83, 134, 169, 201

California State Scholarship and Loan Commission and program, 9, 26-27, 78, 83, 102, 134, 139, 145, 168-69, 201, 221

California State Senate: Bill 33 (1960), 65, 222; Bill 669 (1967), 178, 227; Bill 691 (1967), 181; Bill 851 (1967), 181; Committee on Education, 42, 62

California State University idea, 20, 52, 153-55

Campion, Howard A., 41, 43, 44

Capital outlay. See Budgets; Pay-as-you-go financing

Carnegie Corporation of New York, 44, 212

Carnegie Foundation for the Advancement of Teaching, 27

Carter, Edward W., 33, 229

Casassa, Very Reverend Charles S., 168

Center for Research and Development in Higher Education, 103n, 177

Champion, Hale, 112

Chandler, Dorothy Buffum (Mrs. Norman), 15, 33, 34, 229

Christopher, Warren, 89, 92

Citizens for California Higher Education, 141

Claremont Colleges, 26, 87, 210

Claremont Graduate School and University Center, 159, 173

Claremont Men's College, 168

Clark, George W., 177-78

College Entrance Examination Board, 144

Colorado, master planning, 222

Columbia University, 28, 214

Commission on Financing Higher Education, 212

Committee for Economic Development, 214

242

Harris, Seymour E., 212
Hart, Donald M., 229
Harvard University, 75, 235
Heilbron, Louis H., 229
Heller, Mrs. Edward H., 229
Heyns, Roger, 72
Hibbs, Ben, 87
Higher education: political importance of, 5-6, 63, 65, 67, 216, 223-24; costs of, 36-38, 43, 45, 46
Higher education, California public: competition and tensions, 5, 19-20, 149-65; costs, 9, 31, 36-37, 198-214; studies of, 27-28; year-round operation, 31, 81-82, 83, 202, 221, 227; single governing board idea, 42, 43, 50-56, 103, 223-24, 228; coordination, 49-55; differentiation of function, 49-50, 62-65, 77, 82, 189; superboard idea, 50-52, 103, 225; campus capacities and locations, 82, 83, 95, 103, 149-51, 169-70, 183-84; work-load requirements, 107, 111-12, 127, 202; gift solicitation, 171-72
Higher Education Act of 1965, 94
Higher Education Facilities Act of 1963, 94
Higher Education in A Decade of Decision, 16-17
Hitch, Charles J., 172, 202
Holy, Thomas C., 29, 41, 44

Illinois, master planning, 222
Independent institutions, 8-9, 25-27, 78, 82, 83-84, 139, 166-74, 210, 211, 212-13, 226-27

Joint Advisory Committee on Differentiation of Function, 46, 156
Joint Legislative Budget Committee, 115
Joint Legislative Committee on Higher Education, 68, 118, 147, 162, 216-22, 225, 226-27, 230
Joyal, Arnold E., 46
Junior Colleges: competition for campuses, 5, 30; Master Plan principle, 7, 83, 177, 188-90; enrollments, 8, 25; growth, 20, 177; history, 24-25; diversion of students to, 30-31, 77, 83, 135-36, 177, 188-89; state support of, 30, 78, 83, 113-14, 136, 179-81; limitation to two years, 77; tuition, 133, 136, 138, 146-47, 180; tensions, 151-53; transfers to State Colleges and Uni-

versity, 152, 177, 179; governance, 152-53, 176-77, 178-79, 223-25, 228; image, 181-82, 184-85; relationship to University of California and California State Colleges, 182-84

Kansas City Survey of Higher Education, 45
Keezer, Dexter M., 212
Kentucky, coordinating board, 222
Kern County, 150
Kerr, Clark: elected University of California President, 22; Master Plan Survey, 29, 32-34, 41, 45, 56-61, 86; upon decentralization, 53, 70-74; student demonstrations, 71-72; intention to resign as President, 72; relationship to Coordinating Council, 90, 227; dismissal from University presidency, 99; Budget 1967-68, 118, 122; opposition to tuition, 129; University's Growth Plan, 150, 227; gift solicitation by University, 172; approval of bond issue, 205; general campus doctrine, 207, 224; Carnegie Corporation study, 212; at Joint Committee on Higher Education meeting, 217; *The Uses of the University*, 235-36
Kloetzel, Milton C., 168

Legislative Analyst, 108-10, 112-13, 115, 126, 159, 190
Liaison Committee, 28-31, 40, 41, 43, 44, 45, 64, 90, 169
Liberal arts education, 186-90, 196-97
Lieffer, Don, 69
London, University of, 59
Los Alamos Laboratory, 53
Los Angeles Bar Association, 34, 35
Los Angeles City School District, 41, 44
Los Angeles Normal School, 22
Los Angeles Rotary Club, 34, 35
Los Angeles Times, 96, 120, 121, 128, 145-46, 147, 226, 227, 228
Love, Malcolm, 52, 63
Lowell, A. Lawrence, 75
Loyola University of Los Angeles, 26, 168
Luckman, Charles, 229
Ludlam, James E., 173

Mage, John R., 33
Maryland, coordinating board, 222

244

Master Plan for Higher Education in California: background, 1-6, 24, 28-31; principles, 6-8, 48-49, 137, 170, 186-89; chairman, 32-39; personnel, 41, 43-45, 46-47; procedure, 41-43; press relations, 41-42; structure, 45-47; deliberations, 48-62; name, 61; legislative acceptance, 62-66; achievements, 77-87, 215-16; interest in outside California, 86-87, 222; reexamination, 216-22, 229-30

McClintic, Joseph O., 46

McConnell Report (1955), 28

McHenry, Dean E., 41, 45, 56, 57

McKinney, James, 15

McLain, Fred F., 173

Medsker, Leland L., 177-78

Meriam, Theodore, 229

Meyer, Theodore, 217

Meyerson, Martin, 72

Michigan, Annual Conference on Higher Education, 34

Michigan, coordinating board, 222

Miller, George, 62-66

Millett, John D., 212

Mills College, 26, 44, 168

Minnesota, coordinating board, 222

Missouri, master planning, 222

Morrisett, Lloyd N., 47

Mosher, Samuel B., 33, 229

Mount San Antonio Junior College, 46

Muscatine, Charles, 141

National Commission on Accrediting, 39, 44

National Education Association, 16

The Need for Additional Centers of Public Higher Education in California, 169

Nevada State University Survey, 45

North Carolina higher education body, 87

Occidental College, 26, 32, 33, 40, 41, 44, 47, 52, 74, 86, 89, 95, 168, 173, 185, 210

Odell, Morgan, 173

Orange County School Trustees Association, 38

Oregon State System of Higher Education, 89

Paltridge, James G., 103n

Partisan political influence in public higher education, 23, 87, 99, 101, 219-20, 225, 229

Pauley, Edwin W., 33, 229

Pay-as-you-go financing, 83, 127, 205-206

Peterson, Basil H., 178

Pitzer College, 173

Pomona College, 26, 173

Post, A. Alan, 109-10, 113, 115, 126, 159

President's Commission on Higher Education (Truman), 11-13, 238

President's Committee on Education Beyond the High School (Eisenhower), 13-15, 17, 34, 39, 148, 238

Professional education, 191-97

Professional fields, supply and demand, 102

Programming and Budgeting system, 112, 115

Public and private higher education, 34-36

Quality in higher education, 84-86, 122-24, 200-201

Rafferty, Max, 217, 227

Reader's Digest, 87

Reagan, Governor Ronald: on educational opportunity, 9; crises in budgetary finance, 72, 83, 116; relationship to Coordinating Council, 95-102, 117, 213; Budget 1967-68, 101, 118-27, 201, 204; tuition, 128, 136, 140-47; State Colleges name change to university, 154; State Colleges items not supported, 156; gubernatorial candidate, 162; subsistence grants program vetoed, 168-69; appointment of junior college Board of Governors, 178, 227; approval of state funds to junior colleges, 181; Budget 1968-69, 202-204, 206; attitude toward higher education, 207; task force survey, 214, 223, 226

Redlands, University of, 173

Regional governing boards, 225

Rennert, Leo, 67-68

A Re-Study of the Needs of California in Higher Education, 28

Rice University, 130-31

Richards, John R., 89, 92

Robbins, Lord, 86

Rodda, Albert S., 181

Rothwell, C. Easton, 168

Rubel, A. C., 95-96

Ruffo, Albert J., 218, 229